SEX WORK, MOBILITY AND HEALTH IN EUROPE

Major changes have taken place in the sex industry in Europe. Over the past decade we have seen increasing migration and diversification, along with major shifts in policy towards the industry. There is very little published on sex work in Europe, but the demand is growing for information and analyses of the situation today from people working on health, policy, gender and employment.

The authors of this book examine sex work in terms of economic and social restructuring, concerns about infection and recent policy developments on prostitution.

www.keganpaul.com

KEGAN PAUL
EUROPEAN STUDIES SERIES

THE BATTLE OF THE SINGLE EUROPEAN MARKET
Gilles Grin

SEX WORK, MOBILITY AND HEALTH IN EUROPE
Sophie Day and Helen Ward

SEX WORK, MOBILITY AND HEALTH IN EUROPE

Edited by

Sophie Day and Helen Ward

KEGAN PAUL
London • New York • Bahrain

First published in 2004 by
Kegan Paul Limited
UK: P.O. Box 256, London WC1B 3SW, England
Tel: 020 7580 5511 Fax: 020 7436 0899
E-Mail: books@keganpaul.com
Internet: http://www.keganpaul.com
USA: 61 West 62nd Street, New York, NY 10023
Tel: (212) 459 0600 Fax: (212) 459 3678
Internet: http://www.columbia.edu/cu/cup
BAHRAIN: bahrain@keganpaul.com

Distributed by:
Extenza-Turpin Distribution
Stratton Business Park
Pegasus Drive
Biggleswade
SG18 8QB
United Kingdom
Tel: (01767) 604951 Fax: (01767) 601640
Email: books@extenza-turpin.com

Columbia University Press
61 West 62nd Street, New York, NY 10023
Tel: (212) 459 0600 Fax: (212) 459 3678
Internet: http://www.columbia.edu/cu/cup

ISBN: 0-7103-0942-2

British Library Cataloguing in Publication Data
A catalogue record for this book is available from the British Library.

Library of Congress Cataloging-in-Publication Data
Applied for.

Cover Image:
Kirchner, Ernst Ludwig. Five Tarts (Funf Kokotten), Ruth and Jacob Kainen Collection, Image ©
2004 Board of Trustees, National Gallery of Art, Washington, 1914, woodcut on blotting paper.

Contents

Tables and Figures

Acknowledgments

This book is one result of determined efforts to build networks through which a wide variety of activists can communicate effectively in Europe. In particular, we would like to acknowledge the central contribution of many sex workers, for ensuring that these networks focus on change - to secure occupational, civil and human rights.

As editors of this volume, we would like to thank the contributors, members of the Europap network, participants in and sponsors of the conference we held in 2002, *Sex work and health in a changing Europe*. We thank the European Commission for support towards several contributions in this volume (European Programme of Community Action on Prevention of AIDS and other certain communicable diseases Grant agreement number: SPC.2002288), and also the Wellcome Trust for support towards chapters 1 and 10 (Grant number 053592).

We are grateful to Judith Kilvington, Pascale Martin and Keith Hassell for their administrative and technical support, and to Mark Hoskisson for preparing the index.

Sophie Day and Helen Ward

Contributors

Laura Agustín has a doctorate from the Pavis Centre for Cultural Studies at the Open University (UK). Her research, which will be published as a Zed Book later this year, concerns the connections between migrations of non-European women to Europe, where they sell domestic, caring and sexual services, and the large social sector which proposes to help them. She has worked extensively in *educación popular* both in Latin America and with migrants in various parts of the west and has been an evaluator of social programming for the ILO and the European Commission. She moderates an e-mail list on the sex industry in romance languages. Contact: laura@nodo50.org

Priscilla Alexander has been involved in the sex workers' rights movement since 1976, when she began working with COYOTE in San Francisco. In 1986, she co-founded CAL-PEP, a sex workers' HIV prevention project, going on to work on the issue of sex work and HIV/AIDS for the World Health Organization from 1989 to 1993. Since 1995, she has been working for FROST'D, an HIV/AIDS prevention project in New York City, analysing data. Along the way, she co-edited *Sex Work: Writings by Women in the Sex Industry*, and has authored several papers on various aspects of sex work.

Jenn Clamen has been actively involved with the sex workers movement for four years. Originally from Canada, she spent two years in London, UK actively organizing with the International Union of Sex Workers (IUSW). She now resides in Montreal, Quebec and continues her work with the IUSW as a Canadian representative. Contact: jennifer.clamen@sympatico.ca

Maria Pia Covre, an unrepentant prostitute, was born in Milan and lives in Pordenone, Italy. In 1982, with Carla Corso and other prostitutes, she founded the Committee for the Civil Rights of Prostitutes. She has since become well known for her many initiatives aimed at raising public and political awareness concerning the reality of prostitution and the needs of women prostitutes. A tireless and tenacious activist, she has privately confessed that working as a prostitute was for her a very gratifying experience.

Maya Czajka has been a member of the Board of Directors of the German AIDS-Association since 1999, with responsibility for women's affairs and a range of other issues including the sex industry, drug use and people in prison. A former sex worker, she has been involved in the EUROPAP network since its beginning in 1993. Nowadays her freelance assignments include management consultancy, the provision of expert opinion for family courts, and training in HIV and STI prevention.

Sophie Day is an anthropologist at Goldsmiths College London. She helped found the Praed Street Project in 1986 and has carried out extensive research into the sex industry, both in the UK and Europe. She co-ordinated Europap with Helen Ward (1998-2000), and then became research co-ordinator of the network (2000-2003).

Jo Doezema has worked in the field of gender and development as a policy consultant, researcher and advocate for over a decade, with a specialisation in the areas of sex work, HIV/Aids, feminism and 'trafficking in women'. She is co-editor of the first book to profile the international sex worker rights movement: *Global Sex Workers: Rights, Resistance and Re-definition* (Routledge 1998). Currently, she is carrying out research at the Institute of Development Studies at the University of Sussex, Great Britain, examining the historical development of contemporary debates on trafficking in women. She is the board member for migration of the Network of Sex Work Projects, an international NGO which advocates for the human rights of sex workers. She is also a sex worker, with experience in exotic dancing and street, brothel, escort and window prostitution.

Liv Jessen qualified as a social worker in 1975, and for the past twenty years she has been a director of the Pro Centre, a national resource and social service centre on prostitution in Norway. She is a well-known public debater on all matters related to prostitution in her country.

Hilary Kinnell started the Safe Project in Birmingham in 1987, and managed the project until 1996. She has carried out research into the health and safety of sex workers in the UK, with particular focus on the relationship between vulnerability and legal status. She was the coordinator for Europap-UK from 1998 to 2002, and helped to found the UK Network of Sex Work Projects in 2002. She is currently the national coordinator for UKNSWP.

Don Kulick is professor of anthropology at New York University. He is the author of *Travesti: sex, culture and gender among Brazilian transgendered prostitutes* (University of Chicago Press, 1998), and is currently working on a book entitled *Good Sex in Sweden*.

Ana Lopez is completing her PhD at the University of East London. Her action research investigation has consisted in forming and developing the sex worker collective "The International Union of Sex Workers" and gaining official union recognition in the UK. She has been involved in the international sex workers' rights movement and has worked as a sex phone operator for the last four years.

MAIZ is an independent organisation active in Linz and Upper Austria that has been working with the problems of female migration and the situation of sex workers in Austria since 1994. MAIZ is an organisation from and for migrant women from many continents who are simultaneously protagonists and victims. It is active in the social, legal and employment advice and assistance, health protection for sex workers, education and public work, culture work, working with second generation migrants. Contact: www.servus.at/maiz

Rudolf Mak is a medical doctor and academic at the Department of Public Health, Ghent University, Belgium. He holds a Diploma in Venereology (London, 1984). He started working with sex workers in 1985. He is co-founder (1990) and president of PASOP, a NGO offering health and social services to sex workers in Flanders. He was coordinator of EUROPAP from 1993 till 1997.

Arne Randers-Pehrson qualified as a social worker in 1974 and has worked at the Pro Centre in Oslo, Norway since 1984. He is currently a senior advisor to the Centre, engaged primarily in documentation and the provision of information.

Thérèse van der Helm is a Public Health Nurse and coordinator of the Intermediary project for sex workers in Amsterdam. Together with her staff, including cultural mediators and public health nurses, she takes a leading role in health programs aimed at sex workers. She carried out research among sex workers and their clients in Amsterdam and she trains staff of health projects aimed at sex work in different developing countries. She was the National Coordinator of EUROPAP The Netherlands from 1993 to 2003.

Jan Visser is a sociologist and currently director of De Rode Draad, the Dutch prostitute rights organisation. From 1980–2001 he worked for the Mr A. de Graaf Stichting as policy advisor and researcher. In 1999 and 2001 he did research on the legalisation process in The Netherlands. He coordinated the policy work of Europap.

Helen Ward is a medical doctor and academic at Imperial College London. She helped found the Praed Street Project in 1986, and remains closely involved in its work to promote the health of sex workers. She has carried out research into health of sex workers in the UK and Europe, and coordinated the Europap network from 1998 to 2003. Contact: h.ward@imperial.ac.uk

Introduction

Introduction
Containing women: competing moralities in prostitution
Helen Ward and Sophie Day

Introduction

Prostitution is a significant part of the European landscape: the sex industry is a major employer today, attracting millions of customers. Images of 'the prostitute' shape the gender identity of men and women alike in both negative and positive ways: women may have to avoid red lipstick, longing for red shoes, for fear of being branded a whore; men may have to translate their emotions into hard cash through which they seduce. Men who sell sex themselves are often defined by their bodies, their looks, and they are labelled 'different'. Prostitution promotes a flurry of anxiety about boundaries, around gender, the family, the nation state, Fortress Europe... Since the times of the so-called White Slave Trade, states have implemented policies for controlling prostitution by containing women at home and unpaid as Wives and Mothers who are not allowed an existence independently of men, and containing women as prostitutes in separate zones, brothels or prisons. During the second half of the 20th century, women in Europe broke many of these constraints, making use of economic and social opportunities to join the workforce, live and travel independently. Prostitution appeared less central to the definition of women. Yet, contemporary alarm at the massive influx of women into Europe, called Trafficking, has once more prompted new, often contradictory, policies from states seeking both to defend the nation and restrict the space of prostitution as far as possible. As in the 19th century, prostitution is still

> the Enlightenment in nightmare form – a caricature of universalism, a network of global intercourse, of interchangeable private female parts loosed from the domestic into the public sphere, transforming the particular (my wife, your daughter) into a public woman accessible to all men. (Laura Engelstein 1992:300)

In some respects, the sex industry is more widely accepted today than a decade ago, largely because of the growth of a licit adult entertainment industry. But, in general, sex workers are no more respected than in the past; they continue to suffer abrogation of their fundamental rights. For example, sex workers still constitute a peculiar legal category in the UK, in which prior convictions are admissible in court. This procedure applies to no other defendant; in fact it only applies to women.[1] In other countries restrictions are placed on freedom of movement and employment.

With the growth of the sex industry we have seen a trend to increasing regulation by the state although there is no consensus at local, national or European levels about the most appropriate policies. In the Netherlands, for example, a long history of toleration has led to the formal recognition of brothels, which are now subject to regulations similar to those that apply to any other business. At the same time, the previous toleration of others – foreigners, drugs users, street workers – has all but vanished. Across much of Europe toleration takes a very defined and restrictive form, for example in the street zones where prostitutes must work. In Sweden, concerns about the status of women are cited in justification of recent criminal sanctions against the purchase of sex, and clients (men) as well as prostitutes (women) are now pressured to reform their behaviour. Elsewhere in Europe, public order legislation has been used to further restrict sex workers through fines, deportation, imprisonment and exclusion from public places. Street prostitution has been outlawed in Finland, for example.

Increased regulation has improved conditions of work in the legal sector for some women, who have protection from dangerous and abusive clients as well as managers. At the same time, some women are exploited more as employees than they were as freelance workers and, across Europe, sex workers have expressed concerns that they will be permanently monitored, labelled and stigmatised. Moreover, many in the current workforce are not entitled to work in the growing regulated sector, since a large proportion are migrants. They have no rights to reside or work in the host country and are therefore highly vulnerable to exploitation at work.

In contrast to the general disarray in Europe about the best prostitution policy, there is considerable consensus amongst governments who work together to limit in-migration to national labour requirements. Currently, there is a shortage of skilled workers in many sectors but those who do not demonstrate the necessary skills are aggressively excluded. Many of these excluded would-be migrants are women, often lacking formal qualifications, who want and need to move. They enter countries in the European Union on tourist and student visas, or illegally using agents ("traffickers"). Once in Europe, these women can only work informally, and many join the sex industry. In this way, restrictions on migration have a major impact on the sex industry.

Taken together, these developments have produced a single major debate about sex work today although, at first sight, it comprises two unrelated themes. Arguments to treat sex work simply as a business, subject to normal regulations of financing, profit, taxation and so forth have won support, in part because of the growing appeal of free market principles at the end of the 20th century in Europe. The sex industry is massive and there seems no reason to exempt it from taxation. At the same time, arguments about a double standard for men and women, accompanied by the belief that sex should not be traded as a commodity, have gained ground in the context of unprecedented inequality including the migration of poor people into Europe where they are depicted as victims, if not slaves. The weight of this second view in Europe derives largely from the influence of a feminism in social democracy which defines prostitution as violence against women; in other words, it is inherently and inevitably exploitative. These debates are about toleration (from an 'economic' perspective) on the one hand and abolition (from a 'moral' perspective) on the other. The apparent virtues of neo-liberalism and minimal state regulation, in which morality is left up to market forces, are opposed by those who consider that people cannot be commodities, in particular when these people are women who sell sexual labour.

This debate and the conditions that produced it have marginalised the politics of sex workers' rights and self-organisation. Since the 1970s, sex workers and other activists have organised for change so that sex work can become legitimate, work conditions reasonable and workers come to enjoy universal human rights. Through unionisation, social movements, identity politics and the civil rights movement more generally, sex workers have aspired to a participatory democracy in which workers play a key role. Until the 1980s, unions and other groups made progress on several fronts including opposition to discriminatory laws and attempts to liberalise attitudes to sexuality; alliances were also cemented with other workers, feminists, gay and lesbian groups.

Progress was blocked, however, in the 1980s from a number of directions. AIDS of course deflected activists towards immediate and specific goals. But sex workers also found that the neoliberal principles, which do indeed advocate toleration, worked to the benefit of employers and not workers. Potential allies among brothel owners or business managers in practice opposed unionisation effectively and with great vehemence. More unexpectedly, sex workers also found that feminists opposed idioms of choice in sex work so extensively that it has become difficult to see how a broad feminist alliance could ever be built to improve conditions. Hysteria about trafficked women and children forced to work in the sex industry dominates much discussion of prostitution policy today. In this way, the regulation of migration rather than sex work per se, has had the greatest impact on the workforce.

The European Network for HIV/STD Prevention in Prostitution (Europap)

This book is the result of a long collaboration between health workers, sex workers and academics. In the 1980s, many people assumed that sex workers in Europe would acquire HIV/AIDS and they imagined that sex workers would soon be forcibly tested and licensed in order to control this frightening new disease. A number of health workers and researchers, ourselves included, began to explore these issues and established a research project to look at the social and epidemiological aspects of HIV risk in prostitution. In the course of this research, we found very different levels of service provision and health promotion for sex workers in the different settings, related to the legal and social position of sex workers, as well as variation in health care and AIDS programmes. A group of us therefore decided to establish a network to promote and evaluate health programmes for sex workers. After a period of negotiation, Europap[2] was established in 1993 and funded in part by the European Commission through the Europe Against Aids Programme.

This network thus arose through concerns about HIV in the 1980s, and, in particular, assumptions that sex workers would both acquire and transmit infection. Our initial research, and Europap, were funded largely through HIV monies and not through programmes addressing equity, rights or employment. However, many participants were uncomfortable with this narrow focus, and without underestimating the gravity of HIV, we have successfully broadened the network to reflect equally important issues in sex work including rights, gender, policy and other health issues such as violence. In addition the network reflects positive experiences of the sex industry and the powerful contribution of self-organisation. The network has focused largely on female sex work, as does this book since we did not feel that we could do justice to the very different legal and social circumstances in which men sell sex, and to the differing questions about health.[3]

There have been six different phases of Europap, spanning the last ten years. Europap was initially coordinated by Rudolf Mak at the University of Gent in Belgium, and we (SD and HW) were part of the Steering Committee prior to taking over the coordination in 1998. Europap was successful in extending beyond the initial health and social work focus to include sex worker organisations. In the first two phases we focused on finding out about sex work in the different countries, supporting exchange visits, new health promotion initiatives, and organising regular meetings for people from all the participating countries. This phase culminated in the publication of a book reporting baseline information. (Mak ed., 1996) In the next two phases we worked jointly with Tampep who ran demonstration projects for migrant sex workers in four European countries. We focussed on identifying good practice in health promotion and health care, producing statements on policy, and a manual, *Hustling for Health*, for project workers. (European Network for HIV/STD Prevention in Prostitution, 1999) This has been widely translated and used across Europe.

In 2000, we turned towards new issues at the European level, particularly addressing the impact of major changes such as increased mobility in the workforce and changing policies both on prostitution and migration. The number of countries and projects included in the network has expanded as the European Union has enlarged and we organised a conference of 180 people in 2002 from all the countries of the European Union in addition to states in the process of joining the Union and on its peripheries so as to bring this new network of people together.

This book looks at recent changes in the European sex industry with respect to histories of activism, the increasing mobility of sex workers, policy developments and health, focusing largely on women. Clearly these four themes are intertwined, but we start, after a broad overview of social and economic change in Europe (chapter 1), with a collection of histories from sex worker activists, a recognition of how often they are silenced or marginalised.

Histories

In much of the current discourse on sex work, the voice of key players such as sex workers is missing as others stand up to (mis)-represent their views.

Doezema (chapter 2), in a talk given to our conference on sex work in Europe, reflects on her experience of an apparent culture clash between practitioners who promote health and fight AIDS on the one hand, and activists who fight trafficking, on the other. She has clearly found it relatively refreshing to work on health, where issues of rights and sex worker participation are widely accepted, rather than in the anti-trafficking arena where debates still rage around prostitution as violence and slavery or as work. But she points to the weakness of leaving this anti-trafficking arena for the more comfortable health milieu. Many health workers, and some sex worker organisations, have become immersed in practical issues of preventing AIDS and delivering services, and they often explicitly put 'moral' issues to one side (see, for example, chapter 9). While they distribute condoms and support women in trouble, remembering periodically to oppose laws that get in the way of 'accessing' sex workers, the political playing field has been abandoned to the ideologues of the abolitionist movement. This movement, rooted in Christian churches, social democracy and reformist feminism, has turned from the infertile ground of abolishing all prostitution to the more promising area of abolishing trafficking.

Lopez and Clamen (chapter 3) provide a brief history of sex workers' movements in recent years, and discuss the parallels and overlaps with other social movements and the labour movement. They recount how they formed the International Union of Sex Workers in the UK, their successful fight to gain recognition and affiliation to a major trade union, and effective campaigns in recent years. The trade union model for organisation is a powerful one, and promises to move debates from those around the 'existence' (or abolition) of sex work to that of 'rights' for workers. They discuss the practical obstacles to unionisation, including the difficulties of organising a semi-legal or illegal sector, and the challenge of winning wider sections of the workers' movement to the need for decriminalisation. There are, of course, many limitations to this 'syndicalist' approach to sex work. For example, there is the danger identified by Doezema in the previous chapter with reference to health programmes: organising on the basic economic issues of conditions and contracts will leave the 'moral' or 'political' field to the abolitionists who are steadily making progress with their newfound anti-slavery issue in the form of an anti-trafficking campaign.

One key argument in favour of regarding prostitution as work is that such normalisation can challenge the overwhelming stigmatisation of prostitutes that leads to their abuse. Lopez and Clamen point out, "Eradicating sex work is often proposed as a solution to eliminate violence against sex workers. It is seldom realised that the laws that prohibit activities related to commercial sex . . . stigmatise sex workers which in turn 'justifies' violence against sex workers" (p. 50).

Maya Czajka (chapter 4) describes the complex implications of law reform in Germany, a change resulting from an explicit commitment to 'improve the legal and social situation of prostitutes'. The new law removed the stipulation that a contract between a sex worker and client should be considered an offence against public decency. But the amendment has not lived up to the expectation of many sex workers who lobbied for decades for legal reform – such contracts are still not 'normalised' and sex workers have not gained the same status as other workers. Czajka, an activist in the German Whores Movement since 1989, tells the story of how sex workers have fought for legal recognition, demanding that sex workers have rights and responsibilities like other workers. Sex workers built a movement, forged alliances; they have been promised and then betrayed along the way. Her chapter is a sad but elegant demonstration of the limitations of social movements that become caught up in the tantalising respectability of mainstream political lobbying.

Pia Covre (chapter 5) offers an illustration with her description of prostitutes suffering abuse on the streets of Italy in 1982. The U.S. military, backed by local police, harassed local women until they assembled, protested and formed a committee for the Civil Rights of Prostitutes. In her chapter, Covre recounts the history of this association, from a strike of students in 1984 against 'censorship' of prostitutes, who were not allowed to speak to students, to the recent campaigns against new repressive laws that threaten to criminalise all street prostitution. Once again, the sex workers' movement, preoccupied with improving the lives of sex workers through health work and anti-AIDS campaigns, appears to have been outmanoeuvred on the political front by anti-traffickers, together with powerful interests from the Vatican to the Mafia, who have taken the initiative to contain prostitutes within regulated brothels.

Mobility and migration

In the second section of the book, we consider mobility and migration. Laura Agustín challenges dominant images of women who migrate. Such women are not generally ascribed the resourcefulness of men who travel for work; to the contrary, they are regarded as victims who are trafficked, or otherwise 'forced' by circumstance to leave home. Agustin points to the many other reasons why women, like men, travel. She urges us to credit mobile women with the skills and ambition necessary to get ahead in "strange places" such as the cosmopolitan urban centres of Europe.

There are more words directly from migrant sex workers in chapter 7 from MAIZ. A series of interviews reveal a varied group of women, often with multiple 'stigmata' – being black, sex workers, poor and foreign. These are women who refused to resign themselves to poverty in their country of origin and set out on a path of migration. Sex work is not their goal, but a means to an end; the goal is to establish some financial independence so that they can send money back to their families, and settle in Europe with a degree of stability. These are not 'career' prostitutes, yet they still want to have pride in their work and to maintain self-respect.

In 2000 in the Netherlands, brothels were legalised and registered (see also chapter 15). Therese van der Helm, who has worked as a public health nurse in the Netherlands for almost 30 years, describes the increasing mobility of workers in Chapter 8 and shows how the new legislation has had an impact on the delivery of health care. In a discussion of 'trafficking', van der Helm illustrates contrasting perspectives. A social worker describes what she sees working with Eastern European sex workers, who have suffered "abominable" lives. However Lisa, a 'trafficked' sex worker, offers a different perspective that stresses the iniquities of state systems of control. She repeats the story of debt and money paid to men, but she holds no romantic view of returning home; she is there to stay. "We are survivors", she insists. The new law, purportedly designed to improve conditions for sex workers, is not making Lisa's life easier. Earlier toleration of both migrants in general and sex workers has been supplanted by controls and enforcement that are driving sex workers underground or out of the country. Health services are no longer able to work closely and effectively with migrant sex workers, as van der Helm explains.

Health

In the third section, we address some of the health issues relevant to sex workers in Europe. Ruud Mak, who coordinated a working group on health services for sex workers in the last Europap programme, reports on the wide variation in health care available for sex workers. Where accessible services exist, they often focus narrowly on infection risks and ignore the broader range of health issues linked to sex work, including the results of violence and stigma. This group used available evidence to develop guidelines for health workers to improve the quality of care in different European settings.[4]

We (SD and HW) address the complex interrelationship between stigma and health in the subsequent two chapters. In the first (chapter 10), we look at the way sex work has been represented in relation to disease, and attempt to disentangle the web linking sex work, infection and migration. We report results of empirical research across Europe, on behalf of the Europap health survey group, showing relatively low levels of risk of infectious diseases, such as HIV, in migrants and natives alike. Yet a debate remains – what stigmatises more, research that produces 'facts' that may challenge (or revise?) labels, or a focus on resisting the labels per se, and thus resisting any attempt to research these facts?

In chapter 11 we look at the multiple ways in which stigma affects health. There is the direct impact of stigma that labels sex workers less than human and suitable targets for violence, for example, but there are equally destructive consequences realised over a longer period of time. We report a longitudinal study of sex workers we have known since the 1980s, and propose a model to better understand how stigma affects health.

In the final chapter on health, Hilary Kinnell documents the extent of violence in the sex industry, including the murder and rape of sex workers. This systematic abuse is often overlooked, ignored by the authorities, and justified by the press who distinguish sex workers from 'innocent' victims. Kinnell argues that some feminists have undermined the struggle to expose and oppose this violence: if prostitution is seen as violence per se, then rape is integral and inevitable; the only answer is to abolish prostitution. Indeed, some feminists insist that promoting safety for sex workers is to collude in continued violence since fewer women will be deterred from entering sex work. Kinnell counters this argument as follows: if sex work were recognised and acts between consenting adults no longer subject to state interference, more attention could be paid to interventions that improve the safety of workers, and deal with the perpetrators of serious crimes.

Policy

The final section of the book draws together many of these themes in a consideration of policy. Liv Jessen, a social worker from Norway, provides a personal account of her own journey away from the common belief across Scandinavia that prostitution is inevitably violence against women. Installed at Pro-Centre in Oslo, she describes how she learned from sex workers little by little that this view of prostitution can intensify the problems of sex workers and undermine attempts more generally to improve the status of women. Jessen provides key insights into the national context where many feminists reject images that split women into whores and madonnas, yet conclude nonetheless that whores are still victims in need of protection.

Policy on prostitution has been greatly influenced by different feminisms over the years, and the Swedish government has implemented a legal change to reflect the view that prostitution is violence against women. In most of Europe, it is the sale of sex and its organisation that are criminalised. In Sweden, men who pay for sex are now subject to sanction as well. Such a policy would be seen as a major infringement of civil liberties in most countries, but Sweden has a strong history of state intrusion into what are frequently considered private or domestic spheres. The extensive state provision of services and welfare is linked to a notion of citizenship that defines rights, responsibilities and civilised behaviour; citizens do not smack their children or purchase sex.

Don Kulick (chapter 14) situates the Swedish law in the context of entry into the European Union. He considers it a response to fears of a flood of foreign prostitutes and embeds legal reform in concerns about borders that are becoming permeable to external values and moralities as well as people and money. He also points to the symbolism of the law – it is designed to send a message that "prostitution does not belong in our country" rather than frighten perpetrators. The implementation of the law has been limited, confined to a handful of prosecutions against men, and a more repressive approach to women who are increasingly difficult to reach with health messages.

This discussion of policy is concluded in chapter 15 by the Europap policy group led by Jan Visser. There is no neutral way to discuss policy, and there are as many ways to ask the questions about the 'problem' of prostitution as there are views on the answers. The earlier sections of the book on activism, migration and health demonstrate the importance of labels and of differing perspectives. Nowhere is this clearer than in the field of policy. Visser et al note how changes in prostitution in Europe - the increasingly mobile workforce, drug use, the growth of the adult entertainment industry, more workers, more male sex workers - have led to a larger, more diverse industry that is less easy to control. Hence, there has been an explosion in political debates about reform, which remain largely in the realm of the moral rather than the economic.

We describe the broad approaches that have been applied to prostitution – regulation, abolition, prohibition and decriminalisation – and explain the differences between broad policies, laws and practice. We look in detail at the legal changes in The Netherlands, including the intertwining of debates on immigration and prostitution. By defining a legal sector for local sex workers, the state has granted itself more powers to hunt down and deport dangerous outsiders. Assumptions that such outsiders are slaves (trafficked) help deepen the divide between insider and outsider. As in the case of Sweden, prostitution control is deeply rooted in notions of national integrity.

We demonstrate similarities between the apparently contrasting policies in the Netherlands and Sweden, with the former treating prostitution as work and the latter as violence. In particular, we note increased state powers to control and exclude 'aliens'.

Conclusion

This rather pessimistic note is echoed in the reflections of Priscilla Alexander, a long time activist for sex workers in the USA, in conclusion to the book. Alexander expresses disappointment with the impact of the 'decriminalisation' that has occurred in the Netherlands and, to some extent, in Germany. Commenting on the situation in Europe from a country where the repression of sex workers is extreme, she is also heartened by the debates, the increasing profile of sex workers organisations and the many positive alliances between sex workers and health workers.

We understand and share the disappointment about reform revealed by many of the contributors to this collection. But it is not surprising that legal reforms, self-organisation and projects have not transformed the situation. Prostitution is rooted in both the social *and* the economic organisation of society, and defined in the negative – it is non-reproductive sex, outside the 'accepted' forum of the family – and it does not have an accepted positive definition as work. Deep beliefs linking sex with reproduction persist, underpinning sexism, heterosexism and the oppression of prostitution. At one and the same time, prostitution subverts the family and props it up. Prostitution provides a space, variously controlled, in which men can have extramarital, non-reproductive sex. While there has been considerable liberalisation in views on sexuality, dominant interests still consider commercial sex, where women earn money from men without any long-term commitment, unacceptable. To transform prostitution into sex work, a legitimate profession, would challenge the way we view the family, reproduction, gender and, as we see in the discussions on Europe, national identity. So long as reproduction, and with it sexuality, is contained within a private sphere, and work defined through public exchange, prostitution will continue to be a challenging anomaly. We have a long way to go, but we hope that this collection will be a positive contribution to the debate.

Notes

[1] This legal situation is currently (2004) being reviewed by the British government as part of a broad review of prostitution and the law.
[2] The name Europap was agreed by the largely non-English members of the Steering Committee, and has always been the subject of great amusement to English speakers. Europap was not quite an acronym, the full name being 'European Intervention Projects Aids Prevention for Prostitutes', and has unfortunate connotations of baby food, intellectual rubbish or breast in English! However, the name has stuck, and in the third phase, was elaborated with the sub-heading 'European Network for HIV/STD Prevention in Prostitution.'
[3] See www.enmp.org for more on male sex work.
[4] These guidelines are available in twelve European languages, and can be downloaded from www.europap.net (under services).

References

Engelstein, Laura (1992). *The Keys to Happiness: Sex and the Search for Modernity in Fin-de-Siècle Russia*. Ithaca: Cornell University Press.
European Network for HIV/STD Prevention in Prostitution (1999). *Hustling for Health: Developing Health Services for Sex Workers*. London: Imperial College.
Mak, R ed (1996). *Europap: European Intervention Projects, AIDS Prevention for Prostitutes*. Gent: Academia Press.

14

Chapter 1
Sex work in context
Helen Ward and Sophie Day

Introduction

Sex work is highly sensitive to changes in social conditions, as it is influenced both by economic and employment issues and by the way that families, relationships and sexuality are organised. In order to understand and interpret changes in prostitution, we start with a description and analysis of the major social transformations of recent decades.[1] 'Macro' socio-economic changes of the past two decades include the collapse of the state economies of Central and Eastern Europe and the Russian Federation, the 'globalisation' of the world economy, and related trends in women's employment.

We then briefly describe migration patterns within and into Western Europe, and the related issue of European integration. A summary follows of the changing structures of families and households in Europe, linked intimately to these employment changes, and we consider how these have affected sexuality, including commercialisation and the commodification of sex. This broad background will be used to explore the changes observed in the sex industry, including the size and structure of the industry, the workers, clients and managers involved. Finally we will look at the implications of such changes for health and policy.

Women and the market: experience of transition

In the last two decades there have been more rapid social, political and economic changes in Europe than at any time since the period immediately following the Second World War. The most dramatic change has been the demise of the former state socialist economies through a combination of internal collapse, popular unrest and external pressure. The hopes of the millions who rose up to topple Ceaucescu, to oust Hoeneker or to support Yeltsin in the late 1980s and early 1990s were for freedom, democracy and the opportunities they perceived, rightly or wrongly, in the west. Under the old regimes there was no democracy, heavy repression and limited opportunities. But there were jobs and incomes for most people, and extensive, if poor quality, social provision of schools, child-care and health services.

Secure employment has gone, and women have been particularly affected by unemployment. In a period of history where women's formal employment has been expanding almost everywhere, Eastern Europe is the only area of the world where there has been a decline in the proportion of women in formal employment. (United Nations Development Fund for Women 2000) From 1985 to 1997, women's employment fell by 40 per cent in Hungary, 31 per cent in Estonia, 33 per cent in Latvia, 24 per cent in Lithuania, 21 per cent in Russia, 16 per cent in Slovenia, 12 per cent in the Czech Republic and 13 per cent in Poland. From 1985 to 1997, there was a decline in the proportion of girls going to school in 66 per cent of Eastern European countries. (World Bank 2001)

There is now increasing inequality between men and women. Before 1989, women's wages in CEE/FSU were 20 per cent to 25 per cent lower than men's. This differential has increased: in the Russian Federation, for example, women's wages declined from 70 per cent of men's in 1989 to 55 per cent in 1997. (Russian National Human Development Report, 1999) The loss of formal employment opportunities in the transitional economies[2] is a result of economic restructuring, with the closure of state industries and loss of government subsidies leading to massive job losses. This loss has not been gender neutral: women's unemployment has grown faster than men's.

While the first period of restructuring in the early 1990s saw women losing jobs more rapidly than men, official figures show lower levels of unemployment among women than men in many transitional economies more recently. However, looked at more closely, this shift can be attributed in practice to the withdrawal of women from the formal labour market due to the combination of a lack of formal work opportunities and increased need to work in the home due to declining social and welfare support. (Lim 2002, Ruminska-Zimmy 2002)

Following the initial job losses, the growth of new work opportunities has been generally more beneficial to men than to women. The pattern of women's employment is coming to resemble the west of Europe in that it is highly segregated, lower paid and includes many part time and temporary jobs. Ideological arguments have been advanced in support of this inequality, with right wing parties and organised religious groups promoting the 'liberation' of women from their forced participation in the workforce under state socialism, and encouraging a return to the home and to caring roles. (Ruminska-Zimmy 2002:18) Not surprisingly, these rapid economic changes have led many women to look to the informal sector for work and to migrate. Hence the numbers of women in the sex industry have increased, both within these new market economies and in other European states to which women have moved.

Globalisation

The second major development affecting Europe is 'globalisation'. North American and European multinational companies have lobbied the International Monetary Fund (IMF), World Bank and the World Trade Organisation successfully over the last two decades to open domestic markets to greater inward flows of funds and merchandise. (Stiglitz 2002) National regulatory frameworks collapsed and international trade and investment have increased.

The World Bank and IMF have used their control over loans to ensure production for export and a decrease in public spending in many and, especially, the poorest countries, resulting in the loss of subsistence production and the expansion of agriculture and factories producing commodities for export, many with appalling sweat-shop conditions. Women working in these new factories are forced to change their lives outside work.

One aspect of free trade is that capital – the money invested in factories and stock markets – can be moved anywhere in the world to find the cheapest production costs. Textile production in Europe and North America has declined massively as production has shifted to Latin America and latterly Asia, especially China, where workers have been less well organised, wages are lower and there are fewer laws regulating the exploitation of workers and the environment. Recently, jobs have been exported as massive call centres (telephone service centres) were moved from the UK to India. The mobility of capital is mirrored in increasing mobility among workers but most individuals looking for work have to move illegally in difficult conditions.

When new factories close as quickly as they open and traditional employment has gone, workers tend to look first within their country or in neighbouring countries for some source of income. Today, increasing numbers seek to migrate to wealthier countries of Western Europe and North America (OECD 2003).

In Western Europe, large-scale manufacturing has declined and with it much of the secure, long-term employment that characterised the decades after the Second World War. The drive towards the opening of markets in less developed countries has also affected the European Union. Since Thatcher's radical restructuring of the UK economy in the 1980s, neo-liberalism has gained broad acceptance. Jobs are now less secure, more people are working part time and on temporary contracts, and social welfare entitlement has been cut back. Economic inequalities have increased and the structure of employment for women and men has altered.

Women have continued to participate more and more in the workforce. They have always worked, both inside and outside the home, but now the majority of women, including those with children, are 'formally' employed almost everywhere. This shift in the workforce constitutes one of the most notable developments of the last thirty years. In the European Union, the number of women in waged labour increased from 29 per cent of women in 1970 to 52 per cent in 1998 (European Commission 2000a). The increase reflects the decline in traditional manufacturing and extraction industries, continued growth of the service sector and greater expectations as well as educational achievements on the part of women.

Women's work differs from men's, and includes a large proportion of part-time and flexible workers. For example, 15 per cent of female workers in the European Union are on fixed term contracts, one-third of which are for less than six months. For the under-20s this figure rises to 48 per cent. (Eurostat 2002:1) Many women work part time because of lack of childcare, and women continue to take primary responsibility for their families and homes.

Migration

These economic and social changes have promoted migration into and within Western Europe. In the early 1990s there was considerable migration from Eastern to Western Europe, but this slowed considerably in the mid-1990s as restrictions on movement were introduced. (OECD 2003) During the 1990s, migration from Asia, sub-Saharan Africa and Central and Latin America has also increased. In the early 1990s there was a net in-migration of people at the rate of 3.1 per 1000 population for the European Economic Area (EAA), this fell to 1.7/1000 in 1995-9, and rose to 2.5/1000 in 2000. These official data exclude those who enter as visitors or students.

Towards the end of the 1990s and early 2000s there has been a sharp rise in employment-related migration due to growing skills shortages in many European countries. An increasing proportion of the migrants entering Western Europe are women.

The relationship between migration and sex work is complex. While many migrants enter Western Europe with the right to study and work, others enter as tourists or illegally. For all these groups, economic survival can be difficult; some choose, and a few are coerced into, the sex industry. For migrants with the right to work, openings are restricted. Even official statistics show that legal migrants have higher rates of unemployment than nationals, and migrant women are more likely to be unemployed than men. (OECD 2003) In Belgium, for example, 16.5 per cent of migrant women are unemployed compared with 7.0 per cent of nationals; in Sweden 13.0 per cent compared with 4.6 per cent, Italy 21.3 per cent compared with 13.9 per cent. The work available is often low paid, low status and with little security.

For those without the right to work, including many asylum seekers, there are even fewer options. With no legal papers, they are forced into the informal economy. Sex work is not the only sector; many will work in catering, hotels and domestic service. All these sectors provide work to those without work permits, and the sex industry has provided some with sufficient income and flexibility to create the social capital, for example qualifications and skills, to ensure their longer-term security.

European integration

The countries of the European Union have become increasingly integrated over the last two decades and more countries will join the Union in the near future. Enlargement will have a major impact on internal mobility – millions more people joining the EU will gain the right to move and work anywhere. Yet, at the same time, EU governments and EU institutions are collaborating to restrict immigration, and to put in place some restrictions to health care and welfare rights for the newer citizens.

There are a number of different levels of unification within the EU, ranging from primary legislation that take precedence over national law in the realm of trade, for example, to formal agreements and co-operations. The area of public health is covered by Article 152 of the EC Treaty, introduced by the Treaty of Maastricht and strengthened by the Treaty of Amsterdam, which supports community level action to "focus on the prevention of illnesses, including drug addiction, by promoting research into their causes and their transmission, as well as health information and education". This may involve Community level measures but is generally based on "cooperation", with no requirement of common implementation.[2]

The Women's Rights Committee of the European Parliament has recently considered the consequences of the sex industry for the EU (see chapter 10), but it is unlikely that this will lead to any common legislation on any aspect other than opposition to trafficking. However, the adoption of shared legislation on human rights and business practices may enable some future challenge to be made to the widely varying policies on prostitution within the EU. For example, it is difficult to defend, on human rights grounds, how brothel keeping can result in imprisonment in one EU country while being considered a legitimate business elsewhere. On the other hand, member states are likely to vigorously oppose attempts to impose common laws requiring the recognition of sex work.

The increased cooperation in the field of public health has led to European Commission support for networks such as Europap, Tampep and ENMP which facilitate the sharing of experience.[3] With the end of the Europe Against AIDS programme the future of such cooperation is in doubt.

Changes to family, household and sexuality

A 'traditional' model of the family and household in Western Europe, albeit with clear variations by country, is the nuclear family: a heterosexual couple marry in their early to mid-twenties and they have a couple of children, cared for by the mother who gives up work for several years while the man goes out to earn the money. They then stay together for better or worse until retirement.

This model, never realised in practice by the majority, nonetheless informed social policies until very recently, and still does in some countries. We were expected to live most of our lives in the family or marital home. But this 'norm' is moving ever further from reality.

Many women choose not to marry, and their average age at the time of first marriage is increasing across Europe. Marriage is less popular, with the rate decreasing by almost 40 per cent from 1960 to 1995 (MISSOC 2002). For those who do marry, one in three will now divorce, compared with one in 15 during the 1960s. The number of children born to a woman has declined, stabilising at 1.42, with more of these children being born later in a woman's life (MISSOC 2002).[4]

With a decline in marriage and an increase in divorce, household structures have changed. From 1981 to 1996 in urban centres in Europe, the size of the average household has decreased (from 2.8 people to 2.3), the number of people living alone has risen (from 27 per cent to 38 per cent) and the proportion of lone-parent households has increased (from 6.5 per cent to 7.5 per cent, European Commission 2000b). More people are living in a variety of household arrangements: single people with friends, gay couples and friends, step-families.

These changes, rooted primarily in women's new opportunities in employment and education, have inevitably had an impact on sexuality. Although difficult to measure, a number of surveys have shown that sexual behaviour is changing quite rapidly. For example, with more people spending a greater proportion of their adult life alone, never married, or divorced, they are likely to have larger numbers of sexual partners, either in serial monogamy or concordant relationships.

A large UK survey found that 43.7 per cent of all men were single or previously married. This group accounted for 81 per cent of the new sexual partnerships formed by men. A similar proportion (77.8 per cent) of new partnerships were made by 37.6 per cent of women (Johnson AM 2001). Two surveys found an increase from 1990 to 2000 in numbers of heterosexual partners, the proportion reporting homosexual partnerships and the numbers of concurrent partnerships; young people were having their first sexual experiences at an earlier age than ten years previously (Johnson AM 2001, Wellings 2001).

The major social movements that Europe experienced during the second half of the twentieth century have played a central role in many of these developments, closely linked to, and acting as a catalyst for, the restructuring of work and family. The women's liberation movement of the 1960s and 1970s, while far from achieving even its limited early goals, played a major part in changing women's expectations; women are less likely to stay in abusive or unhappy marriages, they assume they will have equal rights to education and work outside of the home, and expect an enjoyable sex life with a degree of control over their fertility.

Lesbian, gay, bisexual and transgender people are more open about their sexuality and demand respect as well as an end to repression. The growth of the prostitutes' movement in the 1970s is linked to these broader social movements and the successes of the labour movement (see chapter 3).

Changes in the sex industry

How have changes in employment and migration affected sex work as an occupation? How do the changes in family, household and ideology impact on the demand for commercial sex?

Both the increase in migration and the restructuring of internal labour markets have created the conditions for an increase in the numbers of people in Europe who turn to sex work at one or more points in their lives. The sex industry provides flexible and relatively well-paid work to those with restricted employment opportunities. The workforce will include migrants who have come to Europe in search of work since there is little in their home countries, students who cannot afford to live only on a grant or loan, those who have lost relatively well-paid jobs or whose businesses have closed, and young people who no longer have rights to benefits. While sex work is not inevitable for people in these situations, it is one of several options that can be considered more attractive than serious poverty.

There have also been changes to the structure and operation of the sex industry that may have lowered the threshold for entry, making it more accessible. In the past, new recruits often needed some form of introduction, frequently through a friend. Few would simply apply for a job.[5] Today it is easy to register with an agency on-line, advertise using a mobile phone that cannot be traced to your home address, or start work in one of the increasing numbers of virtually licit sex clubs.

However, there are no reliable data on the numbers of sex workers, and most presumptions of an increase are based on anecdotal reports or spurious estimates using police, health service or social work data. Through the Europap network we have developed estimates of the numbers of sex workers in some cities and countries, presented in the table. These are very crude, and range from 0.3 per thousand population in Sweden, to 3.8 in Germany. The average is around 1.4 sex workers per thousand population, which would suggest at least half a million sex workers in Europe. It is important to be cautious with these data, since they are based on extrapolations, and do not share a common definition: some are based on the numbers of people who are actively working at any one point in time, or over a period of time such as a year; others are based on the numbers of people who have ever, or sometimes still do, work in the industry. Some include all sectors, including adult entertainment, while others have a more limited definition of sex work.

Estimates of the numbers of prostitutes in different European countries

Country (city)	Number of Prostitutes	Sex workers per 1000 population
Austria	unknown	
(Vienna)	(6,000)	3.0
Belgium	12,000	1.2
Denmark	6,000	1.2
Finland	4,000	0.7
Germany	300,000	3.8
Greece	10,500 –15,000	1.2
Italy	60,000	1.0
Luxembourg	300	0.7
Norway	3,000	0.7
Sweden	2,500	0.3
The Netherlands	25,000	1.6
United Kingdom	80,000	1.3

Source: Europap country reports and Regional reports 1996 – 2001, available on www.europap.net.

It is even more difficult to find out about trends. Police data, for example, on numbers of arrests for prostitution-related offences will primarily reflect policies and priorities on arrests and prosecution rather than true trends of the numbers working. In the UK the numbers of women arrested for soliciting has declined over recent years due to a shift from street to indoor work, itself the result of intensive policing. Reports from sex work projects suggest an increasing turnover of people involved.

Turning from considerations affecting the supply of sex workers, what of the demand for commercial sex? If there are more people in short term relationships and living alone for longer periods of their lives, is there also an increase in the numbers of people looking for commercial sex?

Most anecdotal reports suggest an increase in the size of the sex industry, but this is difficult to quantify due to the illegal and hidden nature of much of the trade. Data on numbers of men (despite the social changes described above, clients are almost all male) who pay for sex are very limited. The UK survey cited above found that the numbers of men who reported having paid women for sex in the previous five years had doubled from 2.1 per cent in 1990 to 4.3 per cent in 2000. In London the proportion was even higher: in 2000, 8.9 per cent of men had paid a woman for sex in the previous five years. Using population estimates for the UK, slightly more than half a million men aged 16-44 will have paid for sex within the past five years.

The increased proportion of men reporting the purchase of sexual services may be due in part to a greater social acceptability of commercial sex, but it seems likely that there has also been a true increase. A so-called backlash against feminism is widely reported along with an increasingly mainstream use of sexist imagery that contributes to a stronger sense of sex as a commodity. In the 1980s and 1990s 'commodity fetishism' increased, a cult of consumerism fanned by a sharp rise in disposable income.

The high life associated with, for example, city traders and successful entrepreneurs included fast cars, luxury holidays, expensive drugs and, for many, beautiful escorts to share. The growing inequalities in income over the past two decades fuel this trend: more wealthy young single men, and more poor young unemployed men and women redistribute some of the accumulated wealth amongst themselves through the selling and buying of sex.

Within transitional economies, the newly emerging market has also produced increasing inequalities, and more men have spare money to buy sex along with other trappings of western culture. There are widespread reports of a massive growth in pornography and visible prostitution within these countries.

Cheaper international travel and a growth in the number of international cultural, business and sporting events also fuels prostitution. There were an estimated 10,000 additional sex workers in Sydney during the Olympic Games in 2000; the authorities in Athens are proposing to open an additional 230 brothels to cope with increased 'need' for sex workers when the Games are held in 2004 (Smith 2003).

These developments in male consumerism and valued masculinities have most likely combined with the changes described above, affecting both men and women, to increase the supply of male clients in the sex industry.

With more workers and more clients, the sex industry has also diversified. Reports suggest an increase in male, migrant and transgender sex workers and in more specialist services. New technologies have enabled much of the advertising to be conducted through electronic media. In theory, sex workers can now set up their own websites, use mobile phones and recruit clients directly. In this way, they should be able to bypass the endless middlemen and brokers who manage the sex industry at local and international levels.

However, it is clear that businesses have also developed to manage sex work websites, to advise on the new legal issues and to help with promotion and advertising. Escort businesses have shifted to the Internet and many have become global in scope with respect both to the workers they manage and to the clients they serve. Therefore, new technologies have permitted both greater independence on the part of some workers and promoted new business practices that manage and exploit the workforce in different ways.

Legal changes such as the recognition of sex work businesses in The Netherlands, and the relaxation of film censorship laws in the UK, have allowed big business to gain more of a hold over this previously marginalised, albeit massive, industry (see chapter 15). However, in most of Europe, sex work is not legal and businesses making money from the sale of sex work are heavily criminalized and considered morally illegitimate. In such a climate, 'business interests' in the form of corruption dominate all sectors of the industry: pimps and madams manage local areas and larger interests manage the supply of premises, internet sites and even workers in the form of 'trafficking' (whether voluntary or not).[6]

Given the continued fear and stigma attached to prostitutes, a new and deadly sexually transmitted infection was inevitably going to attract attention. Many people assumed that sex workers would be central to the transmission of HIV in Europe at the end of the twentieth century (see chapter 10). They thought to slow the spread of disease by regulating the industry more closely and testing all the workers. Evidence contradicting these assumptions was produced which showed that sex workers have a varied risk, depending primarily on factors other than their occupation, but the argument still continues. [7]

The impact of HIV has been contradictory. It has focussed attention on sex workers, and hundreds of projects have been created to carry out health promotion, including some funding for self-help and peer education initiatives. Through some of these initiatives, including Europap itself, sex workers have been able to advocate a more holistic approach to health in which HIV / STI prevention and care occur alongside more generic occupational health services (see chapters 9 and 10). At the same time, this attention has renewed the process of stigmatisation, often focused on the 'prostitute' who looks most dangerous because she comes from another country, because she is diseased or drug-addicted.

Liberation of exploitation?

The sex industry is larger and more visible across Europe and it has attracted mixed reactions from activists. Conservative religious and moral values associated with the nuclear family, it has been argued, lead only to the repression and denial of sexuality, to violence against women and sexual minorities, and to widespread unhappiness. But the increased toleration of consensual, even commercial, sex in recent years is not necessarily based on an ideology of liberation or happiness.

The same fundamental social relations of poverty and gender inequality apply to commercial sex, as to any other occupation, and access to sexual freedom remains unequal. Some enjoy increased sexual freedom, including those who identified with practices that were previously repressed. Others appear to suffer even greater pressure to conform to a set of sexual stereotypes that still include 'available, passive women' and 'predator men'.

Social movements have divided on these issues. For example, some feminists are opposed to all pornography while others argue for an end to censorship and for more images that will appeal to women. Similar contradictory reactions have greeted changes in the sex industry. Mainstream or liberal feminism is now incorporated into many traditional political parties, parliaments, NGOs and international agencies, and has taken the view that prostitution is simply exploitation or violence against women, which should be opposed at all costs. At the other extreme, sex worker activists and their supporters argue that sex work is a legitimate choice, one that should be respected as a profession, and that sex workers should be proud of their contribution to society. In this debate, some distinguish voluntary from coerced prostitution, but still see little to recommend the former.

As Europe expands still further, we will see how the social experiments in law that have been initiated over the past decade will be expanded, adapted, revised or even reversed. No single reform policy can solve the 'problem' that prostitution represents to European states. The problem is perceived in terms of morality and social order, to be solved through regulation and rehabilitation. But underlying this veneer, prostitution, both in its fluctuations and its persistence, is a reflection of the deep inequalities between men and women, and between rich and poor.

Notes

[1]In this chapter we refer to sex work and the sex industry. Although these terms are increasingly accepted, they are still challenged by some who argue that prostitution is not a form of work, but rather a distinct form of exploitation or abuse. We argue that recent developments have shown more clearly than ever that prostitution is work, that those who sell sex are workers, and that the best method for improving the situation for sex workers is through collective action to win rights, respect and opportunities, as for others who likewise 'work'.

[2]For further information on legal and other agreements in the European Union see http://europa.eu.int/scadplus/leg/en/cig/g4000p.htm#p15

[3]Europap is the European Network for HIV/AIDS Prevention in Prostitution, see Introduction. Tampep is the Transnational AIDS/STI Prevention Among Migrant Prostitutes in Europe (see http://www.tampep.com/). ENMP is the European Network Male Prostitution (http://www.enmp.org/).

[4]With all these figures there are, of course, marked differences between member states of the European Union but, unless stated, the broad trends are similar. For more detailed analysis at a country level, the primary sources should be consulted.

[5]These findings are from our own work in London, unpublished.

[6]For example, most of the sex work flats and saunas in London's Soho area are now run by people from the Balkan states who are also involved in facilitating the migration of young men and women into Western Europe, often involving extortion and gross exploitation. (own data, unpublished)

[7]A European study in 1990 found an overall prevalence of HIV in female sex workers of 1.5%. (European Working Group on HIV Infection in Female Prostitutes, 1993) As with subsequent studies, higher rates were found among sex workers in southern Europe as compared with the north and in particular categories such as male, drug using, and transgender sex workers.

References

European Commission (2000a). *Equal Opportunities for Women and Men in the European Union*.Luxembourg: Office for Official Publications of the European Communities (ISBN 92-894-1213-5).

European Commission (2000b). *The Urban Audit. Towards the Benchmarking of Quality of Life in 58 European Cities*. Luxembourg: Office for Official Publications of the European Communities (ISBN 92-828-9241-7).

European Working Group on HIV Infection in Female Prostitutes (1993). HIV infection in European female sex workers: epidemiological link with use of petroleum-based lubricants. *AIDS*;7:401-408.

Eurostat (2002). *Employment in the EU in 2000*. News releases 86/2002 (19 July 2002).

Johnson AM, Mercer CH, Erens B et al. (2001) Sexual behaviour in Britain: partnerships, practices, and HIV risk behaviours. *Lancet*;358:1835–42.

Lim, Lin Lean (2002). Female labour-force participation. In *Report of United Nations Population Division: Expert Group Meeting on Completing the Fertility Transition*. on http://www.un.org/esa/population/publications/ completingfertility.

MISSOC (2002). *Family Benefits and Family Policies in Europe*. Missoc-Info 01/2002, European Commission Directorate-General for Employment and Social Affairs on http://europa.eu.int/comm/employment_social/missoc.

OECD (2003). *Trends in International Migration 2002 Edition*. on http://www.oecd.org/document/32/0,2340,en_2649_33931_31844576_11969 9_1_1_37415,00.html.

Ruminska-Zimmy E (2002). Women's Entrepreneurship and Labour Market Trends in transition countries. In *Women's Entrepreneurship in Eastern Europe and CIS Countries*. OPA/AC.29/1 United Nations Economic Commission for Europe, on http://www.unece.org/pub_cat/topics/enterprise.htm

Russian National Human Development Report (1999). Moscow: United Nations Development Programme.

Smith H (2003). Olympic city aims to license its brothels. London: *Guardian*, 3 July 2003.

Standing, Kay (2001). Gender and Social Changes in Europe: Women, Employment, Family and Political Representation in the European Union. In *Social Changes in Asia and Europe in the Age of Globalisation*. Lectures from the Fourth ASEF University, Trond Gilberg and Ulrich Niemann (eds), Singapore: ASEF: 121-134. on www.asef.org.

Stiglitz, Joseph (2002). *Globalization and its Discontents*, London: Penguin Books.

United Nations Development Fund for Women (2000). *Progress of the World's Women 2000 UNIFEM Biennial Report*. Geneva: UNDFW on http://www.un.org/Depts/unsd/ww2000/overview.htm.

Ward H, Day S, Green A, Cooper K, Weber J (2004). Declining prevalence of STI in the London sex industry, 1985 to 2002. *Sex Transm Inf* (in press).

Wellings K, Nanchahal K, Macdowall W, et al. (2001). Sexual behaviour in Britain: early heterosexual experience. *Lancet*; 358:1843-50.

World Bank (2001). *Engendering Development: Through Gender Equality in Rights, Resources, and Voice*. Washington DC: World Bank/ Oxford University Press.

Histories

Chapter 2
Culture Clash: anti-trafficking activism or rights and health? [1]
Jo Doezema

Introduction

In 1994 I attended the international AIDS conference in Yokohama as part of the Network of Sex Work Projects delegation. Shortly before arriving at the conference I had heard of a huge UN conference on women in Beijing, and that trafficking in women was going to be discussed there.

At the AIDS conference I asked around and very few people were aware that the Beijing conference was happening or that anything that might be important to sex workers was going on there. The NSWP did eventually put together a delegation to the Beijing conference. But that was when I became aware there were, in a way, two 'cultures': one was concerned with HIV prevention and health work, the other with trafficking 'culture', which is primarily activist. This activism embraces academic and NGO/INGO activity – including projects, writings, email lists, and conferences, – rather than government activity.

The relationship of these two 'cultures' to sex worker politics is the subject of this chapter. The differences between 'health culture' and 'anti-trafficking culture' are described and it is argued that 'health culture' has been more compatible (though a long way from perfect) with sex worker rights. Some possible reasons for this are discussed, taking in some history along the way.

The picture of 'two cultures' is, naturally, a generalisation; in practice, there is a lot of overlap. But there is, nevertheless, a 'culture clash'. What is the main difference between the two approaches? Again, at risk of oversimplifying things, it is the difference between 'politics' and 'practicality'. This difference manifests itself mainly in attitudes towards sex worker rights and, related to this, in attitudes toward sex worker participation.

Political and practical culture

What is the difference between the 'political' and the 'practical' approach to sex work issues? Anti-trafficking activism, rather than health work, has become the primary arena in which ideological differences about prostitution are fought out. This became absolutely clear at the UN negotiations in Vienna around a new

Trafficking Protocol. These negotiations went on for two years, from 1998 to 2000, and government delegations from most of the countries in the UN met to decide how exactly the Protocol should be worded.

It was a very long process because a consensus had to be reached on the final Protocol. Along with other activists from the NSWP and some anti-trafficking activists, I joined a lobby group who went to the meetings to try and convince delegates to keep the Protocol from harming sex worker rights.

Anti-prostitution feminists, who see all prostitution as violence against women, also attended the meetings. Both groups had governments 'on their side', and the resulting ideological clash between those who saw prostitution as work, and those who saw it as violence, nearly caused negotiations to break down. Eventually, a sort of compromise was reached in the Protocol, which unfortunately leaves the way open for governments to adopt repressive measures against prostitution in the name of stopping trafficking.

In 'health culture' the situation is different. With public health at stake, ideological questions about whether prostitution was violence, work or immoral were pushed to the background by the pressing need to stop the spread of HIV.

This was not necessarily a positive development as some health measures can be repressive. And, again, this is only a generalisation – the ideological debates did not melt away. But in general, they were subordinated to the need to stop HIV and get to the prostitutes.

One area where this is very apparent is sex worker participation. While it is not always meaningful, and certainly there is much to be done, the need for sex worker participation is largely taken as given in 'health culture'. That sex workers should have rights, while they may not always be meaningful, is not a contentious idea, nor is that of sex work as labour, or, at the very least, an economic activity. In the 'trafficking culture' these notions are still highly contested.

In many ways, the 'practical' approach comes as a great relief after the draining ideological wars of anti-trafficking. Rarely, when attending health conferences, reading health literature or speaking to those from the health culture, do I have to hear phrases like "prostitutes are empty holes, waiting for masculine deposits of sperm" as I did at a UN meeting on trafficking.

Rarely am I faced with the spectacle of sobbing 'survivors' reliving their horrible experiences time and time again to shocked audiences. However, this doesn't mean that the 'practical' approach doesn't have problems of its own.

The very lack of ideology, the dominance of practicality that makes 'health culture' so refreshing is also the very thing that hinders its effectiveness. The absence of a political perspective, the failure to see the wider context in which health work takes place, is a great problem. The lack of a political perspective can reduce sex worker participation to mere tokenism, and result in only paying lip service to sex worker politics. If there is one thing to be taken from 'anti-trafficking culture', perhaps it is the need to foreground politics. While facing angry feminists is awful work, it does force a consideration of the big issues.

Repressive history

Nonetheless, 'health culture' has been more conducive to sex worker rights. But why? Is it in the nature of the cultural difference itself? That is, is a practical approach necessarily more conducive to sex worker rights than a political one? At first it appeared to me that this might be the case. But the longer I thought about it, the more I began to doubt that this was so. Looking at the history of both approaches, it is clear that both are full of repression rather than rights.

Efforts to combat trafficking have ended up justifying repressive measures against prostitutes themselves in the name of 'protection' for women and children. Modern debates around 'trafficked women' have a long history. At the beginning of the last century, there was a great public outcry against 'white slavery' in Europe and America. This referred to the abduction and transport of white women for prostitution. Many campaigners against the white slave trade saw all prostitutes as victims in need of rescue. Others argued it was important to distinguish the 'willing' prostitute from the victimised white slave.

The situation today is similar. Despite the fact that some organisations have tried to widen the concept of 'trafficking in persons' to include forced migration or forced labour, for the public and policy makers, 'trafficking' continues to be seen as either innocent young girls lured or kidnapped by evil men and forced into prostitution or as illegal migrants sneaking into the country to steal jobs.

This was very clear in the negotiations in Vienna, where our lobby strategy to move the emphasis away from prostitution and to forced labour in general had very limited success. There was a general reluctance to see prostitution in the same light as labour. For many delegates and for other lobbyists, forced labour was one thing, and trafficking in women something quite different. As a result, the new Protocol does nothing to protect the rights of sex workers.

The ideological culture around 'trafficking in women' undermines the idea of prostitution as a legitimate profession. If migrant sex workers are 'victims of trafficking' who only ended up in prostitution because they were forced, then labour rights are seen as unnecessary. If they are hardened prostitutes who crossed the border to ply their trade then they are illegal migrants who should be jailed or deported.

This is why the NSWP initially called for the Protocol to be rejected completely and why I believe that the 'anti-trafficking culture' presents a great threat to sex worker rights.

Efforts to protect public health through curing or preventing STIs or, as they were called, 'social diseases' among prostitutes similarly have a long and less than illustrious history. From the eighteenth century the so-called 'regulationists' believed that the 'necessary evil' of prostitution should be controlled by stringent state regulations.

Dr. Parent-Duchatelet, whose 1836 study of French prostitutes in the nineteenth century provided a model for regulationists, wrote: "Prostitutes are as inevitable in a great conurbation as sewers, cesspits and refuse dumps. The conduct of the authorities should be the same with regard to each" (quoted in Roberts 1992:223).

Harnessing rational scientific arguments to moral disapproval, 'regulationists' argued that state regulation was the only way to control social disease. 'Innocent' women and girls needed protection from immorality; however, once fallen, it was society that needed protecting from the immoral woman.

The best way to protect society, argued regulationists, was not to criminalise prostitution, but to register and medically control them, and forcibly detain prostitutes. This ideology is by no means dead; in many places, public health measures have led to repression in various forms, including mandatory health checks and imprisonment of infected sex workers found to be working. However, these repressive approaches are largely discredited in the health culture, from the WHO down.

Conclusion

So both cultures have in common a history of repression, and both carry a huge metaphorical and symbolic weight. From syphilis to AIDS, white slavery to trafficking in women, prostitution has always stood for vastly more than just the rather mundane, practical business of getting on with making a living.

Why has one managed to change its history and the other not? There may well be a number of answers. But one obvious direction to look in is the role of sex worker activism. It is certainly true that sex workers have been more politically active in the 'health culture' than in the 'anti-trafficking culture'.

But this, of course, begs a further set of questions. If sex worker rights have had more influence in the 'practical' culture of health provision, and if sex worker activism was responsible for dislodging the historical weight of repression, the questions need to be asked, how and why has this happened?

Why has 'health culture' changed and can it be done within 'anti-trafficking culture'? Given the current political profile of anti-trafficking, the number of new national and regional laws being drawn up, the plethora of new projects springing up everywhere, and the great sums of money available, these questions are extremely pressing.

Notes

[1] This paper was presented to the Europap/ENMP Conference, *Sex Work and Health in a Changing Europe*, 18-20 January 2002, Milton Keynes, UK

References

Roberts N (1992). *Whores in History*, London: HarperCollins: 223

Chapter 3
Why we need a sex workers' union
Ana Lopes and Jenn Clamen

Introduction

In his introduction to *Sex For Sale,* Weitzer (2000) points to the need for more research on sex work lobbying groups or organised sex work, in which the central focus is not the individual. This article traces the history of the movement for sex workers' rights internationally and, in particular, in the UK.

It focuses on unionisation attempts and the successful union recognition of the International Union of Sex Workers in Britain. We discuss the importance of this move, the difficulties faced by the new union, its victories and the main issues of the sex workers' rights movement.

A New Social Movement

The sex workers' rights movement is, to a certain extent, what could be called a new social movement. Its most organised and visible forms appeared after the 1960s; it is oriented towards challenging the values within society, creating a lifestyle and an identity, thus pushing back the boundaries of the social system. Like a citizens' rights movement, sex worker organisations are aimed at reclaiming rights that are granted to the majority of the population but have been systematically denied to those working in the sex industry.

Most organisations within the sex workers' movement correspond to what researchers describe as the characteristic form of organisation of a new social movement: oscillation between periods of high and low activity; fluid hierarchy and loose systems of authority; shifting membership and fluctuating numbers, often held together by personal or informational networks — newsletters, etc. (Scott 1990).

However, there has been, unfortunately, an absence of coalitions between sex worker activists and other new social movements. This is probably due to a lack of communication between groups; it has, however, certainly been challenged in the UK where sex workers' rights events have been supported by a wide coalition of anti-capitalism activists.

Some sex workers' organisations have attempted to unify the traditional labour movement (including trade unions) with the new social movement. The main issue for these organisations is painfully similar to that within traditional labour movements: the need to change domination within the relations of production.

Unlike most other contemporary social movements, the sex workers' rights movement links people by their occupation, by their insertion in a certain industry — the sex industry. It is fitting, therefore, that sex worker activists reclaim the language of the workers' movement and class struggle. The fact that sex work issues have been, until very recently, completely ignored by the labour movement is therefore disconcerting.

The international movement

Sex workers have organised internationally to claim rights traditionally denied to them. The most visible organisation within the movement is the global umbrella organisation, The Network of Sex Work Projects (NSWP). The NSWP was founded in 1991 and emerged as an informal group of activists that met each year at the International AIDS Conference. The NSWP is comprised of individuals and organisations in over 40 countries.

The Network first appeared at a time when international organising was difficult, especially for an informal group lacking funding. The arrival of the internet facilitated networking and the emergence of an on-line discussion group that allowed contact between international sex worker activists. In 2001 the NSWP received funding from the International HIV/AIDS Alliance, and has since become a formal, legal NGO. Yet the NSWP's greatest source of pride is that it continues to voice sex workers needs and demands at events like the International AIDS Conference.

The North American and European movements have also successfully organised several international sex workers' conferences. The first of these conferences, the First World Whore's Congress, in Amsterdam in 1985, led to the establishment of the International Committee for Prostitutes Rights (ICPR). Sex workers from nine different countries (mainly from industrialised countries but also from countries such as Singapore, Thailand and Vietnam) prepared a charter of demands that would be released on February 1985 (Pheterson ed. 1989: 33). This document has been seen as the movement's manifesto. The Second World Whores' Congress took place at the European Parliament in Brussels, in 1986 where AIDS was a hotly contested topic (Pheterson ed. 1989: 49-50). A few years later another international conference took place in the USA, the International Conference on Prostitution (ICOP).

In 1973 Margot St James, a former prostitute, founded COYOTE in San Francisco, USA. Today, COYOTE has branches in several cities in the United States. Several other sex workers' rights organisations exist throughout the USA. The National Task Force on Prostitution (NTFP) was founded in San Francisco in 1979. In 1993, to mark the inclusion of Canada, the organisation changed its name to the North American Task Force on Prostitution. Today the North American Task Force on Prostitution, based in New York, is an umbrella organisation for sex workers' rights organisations in different parts of the United States. Hooking is Real Employment (HIRE) was founded in Atlanta by Dolores French, a prostitute and escort.

Although the North American and European sex workers' movement is more documented, sex workers have organised very successfully in other parts of the world. The Indian Durbar Mahila Samanwaya Committee (DMSC) is perhaps the most impressive sex workers' organisation today. The organisation started as a service provider for sex workers in the Sonagatchi area – Calcutta's oldest and largest red light district – in particular the STD/HIV Intervention Programme. After attending and presenting research findings at International AIDS Conferences and networking with sex workers' activists, coordinator Dr Smarajit Jana encouraged sex workers themselves to lead and take ownership of the project.

The DMSC's membership is made up of 60,000 female and male sex workers. Together with their children and supporters they organised the first National Conference of sex workers in November 1997. Since 2001 they have organised a carnival or gathering called "The Millennium Mela" in a sports compound which brings together thousands of sex workers from India and other countries.

Having established the carnival during 3 to 6 March each year, the DMSC has called for 3 March to be recognised as International Day for Sex Workers' Rights. The DMSC provides different services: a drop-in centre in the red light district; an outreach and peer educators' programmes; a workers' union and a credit union.

There are numerous sex workers' rights organisations all over the world, from Australia to Delhi to South Africa. All these organisations, despite variations, campaign for the repeal of anti-prostitution laws, the end of the stigma attached to sex work, and the provision of resources to those working in the sex industry so as to empower them – in education, HIV and STI information, for example. They also function very successfully as support groups (Overs 1997).

The sex workers' movement in the UK

The sex workers' rights movements in Europe became visible in 1975 when prostitutes occupied a church in Lyons, France, to draw public attention to police harassment and the injustice of existing laws. Shortly after, Claude Jaget (1975) published a key work on prostitutes' rights: *Prostitutes: Our Life*.

By 1975 Helen Buckingham established herself as a spokesperson for prostitutes in Britain. She was a highly-priced escort providing services to the rich when she was made bankrupt by the Inland Revenue, who demanded tax payments based on her earnings from prostitution. Buckingham claimed that if the government could tax her it must also allow her to work legally. She became a researcher and one of the main subjects for Jeremy Sandford's book *Prostitutes* (1975).

Inspired by the launching of this book, herself and others involved in the research launched PUSSI (Prostitutes United for Social and Sexual Integration). The group later changed its name to PLAN (Prostitution Laws Are Nonsense). Helen Buckingham later allied herself to Selma James to form the English Collective of Prostitutes (ECP). The ECP grew out of the Wages for Housework collective to campaign for legal, civil and economic rights for prostitutes.

In 1976 a group of prostitutes, social workers and a lawyer established PROS in Birmingham, to campaign on behalf of street prostitutes and abolish imprisonment for loitering or soliciting.

Unionising in the sex industry

Davidson (1998) argues that prostitutes' organisations are bound to have limited success in action and that they will always resemble pressure groups rather than trade unions, although she supports campaigns for legal reform. This distinction between pressure groups and trade unions is crucial in defining the potential for collective resistance by prostitutes.

According to Davidson, such organisations cannot attain real change because there are more differences than similarities between sex work and other labour. Firstly, the prostitute-client relation is one of consumption, not of production so clients are interested only in haggling over the price — they do not have any economic interest in maximising sexual 'value' or productivity. Secondly, prostitutes have no bargaining power because labour markets are not strict and workers lack rights to legal protection. Finally, the state benefits from prostitution and therefore it has no interest in mediating conflicts of interest between prostitutes and clients or third parties.

In a critique of Davidson, West (2000:18) argues that Davidson is too pessimistic about short or medium-term change. While she agrees that the problems of political mobilisation around prostitution are certainly "enormous":

> the fact that capital in other sectors can draw on cheap indigenous, or migrant labour does not itself inhibit workers or their unions from taking any action at all.

The very existence of successful sex workers' unions supports West's argument.

Why we need a union

The globalisation of the sex industry has proved very profitable for a minority of people who control the industry. Though the sex work industry has expanded, sex workers' control over the industry and sex workers' legal and occupational rights have not. Archaic laws govern the industry across the world and discrimination against sex workers abound. A growth in the community of sex workers has accompanied this economic expansion, however. As a community, we respond to the unequal treatment of sex workers at a global level: health care, social care, access to mainstream services, and equal treatment under labour law. Addressing these issues is the goal of a sex workers' union as well as increasing workers' control over the industry.

The struggle for sex work law reform is not a new one. In the 1970's Margo St. James drew attention to the need for decriminalisation of the entire industry. While decriminalisation is a priority and overall spur for sex worker activists, our immediate and pragmatic concerns are the need to reinforce and introduce labour laws that allow sex workers the same freedoms as other workers. Enforceable contracts, entitlement to sick pay, and equal treatment in the workplace are only a few of these demands.

Recognition of sex work as legitimate employment is a primary focus of a sex workers' union. Therefore, removing the debate about sex work from a moral framework and placing it in the framework of labour rights is essential to aligning sex workers with other workers.

Establishing a sex workers' union implies a demand for a regulated industry. Through a sex workers' union, sex workers themselves necessarily govern how this regulation should be shaped. Unlike other types of associations, unions cannot be directed by any outside agency. They provide a way for experience to determine the parameters of sex workers' conditions of employment.

Sex workers' unions have already been established in several countries. In 1995 the Associacíon de Mujeres Meretrices Argentinas (AMMAR) was established in Argentina. AMMAR has since affiliated to one of the three main national trade union federations in Argentina – the Central de Trabajadores Argentinos (CTA) which has 1.5 million members. AMMAR has five branches and offices in five different regions of Argentina. The association is led by sex workers but receives the help of technical and professional consultants.

AMMAR is also part of the Latin American Network of Sex Work Projects created in Nicaragua in 1997. The association was present at the Convention of Sex Workers of the Cono Sur that took place in March 2001, which brought together participants from Uruguay, Chile and Brazil.

The Lusty Lady is a unionised nude theatre in San Francisco, USA. After complaints to management about a lack of security that allowed clients to photograph and film dancers without their knowledge or consent, dancers requested support from the Erotic Dancers Alliance (EDA) — a sex worker advocacy group based in the city. After much negotiation, they were allied with a local branch of the Service Employees International Union. Management removed the one-way glass that put their anonymity and safety at risk. Other problems, however, pervaded in their workplace, as it does in many peep shows and clubs where exotic dancers work: favouritism toward certain dancers, lack of sick pay, and the dismissal of workers on dubious grounds, to name a few.

In 1996 the Exotic Dancers Union, the theatre's union was formed, and soon afterwards members started negotiating contracts with the company. A union-backed day of protest some months later expressed their frustration at the way their employer, The Lusty Lady, refused to take responsibility for providing safer working conditions. During "No Pink" day dancers continued to dance nude but kept their legs "demurely closed" (Miss Mary Ann 2000:5). The management responded by firing one of the dancers who took part, to which the dancers retaliated by picketing the club for two days. The dancer was later rehired and subsequent negotiations were undertaken in a more cooperative atmosphere.

Threats about firing long-term dancers were replaced by an offer of a pay rise (Miss Mary Ann 2000)!

This collective action is a fantastic success story of the strength that a sex workers union can bring to the labour movement.

The International Union of Sex Workers (IUSW)

The International Union of Sex Workers (IUSW) arose as a small coalition of people working in the sex industry, and their supporters. Members were brought together in the throes of a planned demonstration against the proposed 'clean up' of London's red light district in Soho by the local Westminster Council. The English Collective of Prostitutes initiated a strike on behalf of all sex workers, as part of the 'Global Day of Women's Action' on International Women's Day 2000. Assisted by members of the Sexual Freedom Coalition, the IUSW paraded through Soho's streets publicising the action and adding a carnival atmosphere to the event by providing a samba band and dancers to accompany an evening procession.

Our celebratory approach was purposeful and intended. The democratic environment that we wish to nurture within the IUSW celebrates the pride that sex workers can take in what they do and works towards acceptance of sex work rights. We invite solidarity from people who work for safer working conditions and we strive for a strong collective that rejoices in sex workers standing up for their rights and in their ability to create social change.

The international collective of sex workers' struggle to unionise has been long but fruitful. Our campaigns spanned two years and in that time we established links with sex workers' organisations in other parts of the world and became members of the International Network of Sex Work Projects. We have also published a bulletin entitled RESPECT! – Rights and Equality for Sex Professionals and Employees in Connected Trades.

We sought from the outset to secure recognition by the Trade Unions Council (TUC). After researching the matter we concluded that it would be far easier and more realistic to join an existing union rather than attempt to match the pre-requisites for recognition as a separate union. To pursue this we attended the TUC Gay and Lesbian Conference in 2000. Our rationale was that Gay and Lesbian Union Officers would be more open and sympathetic to our cause than other officers, since they had been through a similar process of fighting for rights and acceptance. The approach was successful and we took the opportunity to lobby officers from several different unions. They all supported us individually, but either lacked the courage to take the matter further within their own unions or received a negative response from their senior officers.

Demands of the International Union of Sex Workers:

Decriminalisation of all aspects of sex work involving consenting adults.

The right to form and join professional associations or unions.

The right to work on the same basis as other independent contractors and employers and to receive the same benefits as other self-employed or contracted workers.

No taxation without such rights and representation.

Zero tolerance of coercion, violence, sexual abuse, child labour, rape and racism.

Legal support for sex workers who want to sue those who exploit their labour.

The right to travel across national boundaries and obtain work permits wherever we live.

Clean and safe places to work.

The right to choose whether to work on our own or co-operatively with other sex workers.

The absolute right to say no.

Access to training — our jobs require very special skills and professional standards.

Access to health clinics where we do not feel stigmatised.

Re-training programmes for sex workers who want to leave the industry.

An end to social attitudes which stigmatise those who are or have been sex workers.

Disappointed with the response, our work as a pressure and campaigning group continued. It was only five months later that one of us met the men who would provide a way into the unions. In November 2001, Martin Smith gave a speech at the No Sweat annual conference. No Sweat is an organisation that campaigns against sweatshops and Martin spoke about the GMB's (Britain's General Union) efforts to organise sweatshop workers in East London.

Soon after that negotiations began between the IUSW and the GMB, the third biggest trade union in the UK, with the view to forming the first sex workers' union branch in Britain. The first meetings underscored the professionalism of the union officers. Supported by the Regional Secretary Paul Kenny, they maintained their mission was to support workers in organising, regardless of what their work is. Much was to be learned by both sides. We in the IUSW knew little about real union organisation and structure; on the other hand, the GMB officers who helped get the branch off the ground (Martin Smith, Lisa Venes, Rose Conroy among others) knew little about the realities of the sex industry and the needs of sex workers.

As the IUSW did not feel it was in itself representative of all sex workers of all sectors of the British sex industry, an open meeting was called in which the proposal to affiliate to the GMB was debated among sex worker activists, academics, supporters, business owners and even clients. Sietske Altink, from the Dutch sex workers' union, the Red Thread, prepared us for some of the problems we were bound to face, such as the difficulties of reaching an agreement on issues such as decriminalisation and tax payments. We also needed to account for whether a union can represent workers in illegal sectors of the industry or illegal migrants. In the event, our IUSW branch resulted from a unanimous vote to affiliate to the GMB London Region.

By joining the GMB we have established one basic labour right for all sex workers in the UK: the right to join and be represented by a recognised union. Two months later we celebrated our first Labour Day as an official union. On Mayday 2002 we proudly marched through the streets of Soho with banners that read "Sex Workers Pride" and "Sex Workers of the World Unite!", with other national unions in the official trade unions Mayday march. Pride in ourselves and in what we do is a pre-requisite in our struggle to establish our rights.

The new union branch is open to all sectors of the industry, sex workers, small business owners, support staff, service providers (like health project workers) and supporters. Recruitment is fundamental to the branch at the moment since our continued union status is threatened if affiliate numbers drop below a certain minimum. Although membership has grown steadily since March 2002, we have recognised reasons why some sex workers are reluctant to join.

Unionising involves a form of regulation, one that many sex workers do want for their industry. With regulation comes restrictions on work; although this would bring a lot of the underground industry to the surface and make many of the conditions safer and more just, many sex workers, understandably, would rather continue to work within the conditions they have already established and become accustomed to.

Being a union member, in most contexts, requires outing oneself or becoming affiliated with other members in some way. Most sex workers, out of necessity, would rather remain anonymous and therefore their privacy precludes union membership. Although the IUSW branch of the GMB permits this confidentiality, joining a union would require some sex workers to commit to the struggle for better labour conditions; some are just interested in working.

Many men, women and transgender sex workers do not identify as sex workers. This includes exotic dancers, masseuses, and a whole range of people working in the industry. Selling sex is usually the first thing associated with sex working and because not all workers in the sex industry sell sex, this creates a perceived obstacle to their membership.

Many in the sex industry are 'passing through'. They consider their time in the industry to be brief and as a result do not consider it worthwhile to become active or take part in union activities.

All of these barriers are ones that sex workers have identified throughout the establishment of the IUSW. These barriers, however, are counteracted by sex workers that do join the union and can work towards creating a safer environment for all sex workers, including those that are not members of the union.

These barriers are caused by the marginalisation of sex workers and the stigma attached to our industry. Once we claim our rights, there will be no reason why sex workers should not be proud of themselves and join a union or professional association. One of the aims of any sex worker organisation should be to promote self-respect and pride – without which no one is able to stand up for their rights.

Benefits

Unionisation offers a degree of protection thus far denied to those working in the sex industry. Free legal advice and representation,

48

tax and employment rights advice are some of the benefits union members enjoy. The sex industry branch of the GMB has also worked to adapt the general benefits offered by the GMB to fit sex workers' needs. For example, we looked for educational activities we could subsidise, like general workshops about the sex industry, strip tease and pole dancing courses and self-defence courses. We also subsidise courses that enable sex workers to have alternative professions, if they wish to do so, like I.T training, or help with putting together a C.V.

While it is easier to organise legal sectors of the industry, benefits such as legal advice can be enjoyed by all. Many sex workers see themselves as self-employed and the union can protect their rights as self-employed workers. Data collected by the union (for example, names and addresses) are totally confidential, which means that sex workers can enjoy the benefits of union membership regardless of their immigration status and do not have to fear their details being passed on to any authorities, such as the immigration service or police.

The strength of a union branch and the extent to which it can successfully press for changes in the industry or particular work places depends on the number of its members. Trade union legislation requires that when 50 per cent of the workers at a certain company or work place are affiliated to a union, management is obliged to sign a recognition agreement with that union. So far, we have achieved this in a couple of table dancing clubs.

This has been a major victory and a historic step. With the help of the GMB, workers at these clubs have negotiated codes of conduct and grievance procedures with management; workers have elected union representatives who will be trained continuously by the GMB; union officials have the right to go into the work place at any time and management is bound by the recognition contract to inform the union of any changes to its policy. These measures have significantly improved the working conditions at the clubs and workers feel that they have a level of protection, at present lacking in the majority of similar establishments.

There are four main issues that sex workers and sex worker activists face globally: legislation, migration, violence and health (especially the spread of HIV/AIDS). We address two of these below.

Legislation

The campaign for the decriminalisation of sex work has been a central concern for many sex worker activists for decades, and is a key issue for the IUSW. Proponents for decriminalisation of the sex industry believe that current laws create a cyclical pattern of violence and poor health and safety conditions for people working in the trade. The decriminalisation of sex work would effectively remove laws against sex work. A total decriminalisation would involve the repeal of laws against consensual commercial and non-commercial adult sexual activity.

Although we want sex work to be decriminalised, we would not be opposed to some kind of regulation, provided sex workers have a prominent role in the drawing up of such regulations and they do not lead to a further breach of sex workers' human, civil and legal rights.

However, we reject legalisation of the sex industry because countries that have adopted such a legal framework have increased state control over sex workers and limit their rights. Where sex work is legalised, as in the Netherlands, health and safety regulations are imposed that do not necessarily reflect the needs of sex workers. The requirement to hold a license to work and for mandatory health checks creates a two-tier system within which legal or licensed workers are protected and illegal workers, those without a license, are further marginalised and made vulnerable.

Since it has affiliated to the GMB, the IUSW has attempted to use the union's political clout to trigger a debate about sex work legislation and ultimately achieve law reform. We recently made history at the TUC Women's Conference by securing enough support to get a motion passed calling for the decriminalisation of prostitution, the right to full labour rights and voluntary and non-judgemental medical services for all sex workers.

Violence

Eradicating sex work is often proposed as a solution to eliminate violence against sex workers. It is seldom realised that the laws that prohibit activities related to commercial sex (e.g. soliciting and working together from premises) are very much responsible for the vulnerability of sex workers. Furthermore, these laws stigmatise sex workers which in turn 'justifies' violence against sex workers.

Through unionisation in the sex industry we aim to eliminate such laws and, by having sex work recognised as real work, to challenge the stigma associated with the industry.

Many sex workers who are attacked are very resistant to reporting incidents to the police. This is due to the semi-legality of some sectors of the industry and to the widespread belief that the police and courts do not take violence against sex workers seriously. Although police attitudes are changing, there is in general a lack of education and awareness of sex work issues among several police forces. The application of the law is also inconsistent with regards to sex workers and recently sex workers have been charged under other laws, for example Anti-Social Behaviour Orders can effectively mean house arrest for sex workers – a punishment not routinely meted out for sex work itself. The new union branch has worked with several police forces in order to address this issue. As part of a wider advisory group to the Metropolitan Police on sex work issues, the union has participated in the production of a leaflet pack on safety and violence for sex workers. It is also helping to organise a training day for police officers.

The future

Unionisation of the sex industry in the UK has only just begun and we have a long way to go. In fact, we need to catch up with most industries which have been unionised for more than one hundred years!

The branch will continue to recruit sex workers and secure recognition in other work places. At the moment, most of our members are located within the London region but the idea of unionisation is gaining acceptance around the UK, passing from sex worker to sex worker, from sexual health professionals to sex workers. The idea is also spreading to other countries. In Sweden, an informal network of sex workers has recently requested the assistance of the UK union in attempting to unionise. The process is under way and the network will soon be affiliated to a fully recognised union.

The union will continue to make efforts to place sex work issues on the labour movement's agenda, both nationally and internationally. After our victory at the TUC Women's Conference, we are eager to pass similar resolutions at the TUC Annual Congress and ultimately at the International Labour Organisation (ILO) Conference.

Conclusion

Sex workers have been organising and campaigning for their rights for years. In some countries, as in the UK, such organisation has taken the form of affiliating to recognised trade unions, expanding sex workers' rights and further legitimising sex work as labour. The focus on labour rights has provided a forum where sex work is assumed to be a legitimate form of labour, thus shifting the debate on from a struggle with abolitionists. This approach has lent itself to a struggle for rights rather than existence.

References

Davidson, J O (1998). *Prostitution, Power and Freedom*. Cambridge: Polity Press.

International HIV/AIDS Alliance. *Sex Work: The Sex Industry in Context*. Brighton: International HIV/AIDS Alliance (in press).

Jaget, C (ed) (1975). *Prostitutes: Our Life*. Bristol: Falling Wall Press.

Overs, C (1997). Red Lights: a brief history of sex work activism in the age of AIDS. In Oppenheimer and Reckitt (eds). *Acting on AIDS: Sex, Drugs and Politics*. London: Serpent's Tail.

Pheterson, G (ed) (1989). *A Vindication of the Rights of Whores*. Seattle: Seal Press.

Sandford, J (1975). *Prostitutes: portraits of people in the sexploitation business*. London: Secker and Warburg.

Scott, A (1990). *Ideology and the New Social Movements*. London: Unwin Hyman.

Weitzer, R (2000). Why we need more research on sex work. In Weitzer (ed.) *Sex For Sale*. London: Routledge.

West, J (2000). Prostitution: Collectives and the Politics of regulation. *Gender, Work and Organisations;* **7**(2):106-18.

Websites

Miss Mary Ann (2000). Labor Organizing in the Skin Trade: tales of a peepshow prole. http://livenudegirlsunite.com/story.html (accessed January 2004).

Network of Sex Work Projects (2002). The anti-sex work anti-trafficking agenda: a threat to sex workers' health and human rights; Statement from the Network of Sex Work Projects at the XIV International Conference on AIDS, Barcelona, July 2002. http://www.nswp.org (accessed January 2004).

Chapter 4
A new era for sex workers in Germany?
Maya Czajka

Introduction

On 1 January 2002, new legislation regulating prostitution in Germany came into effect. The 'ProstG' (Prostitutionsgesetz) law will operate provisionally until the end of 2004 at which point parliament and the government intend to assess its effects and possibly table improvements. It is therefore difficult to judge whether or not the law will come into final effect in 2005 in its present or in a modified form. Indeed, no one can be certain that the new legislation will not, in the end, be thrown out in favour of the former status quo.

So what is it about, this new law, for so long an object of desire and passionate struggle? What does it achieve? Does it bring the hoped for improvements? Does it turn workers in the sex industry into 'respectable' professionals at last? Does it help sweep away stigma and discrimination? Let us take a closer look.

Considering the mountains of files which were produced over the fifteen years that it took to formulate the new law, it is amazing to discover there are only three clauses in the legislation, which together barely fill one sheet of A4! It's true that the German federal government did add a further three ponderous pages of explanatory comment, which sets out how they assume that the apparently 'oldest profession' might henceforth be regulated.

The legal changes

The intended effect of the three clauses is obviously more wide reaching than one might suppose at first glance. Clause 1 seeks to enable sex workers to make legally binding contracts with clients and also to make employment contracts with the management of brothels and similar establishments. A contract struck between a sex worker and a client will no longer be considered an offence against public decency. The law spells it out as follows:

> When sexual acts are entered into in respect of a previously negotiated fee, this agreement in itself constitutes a legally binding claim.

Sex workers are accordingly able to file a claim in a Civil Court now for fees agreed upon but not paid. A novelty, indeed. However, sexual servicing has still not been brought into line with other service work. In the final instance, (to quote the explanatory comments) "the legislature is concerned with the legal claims of prostitutes, and not with claims arising from clients or from managers of brothels and similar establishments...." (ProstG 2001, Explanatory comments).

Faced with the dilemma of, on the one hand, having somehow to assure the enforcement of contracts, but anxious, on the other hand, to avoid a situation in court or before an industrial tribunal where the type, extent and exact nature of a sexual service would be under debate, the government and parliament prevaricated. This allowed them to keep one foot in each of the contradictory camps. An agreement between a whore and a client now constitutes a contract that is "legally binding for one party only". A whore is thus able to file a claim. A client, however, is unable to sue for agreed services not duly rendered.

Clause 1 has a further consequence. According to the letter of the new law, sex workers are able to negotiate employment contracts with owners of brothels, saunas and escort agencies and are thus in a position to file a claim for outstanding wages before an industrial tribunal even though they may have resigned without giving notice or stating grounds, and even though they might have refused to provide particular services or have done their job poorly.

Clause 2 're-defines' pimping as a punishable offence but otherwise amounts to nothing more than a few new headings and additions thrown in for good measure. Some of the old legislation is gone, apparently just left out. Those familiar with the old legislation perceive little change and much confusion. Sex workers' employers can still be charged with procuring/pandering, albeit less easily than before. Clause 2 does however state that to act simply as a third party agent for sex workers and clients is no longer a criminal offence.

Clause 3 simply lays down the date on which the law should come into effect.

To what extent has the new legislation changed sex workers' situation? How did things look before these legislative changes?

Back in the good old days before 2002, whores had always honoured the age-old tradition of getting their cash up front. The agreed fee was pocketed before any sexual service was rendered.

The reason for this practice can be found in Paragraph 138, Article 1, of the Federal Statutory Code (BGB, Art. 138). This stipulates that any agreement, contract or other transaction which offends public decency is not legally binding (Palandt 2002). In 1989, the German Federal Court (BGH, the supreme court of Germany) had decreed that "a legal transaction between a prostitute and client offends public decency and is thus not legally binding", and stated that prostitution "is an offence to all fair-minded and decent citizens" (BGB, Art. 138). A sex worker therefore had no chance of suing a client for non-payment.

Paragraph 138 effectively made contractual agreements impossible for sex workers. Consequently, no contracts with clients, for tenancy or for employment in bars and strip-clubs were ever made. Whores had no rights because their occupation was seen to be in conflict with public decency.

A sex worker's dissatisfied client, however, was able to sue for fraud. The Criminal Code assured a money-back guarantee to any client "who had not received the service negotiated" (Criminal Code (StGB), Art. 180a, 181). Quite apart from the double standard upheld by this Paragraph, it also prevented sex workers from registering their business and from accessing private or state health insurance schemes. Income tax was nonetheless levied at the usual commercial rates.[1]

One other Civil and Social Code law still relevant today to the sale of sexual services is the OWiG law on grossly indecent acts and acts of public nuisance. Its prohibition on advertising for sexual services is applied only in certain federal states, and then, rarely. In other states, such advertising is tolerated and also costs considerably more than other commercial advertising. The OWiG law also criminalises responsible advertising containing references to "safer sex", for example (OWiG, Art. 119, 120).

The OWiG law continues to discriminate against sex workers. They are unable to carry on their profession legally and are deprived of the rights afforded to workers in other occupations. It is also clear that sex workers have to work overtime to pay the fines arising from this law.

Further restrictions on the sale of sexual services were contained in the paragraphs 180a and 181a of the Criminal Code (StGB), and Article 297 of the Introduction Law to the Criminal Code – statutory order law (EGStGB).

The organisation of prostitution was sanctioned by these paragraphs, which were formulated on the assumption that women must be protected from coercion, pimping and exploitation. According to this so-called 'Pimp Paragraph', prostitution could legally be provided, but any further measures were illegal. The place, time, type and extent of services could not be designated.

In practice these regulations did not protect sex workers. They were a further obstacle to sex work being recognised as a regular form of employment and prevented sex workers from gaining access to federal employment rights and to the federal social security system (Molloy 1992:29).

Court verdicts were handed down which determined that all forms of decent working conditions in brothels and similar establishments promoted prostitution and were therefore illegal. This applied, for example, to adequate sanitary provisions and to sex workers' representation in negotiations with management concerning their working conditions. The reasoning behind such verdicts was that humane working conditions would discourage women from abandoning their 'deviant' lifestyle.

Even the provision of free condoms was considered criminal. The management of brothels and other sex work establishments were consequently disinclined to improve their employees' working conditions. Measures to prevent HIV infection and other STD were made practically impossible.

Article 297 of the Introduction Law of the Criminal Code enables the creation by Federal State governments of specific 'no-go' areas for prostitutes. In conjunction with the above cited Paragraph 120 of the OWiG law, Article 297 means that sex workers who infringe this ruling face fines of up to €500 for a first offence, and up to six months imprisonment or higher fines for repeated offences, which constitute a criminal act.

One effect of this law has been to increase the number of bribes of public administrators in 'no-go' areas. Experience with strictly controlled 'no-go' areas (for example, in Hamburg, Munich and Frankfurt) shows that, in addition to the problems of real estate speculation, ghettoisation and 'barrack-style' brothels, sex workers quickly lose economic ground to the pimps working there.

'Barrack-style' prostitution – the concentration of sex-workers in 'industrial' brothels – is also a direct result of 'no-go' area legislation and drives sex workers out of traditional districts. Large brothels and Eros Centres can afford to occupy the few legal zones and maximise their profits through the commercial provision of sexual services. Stiff competition in the 'tolerance zones' and the threat of high fines in prohibited zones keep the sex factories full, despite the exploitative conditions.

Sex workers who will not or cannot accept the conditions in the 'barracks' find themselves condemned to the outskirts of the city and, hence, to worse exploitation: higher rents for hotel rooms; 'protection money' for pimps; increased danger due to isolation; and often a complete lack of infrastructure, such as bars, toilets and telephones. Counselling centres and aid agencies have observed that immigrants, drug users and drug addicts are adversely affected by the 'no-go' area legislation.

In cities such as Berlin without 'no-go' areas, pimping is much less prevalent and 'barrack' brothels and Eros centres do not exist at all.

Criticism

Such a law did not of course fall out of the sky. A government does not consider reviewing legislation until pressure has been exerted. Concerned parties must have voiced their needs and demands. Indeed, they did. All that, and more besides!

The long road to this law was paved largely by a small, angry and very active group of women. Whores and their supporters began in 1986 to campaign for employment rights for prostitutes – as they were then still known. In 1989, I became part of this young movement.[2]

In the course of small group discussions about discrimination (and later about stigmatisation), whores increasingly took issue with their reputed status as victims. We perceived and described what we did not as deviant behaviour, but as work. It was obvious that we should stop referring to ourselves as 'prostitutes' and adopt the term 'sex workers'. Nor did we 'practice prostitution'. It seemed logical to introduce the concept of 'working in the sex industry'. We considered ourselves to be workers in a particular service sector, in which women faced particular discrimination. Our criticism of the ProstG is based on this premise. Let us take a closer look at the individual Clauses of the ProstG.

When we activists saw the first draft of Paragraph 1, Clause 1, we were speechless. What exactly was meant by 'sexual acts', if you please? Had we not for years already been talking about work, about a service industry, about exploitative economic conditions? 'Entering into sexual acts' – my foot! We do not 'enter into sexual acts' (at least not with clients) – we WORK. And precisely because what we do is work, and should be called work, we demand access to all the rights afforded other employees. And it matters not at all whether we are freelance or employed – in either case we are working – and that is, and always has been, the point.

And where in hell's name was there any gain for us? Our traditional 'money up front' approach had always worked.

We had campaigned for the same rights afforded other employees in service jobs – not for a 'Special Decree'.

The claim that Clause 1 of ProstG succeeds in aligning sexual services with other service industries remains, for us, utter nonsense. This had never really been parliament's intention (see the website http://www.highlights-berlin.de/ for comments). The law does not want to be seen to be encouraging women to offer sexual services. Nor is the legislature in any position to ascertain or investigate whether women "exercise their profession voluntarily" (Minutes from Expert Hearing of the draft Prostitution Law, June 2001, Berlin, http://www.spdfraktion.de/cnt/rs/rs_dok/).

It appeared, nonetheless, as if the new law would in some way make it possible for whores to have an employment contract. The explanatory comments on the law include the terms "occupational relationship", "dependent activity", and "limited rights of supervision". We grew suspicious. What was that supposed to mean? Do such laws exist for other service jobs?

Our suspicions were justified. The legislature continues to infer that women who work in the sex industry are in need of special protection. The legislature believes that women do not autonomously decide to offer and sell sexual services, and that they therefore need to be protected against coercion and exploitation by a special law.

The legislation states that 'the prostitute':

- can resign without serving notice
- not be obliged to undertake sexual services or be   reproached for apparently "poor performance"

- not be subject, beyond definition of time and place of service, to further directives from brothel management (See Appendix, ProstG 2001: Explanatory comments).

For brothel management, employment contracts would basically amount to the following:

The management might define when and where sexual services were to be assured, but not the type or nature of these services. Compliance with 'safer sex guidelines' and the use of condoms, for example, would remain mandatory. Brothel management could not sue for non-compliance with agreed terms of employment, with the exception of the working hours agreed upon. Even if sex workers had agreed in a contract to provide certain sexual services, this agreement would not be binding. A sex worker might resign at any time, without serving their notice.

Equal rights or stigmatisation? Might? Would? Could? Why have I written this in the subjunctive tense? Simply because the whole issue of employment contracts remains purely hypothetical. They do not exist. In workshops hurriedly convened by the Ministry for the Family, Pensioners, Women and Youth in February 2002 and April 2003, reports flooded in from throughout Germany stating that the law had done nothing but create insecurity, hesitation and confusion (unpublished minutes of workshop convened by the Ministry for the Family, Pensioners, Women and Youth April 01st, 2003).

Representatives of state pension and health insurance schemes reported that enquiries had been made (a total of six in 16 months), yet none had led to contractual agreements.[3] The largest European trade union for service industries, *ver.di*, which also participated in the workshops, convened a national working party to develop blueprints for a standardised employment contract. The question of just what might be standard in such contracts, however, remains a riddle even for seasoned lawyers.

In southern states of the Federal Republic, that is, the Federal States of Bavaria and Baden-Württemberg, opposition to the law has led to all drafts being forwarded first to the State Prosecutors of the various local authorities which licence local brothels in order, in theory at least, to be on the safe side of the law. For example, the State Prosecutor for Munich announced that any contractual employment agreements, which come to their notice, will constitute grounds for investigating possible contravention of articles 180a and 181a of the Criminal Code (StGB).

> Legislation on the protection of employees regarding summary dismissal, hours of work, maternity leave and industrial injury, industrial representation and access to unions is long overdue in the unprotected area of women's work, prostitution. Whilst regular employment contracts would indeed be lucrative for only some female sex workers, the recognition and 'normalisation' of their occupation would have a clearly destigmatising trickle-down effect for self-employed sex workers too. -Cora Malloy (Molloy 1992).

The ProstG made the job of an employer, with attendant rights to give orders and supervise service, impossible. It prevented a normalisation of employer/employee relations, and did not even begin to destigmatise sex workers.

With the introduction of the above mentioned 'contract that is legally binding for one party only', the legislature expressed all too clearly its distrust of the fact that women are able to decide for themselves what they want to do with their lives. During parliamentary debates, the supporters of these 'protective paragraphs' (almost exclusively men) repeatedly drew on arguments common in debates on human trafficking. It was a discouraging and victimising debate.

It should be appreciated also that all issues covered by the Aliens' Law (Ausländergesetz) are completely unaffected by ProstG. The law applies only to nationals. It was decided explicitly, "this law would not and should not regulate questions relating to aliens. These remain questions for the Immigration Law". One participant of the workshop in April 2003 said: "With regard to the legal status of non-nationals, there can be no question that a residence permit should be issued in order to practice prostitution". All colleagues who do not enjoy the privilege of having an EU passport, or of being married to someone who does, are thus illegal residents with all the negative consequences that this entails.

Paragraph 2 states that to act as a third party agent for prostitutes and clients – formerly defined as 'procuring with intent'/'pandering' - is no longer a punishable offence. Due to the enormous difficulties involved in producing conclusive evidence of this charge, such cases have not been fought in Germany for some decades. But at least this one aspect of the new law doesn't do sex workers any harm.

The trade unions, on which so many of us had pinned great hope, have no idea what to do and, as a spokeswoman for *ver.di*, the world's largest trade union branch, confirmed: "there is no demand for employment contracts". (unpublished minutes of workshop convened by the Ministry for the Family, Pensioners, Women and Youth April 01st, 2003)

The effects of Clause 2 are so negligible as to be irrelevant. The new version does not exclude the possibility of employers (brothel owners, etc) being charged with procuring/pandering. This merely cannot happen quite so quickly as in the past, "For example, the State Prosecutor for Munich announced that, in their view, a contract of employment including agreements reached voluntarily on the time and place when and at which prostitution might be practised constitutes grounds for an investigation of the employer on suspicion of procuring with intent".[4] Opposition to the law may not be able to stop parliament approving the new legislation, but it is still a force to be reckoned with, at least in Bavaria and Baden-Württemberg.

Federal and local perspectives still conflict. For example, a brothel owner who offers his/her sex workers pleasant working conditions is no longer committing a criminal offence - at least not from the perspective of the federal republic. At a local level, she or he may be.

What led to the ProstG?

The Prostitution Law had a long and troubled history before it reached parliament in 2001.

AIDS hysteria put sex workers under increasing pressure in the 1980s, with the result that more and more groups and associations formed. We began to organise politically to defend ourselves against the massive increase in discrimination.

The image of a whore plague, which was infecting innocent family men with AIDS and spreading death and decay, loomed large at this time. In the mid-1980s, programmes were hurriedly conceived which would enable whores to give up their job to claim social security without the usual lengthy paperwork. Subsequent government-funded job creation schemes sought to integrate ex-whores. Huge sums of money were invested to save society from fallen women. To qualify for these programmes, it sufficed that a whore claim to be 'afraid of AIDS'.[7] And who was better placed to undertake the 're-training' and social work than the whore movement activists? Thus our self-help groups were gradually transformed into more or less well-paid state-funded organisations with their own counselling centres.

In 1986, the newly founded Green Party started to discuss a draft law aimed at abolishing discrimination towards women in German society, raising our hopes. We, who were active in German sex worker organisations, also hoped that the new Party would help reform Germany's prostitution and gender policies.

A look at the draft Anti-Discrimination Law quickly told us that the Green Party had completely overlooked the needs of sex workers – we were simply not mentioned at all in the draft. Sex worker organisations had no choice but to seek out the Party and draw their attention to the fact that whores 'were just ordinary women too',[5] and deserved to be taken into account in the same way as other women.

The Green Party was forced to reconsider and began to do some homework. After extensive discussions with the sex workers' movement, an 'Anti-Discrimination Law Part III'[6] was presented in Spring 1990. This draft complied to a large extent with the demands drawn up by large sections of the whore movement, and was supported mainly by a few liberal feminists within the party, alongside sex worker organisations and autonomous whore activists.

We had engaged in long debates with the Party, about condoms, STIs, about AIDS, about self-determination, free enterprise in the sex industry, about exploitative working conditions. We had discussed economics, politics, stigmatisation and victimisation. We had, however, forgotten to talk about sexuality, sexual practices and about - men - the men involved with those liberal feminists, as it turned out.

In the long-term, it proved to have been a fatal mistake to have worked only with women in the Party. This became evident during heated fights with Green Party members of parliament during the draft's first reading in March 1990. Most people still held on to their image of women forced into prostitution. Hardly anyone seemed able to imagine that women might make a conscious and voluntary decision to enter sex work. To come face to face with us - not beaten black and blue and able to most eloquently express our own thoughts and needs – was obviously an unexpected novelty for most 'Green Party' men (and women). We didn't give the impression of needing to be 'saved', nor of women who were forced and beaten into brothels every day by 'vicious and mean pimps'. Nor did we appear to have an omnipresent, international gang of villainous traffickers at our backs.

So we embarked in March 1990 on a discussion with liberal feminist women who were to some extent supportive and felt that something had to be done about discrimination against whores. However, they did not want to hear that their very own partners, being emancipated, liberal men helping with household affairs and the education of their children, might actually visit whores at night. We also talked to a few 'greeny' men who had naturally never visited a prostitute but who all knew someone – either a friend, a brother, a colleague etc. – who had visited a whore at least once. These 'friends' had in turn provided those emancipated liberal men with 'first-hand accounts' of the visits. We found that these 'green' men were and are not different from other men who claim never to have made use of sexual services but are somehow very well informed about the life and working conditions of sex workers.

The 'green' men were no different – and are today no different – than other men. They claim never to have bought sexual services from women, and that they would never do so. Nonetheless, they are extremely familiar with the lives and working conditions of sex workers!

The few members of parliament who dared grace this public hearing - most did not even attend - had to justify their support for the sex workers' cause in front of a large number of journalists. At the same time, we became angrier by the minute because what we had achieved in long and tiring negotiations with the Green Party feminists were weak compromises. We had a hard time defending these because we were not really whole-heartedly in favour of these compromises ourselves.

When the issue of sex workers' exclusion from the social security system came up, a 'green' man jumped up and cried out utterly distraught: "I didn't know that, I really didn't know that. How terrible for the women, something has to happen immediately. What will they do when they need to see a dentist?"

A young man with a sense of the practical things in life. Unfortunately he was so preoccupied with weeping that he was unable to continue in the hearing, and was comforted and accompanied outside by some (male) colleagues, and never seen again. (Nor did his colleagues return).

Understandably we were ambivalent about that hearing. On the one hand, we were satisfied because it was the first time in German history that a party represented in German parliament discussed the issue of prostitutes' rights. On the other hand, we were totally frustrated and disillusioned by the double standard and hypocrisy of MPs and the media. The few Green Party women who had actually understood us felt the same as we did. The draft legislation had not withstood its first trial by fire. On the contrary, it had caused a huge rift to open up.

In October 1990 Germany's historic reunification united the Federal Republic of Germany and the German Democratic Republic. For a short while the Green Party was not represented in parliament. In the legislative period following reunification, the party re-emerged with a new face: as a union of the West German Green Party and the former East German 'Alliance 90' (Bündnis 90). The contract regulating the integration of the two parties identified the 'Anti-Discrimination Law III' as an unresolved issue. In the first weeks after the inauguration of the new German parliament, the issue was dealt with – along with other 'miscellaneous' topics - in a single session: and then disappeared completely from the parliamentary agenda.

We were extremely disappointed and felt utterly betrayed. We wept a bit, cursed wickedly – and then reformed for the next offensive.

In the wake of public interest that followed the hearing in 1990 many students and academics discovered a potential research subject in the topic of prostitution law reform. Such a 'fascinating topic' promised academic laurels. Our organisations and offices were flooded with requests for material and information to facilitate master and doctoral theses. Women's associations, Christian organisations and schools turned to us with their questions. Even journalists started to develop an interest in the issue. For a period in the early 1990s, every talk show featured an interview with a whore or ex-whore.

We talked about everything then, trying as best as possible to protect our own biographies and families and simultaneously provide an overview of the situation of the German sex industry in general and the economic situation of prostitutes. We did earn quite a bit of additional money out of those shows, too!

However, what the audience and chat show hosts really wanted to know was why such young, pretty and obviously intelligent women earned their money by spreading their legs. They suspected deep-rooted childhood traumas lay behind our decision and wondered openly whether we would not rather be cleaning women, wives, mothers – anything 'respectable'!

At some stage the media and the audience tired of listening to the 'intellectual hooker' and wanted to hear about the 'real hooker'. They wanted us to tell how we were beaten and coerced, how we had tried repeatedly to escape the regimes of pimps and how desperately we tried not to spend all our money on luxuries.

During this period, some of us made even more money through this new role.

Nevertheless, we simultaneously devoted ourselves to working on a new draft law. This time, we avoided political parties and worked with a few lawyers and social workers sympathetic to our cause. We included everything that was important to us, leaving it to the political parties to decide whether to support us and which issues to support. We were determined not to settle on the compromises we had agreed before when working with the Green Party. We did not want to dilute the demands that were so important to us, for example, that we should have duties without any corresponding rights and pay taxes without enjoying any access to the social security system.

Our draft was comprehensive – over 50 closely written sides – and we had carefully examined all legal areas which pertained in any way to the sex industry: Civil Code, criminal law, public order laws, the law on the regulation of sexual diseases and the federal law on epidemics.

In the meantime, in the autumn of 1998, after sixteen years of conservative-Christian-liberal-democratic majority rule, Germany at last saw a change of government. The 'Greenies' (our former friends) formed a coalition government together with the Social Democratic Party. "Yeah! "(we thought). At the outset of their term of government, both parties agreed in writing in their coalition contract to "improve the legal and social situation of prostitutes" (Coalition Contract, 1998).

All of us, throughout the country, were excited, aroused, even overjoyed! We thought we would be outcasts no more, that we had seen the end of humiliating working conditions, of catastrophic health provision and of endless discrimination. At last we would truly be able to claim with pride that "We are women, just like the rest of you".

When at last, after lengthy negotiations, the coalition agreement was signed during the night of 19/20 October 1998, champagne corks popped in self-help projects, in associations, in counselling centres (and in a few brothels). We had (we thought) succeeded!

In the weeks following the elections and during the long drawn out negotiations between coalition partners, we spoke repeatedly with women and men in both parties whom we either knew or who had been assigned to this issue. We often waited for hours outside closed doors for discussions to end, just to make sure that our demands had not been overlooked in the course of the negotiations and that they would be mentioned in the final coalition agreement. We wanted to make sure that something would change at last.

This one single sentence: "We will improve the legal and social situation of prostitutes" made us almost crazy with joy. I remember how I sat alone at my activist's desk in our association office and frantically searched the internet for the relevant passages in the comprehensive agreement. Once I'd found them, I didn't know who to ring first, who to meet where, which party to go to. I believe I even wept for joy. Since then, the tears have given way to rage.

Those of us who had been campaigning over the previous decade knew any improvement to the legal framework would require lengthy debate in parliament. So, like good Girl Guides, we prepared. We kept a close eye on every development, however minor; we combed the press, as well as party and government publications. We maintained permanent contact with MPs, and waited.

We assumed in fact that no legislative changes would ensue until we, the experts, had been consulted. Half way through the parliamentary period, it dawned on us that time was running out. Procedures in parliament are complicated and all significant legislative change requires the consent of the Federal Council. How was it all to be done in time? Nothing was happening. Surely, they should have long since started expert panels, workshops and hearings. Had the government we elected, of which we had such great hopes, simply forgotten us?

We slowly began to suspect what we know today for sure: the whole law was to be nothing other than a badly done cosmetics job.

When the 14th German Parliament (Bundestag) dealt with the issue of sex work in Germany in spring 2001, we once more had to endure a typically uninformed discussion: trafficking in humans, migrant workers in the sex industry, drug-addicted street hookers, child prostitution, women who chose professional prostitution and AIDS were all thrown indiscriminately into one big pot. And that was it.

The coalition agreement's promise to improve the legal and social position of prostitutes had become a burden and was conveniently shrunk to a size compatible with the rapidly dwindling legislative timetable. The election campaign for the subsequent parliament was about to begin. And so we were fobbed off with pathetic excuses: "You have to understand - it's just not an issue any party wants to fight an election on", or " We're doing everything we can – but you must understand, it's a difficult issue".

Cold comfort. No one had time; no one wanted to talk to us. The little that we did find out was certainly no cause for joy; there was to be a "short draft, formulated in quite general terms". From circles within the Alliance 90/Green faction, we heard: "one didn't want to run the risk of a too daring draft failing due to resistance within the party's own ranks." We were furious.

The whore movement mobilised all that remained of its energies. We had endured fifteen years of debates, of defending ourselves, of exclusion, of struggle. We wanted adamantly to be involved in formulating and influencing this new law.

But not all veterans were still 'on board'. Some had given up years before because they had other priorities in their lives, because they had grown disillusioned and tired or because they had made an uneasy peace with the existing situation. Everyone had their own reasons for the decisions they made and all were valid in their own way.

After the events of 9/11 in the USA some of us old activists began to hope that all legislative business might be postponed to the next period, due to the political climate. We were afraid that any law, however vague, might cement a status quo that it would then be impossible to overthrow for the next thirty years. This much we had learned from history: when once a parliament has 'dealt with' an issue it is usually in no hurry to do so again.

Others were of the opinion that even such a miserable law constituted progress of sorts. Should the law be passed in this diluted, superficial form then we would have to trust judges and prosecutors to interpret it widely. Those of this mind said we had fought to make parliament deal with this issue for far too long to just call off the reform when something, however small, might yet be achieved.

Now, seventeen months later, this discussion is over for the law is in place. And we are all still sitting around the ministerial desk, thinking that perhaps there is something to save, to smooth out, and to influence, at least regarding the interpretation of the law. For we know (we did after all listen very carefully to the parliamentary debates in 2001) that the government is expecting a report after the trial period of three years, a report in which conditions faced by sex workers under the new law will be set out.

And in order that this report be authentic, in order that this report serve our interests, what's left of our movement sit dutifully at this desk - smartly dressed, prim and proper, and demure. We have fallen into the trap of being institutionalised by a political machine that only pays lip service to our demands. We can still be seduced into believing in the outside chance that we can exert some influence, just like any other social movement. We are no exception.

The whore movement – a myth?

The whore movement is one of those modern myths, a social movement that is supposed to function as a political party or pressure group and bring about change but, in reality, demonstrates only the boundaries of 'tolerance' by established interests in the name of social pluralism. The survival of the mythical 'whore movement' serves 'the authorities' both within and beyond its own ranks.

In reality, from its beginnings through to the early 1990s, the whore movement was manifest more or less exclusively during the National Congresses of Whores. Throughout the 1980s, the Congress was open only to bona fide whores. Great efforts were made to screen participants. Bogus whores and bogus street hookers were immediately thrown out and investigations were instantly instigated to determine how they had managed to gain entry at all.

However, 'bogus' participants who were there under the aegis of some powerful figure in the whore camp were allowed to stay. Any whore found responsible for bringing an 'alien' into these hallowed ranks had to explain his/her reasons and, were these to be deemed deficient, then she or he too might be asked to leave. Rounds of introductions took up an enormous amount of time at every Congress. Is she or he a whore, or not? Why not? Is that a journalist/ a brothel owner/ or (horror!) even a social worker?

When AIDS hysteria peaked in the mid-1980s, federal, regional and local authorities in Germany were anxious to prevent the spread of HIV by prostitutes. Counselling centres for prostitutes and research by expert whore activists received generous funds.

Activists within whore self-help groups and associations, until then largely voluntary organisations, suddenly found themselves in paid work as counsellors, able to meet the growing demand for advice and offer regular service. Prior to this development many women had begun to study social work, sociology, theology and education. The whore movement grew – there was a lot to be done!

The improved financial and theoretical basis of the whore movement led gradually to the Whores' Congresses being taken over by the sponsors who funded them, and they were planned by voluntary or paid, usually badly paid, staff.

The movement criticised this development from many perspectives and made a particular issue of the creeping exclusion of whores from their Congresses. This critical faction found itself eventually excluded, or chose to attend no longer. Interestingly, the exclusion of critical voices was vigorously undertaken by whores and other Congress supporters but, ultimately, the critical whores were not literally thrown out; they were no longer welcomed.

The critical women maintained informal contact with each other so as to compensate for the psychic stress and lack of appreciation experienced at the Congresses. They were anyway of the opinion that a unity amongst whores had never existed, (and certainly never as a unified movement) and that expediency simply makes for strange bedfellows. This was the internal drama: the activists slumped into depression, the social workers started to realise the importance of social counselling markets for sex workers, and the politicians realised that there was no need for funding or networking – 'make-up' for the media would be enough.

In recent years numerous projects have disappeared without a trace: Hamburg, Braunschweig, Essen, Düsseldorf, Münster, Köln, Stuttgart, Leipzig. They suffered the same fate as many other private, social work type projects which devote themselves to marginalised groups but which fail to make the transition to becoming socially integrated, established projects. This is partly because they worked in isolation, partly because they worked on their own particular issues, and partly because of negative government policy and media images.

Counselling centres, which employed a number of sex workers, have acquired a poor public image because state funding has been cut, often drastically, and political differences between sex workers, sponsors and supporters have proved increasingly difficult to negotiate. Sex workers are no longer seen as experts. They have to glean information on the next policy steps and current debates from the daily press. No longer do we vote on how to proceed collectively and the whore movement, insofar as it exists at all, reacts to developments rather than taking the initiative.

The view that whores have disappeared from politics, to be replaced by social workers, is certainly true in some respects. There were many more whore projects and associations a few years ago, and many more active 'unorganised' lone fighters. Above all, there were more whores committed to political struggle.

Within our ranks, certain personalities emerged, who acquired cult status. This phenomenon served our purposes in campaigning and those of the authorities in demonstrating political inclusiveness. The motherly colleague with the ample bosom, neat bun at the nape of her neck and a heart of gold was always available to journalists.

The intellectual with a bunch of kids - her absolute first priority - took these along to parliamentary hearings. She also got worked up (and derived some pleasure from) answering banal chat show questions, preferably from moral theologians and Christians, while the kids would be waiting in the wings, along with her husband.

Those of us able to slip into the role and make humorous, witty and ironic appearances did so at every opportunity – and had fun doing so. We could always find a reason, if we looked hard enough, to pop a few champagne corks.

Everyone involved is thus under increasing pressure, and we are exposed to enormous stress in our dealings both with funding bodies and other parts of the movement. It is as if activists had struggled to cross a great ocean of treacle. Having arrived, exhausted, at the far shore, they look back onto an ocean that lies smooth and unchanged behind them: their passage has left not a trace. The system has resisted attack and survived.

Mutual, institutional and public appreciation is minimal or completely lacking. And what we did was never enough, would have had to have been more, and could have been more. What did it matter if we were quoted in the press when they misquoted us half the time or used information misleadingly?

What use was praise from local authorities and government ministries "for our support of women wishing to give up prostitution" when they wouldn't guarantee our funding?[8] How did it feel for us, as politically committed women, to have to pretend that we were only counselling women who wanted to get out of sex work, when in fact we were counselling women on how to start up in it, something that we could not mention?

As well as all this, conditions generally within the sex industry were changing for the worse. More and more women are going into it, not because they love the milieu, because it turns them on, or because a pimp drags them by their hair to a brothel. No. They are driven into sex work by poverty.

Migrants in Germany in search of an income, and downwardly mobile German women alike are taking up sex work. There is little time for political commitment in such a climate.

Those social workers involved in the whore movement are now determining the nature of whore self-help. The (few) whores in the associations are those who expect more commitment and unconditional devotion to the cause from social workers, because the latter profit from the stigmatisation and discrimination of whores. At the same time, social workers make no secret of the fact that they expect the whores themselves to organise campaigns that further the interests of social workers.

A lot of energy will be expended during this discussion on the road to emancipation. Whether, in the current conditions, we shall ever get there remains to be seen.

After almost one and a half years of ProstG only one fact is glaringly obvious: the law has not improved the situation for men and women working in the sex industry. On the contrary, the situation in the industry has worsened due to prevailing uncertainty. It is doubtful whether - as in homeopathic practice – it is a temporary phase during which symptoms have to get worse before they can get better.

De facto, nothing has changed. The whores still get their wages up front, the stigmatisation continues, and as well as all this, we are now faced with endless discussions with concerned clients who "have heard that we now have the right to a pension".

The brothel management does not sign employment contracts with their employees and whores are in the same dreadful situation.

This latest law continues to underwrite a basic lack of autonomy in men and women working in the sex industry. It is assumed that they can be exploited, embezzled, unduly influenced and still require the special protection of the criminal justice system in a way that differs radically from workers in other service jobs.

The authorities, operating a misguided, paternalistic double standard, have created a lamentably incompetent piece of legislation. "Let's make an omelette without breaking eggs" must have been the guiding motto of all the debates and research evaluations, which led to this law being passed by parliament.

Those whores, brothel owners and supporters who are determined to grab the opportunities presented by this law and make the best of it are not to be envied. They continue to form working parties and discuss what is to be done, invest enormous amounts of money on advice from lawyers and accountants...and hope.

We shall see what happens – or rather, whether anything will happen at all.

Abbreviations

ADG III	Anti-Discrimination Law
AuslG	Law on the Immigration and Residency Rights of Non-Nationals in the German Federal Republic
BGB	German Civil Code
EGStGB	Introduction Law to the Criminal Code – statutory order law
EStG	Federal Income Tax Law
OWiG	Civil and Social Codes
ProstG	Law on the Rights of Prostitutes
StGB	Criminal Code

Notes

[1] Income deriving from sex work is taxed as "Other Income" at a considerably higher than average rate (EStG Article 15).

[2] In 1989, whilst researching my student dissertation, I met the "Whores' Mutual Self-Defence Group" (HWG) in Frankfurt. My interview partner, Cora Molloy, immediately identified me as a colleague and invited me to the next Whore Congress. I had been working in the sex industry for five years. This was my first contact with politically organised colleagues.

[3] When the Workshop ended on 01.04.2003, (fifteen months after ProstG came into effect), it was clear that no employment contracts had been made in the German sex industry.

[4] These comments come from: "Statement of the Legal Study Group of the German Whore Movement in April 2003 on "One Year ProstG" and from results of the "Second Workshop on the Prostitution Law", convened by the Federal Ministry for Family, Pensioners, Women and Youth in April, 2003.

[5] The slogan echoes the title of Pieke Biermann's book, *We Are Women Just Like Any Others! – Whores and their Struggle*, 1980.

[6] Anti-Discrimination Law Pt.III- (ADG III). The Green Party initiated the first Anti-Discrimination Law in Parliament in 1986.

[7] During a period of AIDS hysteria, claiming to 'be afraid of AIDS' enabled hundreds of women (for example in Berlin) to quickly claim Social Security and then move into state-funded jobs outside the sex industry (Hydra Nachtexpress 1988/89).

[8] Funding for counselling centres was available for HIV prevention programmes and to support women who wanted to give up sex work. Very few counselling centres obtained funding for alternative information campaigns.

References

Biermann, Pieke (1982). *Wir sind Frauen wie andere auch!*, (*We Are Women Just Like Any Others! – Whores and their Struggle*). Reinbek.

Civil and Social Codes (OWiG) from 24.05.1968, redraft by public announcement 19.2.1987; last redraft on 22.08.2002, (publ'd in Berlin in Official Federal Gazette, 2002), Translated into English by Jill Denton (2003), Berlin.

Criminal Code (StGB) from 15.05.1871, redraft by public announcement 13.11.1998; last redraft on 22.08.2002, (publ'd in Berlin in Official Federal Gazette, 2002), Translated into English by Jill Denton (2003), Berlin.

Drößler, Christine (ed) (1994). *Prostitution – Ein Handbuch*, Schüren Presseverlag: Marburg.

German Civil Code (BGB) redraft by public announcement 02.01.2002; last redraft on 24.08.2002, (publ'd in Bonn in Official Federal Gazette, 2002).

German Federal Parliament, 14th Electoral Period, Publication Nr:14/5958, explanatory background on the Federal Legislation, 2001, Pt.1 Nr. 74, publ'd (in Bonn on 27.12.2001).

Hydra Nachtexpress, *Zeitung für Bar, Bordell und Bordstein*, Special Issue, Vanity Press: Berlin, 1988/1989.

Hydra (ed) (2000). *Das heimliche Treiben der Männer*. Verlag am Galgenberg: Hamburg.

Introduction Law to the Criminal Code – statuary order law (EGStGB), redraft by public announcement 02.03.1974, (publ'd in Bonn in Official Federal Gazette, 194).

Law on the Rights of Prostitutes - ProstG (Prostitutionsgesetz – ProstG) from 21.12.2001, Federal Legislation Year 2001, (publ'd in Official Federal Gazette, Bonn on 27.12.2001, Printed Legal Matter No.14/5958, Berlin).

Law on the Immigration and Residency Rights of Non-Nationals in the German Federal Republic (Ausländergesetz – AuslG), from 09.07.1990. Last amended on 16.02.2001 by the Law to End Discrimination against Same-Sex Partnerships (publ'd in Berlin in Official Federal Gazette, 2002).

Molloy, Cora (1992). *Hurenalltag. Hurenalltag. Sperrgebiet, Stigma, Selbsthilfe Sperrbezirke und ihre Auswirkungen am Beispiel Frankfurt am Main*. Frankfurt, Materialien zur Sozialarbeit und Sozialpolitik, Band 34, Fachhochschule: Frankfurt am Main.

Palandt, Otto (2002). *Legal Commentary to German Civil Code*, 61st Edition, München.

Social Democratic Party and the Alliance 90/Green Party, Coalition Contract 1998. (First Steps to Renewal – Germany's Path into the 21st Century, publ'd in Bonn 20.10.1998 by Federal Centre for Political

Chapter 5
Twenty years of action: Committee for Civil Rights of Prostitutes, 1983-2003
Pia Covre[1]

While waiting for clients one hot summer night near the municipal park of a town in northern Italy, a group of street workers decided to protest about the behaviour of US personnel from the local US Air Force military base. The prostitutes found the continual verbal and physical abuse from young American soldiers unacceptable. So was the behaviour of the local police.

It was 1982. A short, incisive press release issued by these prostitutes in the national press attracted a good deal of public attention, and the episode became a *cause célèbre*.

In 1983, this informal group formed a legal association under the name *Comitato per i Diritti Civili delle Prostitute* (Committee for the Civil Rights of Prostitutes). An official political manifesto was prepared and posted on the town walls. This was a manifesto for the rights that prostitutes had been denied as citizens. It demanded a complete revision of prostitution laws.

Media attention broadened the original prostitutes' network, which came to include transgender groups and prostitutes' groups from other cities. Our cause became so popular that it was taken up by political parties, some of which proposed to revise the laws in line with our demands. This raised the issue more widely in popular discussions and promoted a debate among feminists. We sought to decriminalise prostitution and respect the right of self-determination of those who chose freely to work as prostitutes.

Attempts to reform the law have always been difficult and controversial in Italy. The 1958 prostitution law[2] for example, was a victory for prostitutes as they gained the freedom to work outside brothels. However, abolitionism has always meant that prostitution is viewed with ambivalence, and those who choose to work as prostitutes have never been fully respected.

In 1983, *Comitato per i Diritti Civili delle Prostitute* made contact with the English Collective of Prostitutes and the Dutch group, *Rode Draad* and began to organise internationally. Since then, we have campaigned actively for the freedom of sex workers both nationally and internationally. This has involved conferences, initiatives against prejudice and discrimination, information campaigns, sit-ins, and protests in the media about the stigma and social exclusion of prostitutes, including transgenders.

Public appeal for Prostitutes' Rights, Comitato per i Diritti civili delle Prostitute. September 2000, Pordenone.

For the respect of the civil rights of prostitutes

Because as long as we are perceived as quiescent prostitutes or informers who are the victims of extortion and exploitation, we are tolerated. Yet, whenever we pretend enjoyment of the same rights granted to all other citizens, we are then persecuted and threatened.

For the freedom of self-determination of sexual choices

Because sexual liberty cannot be bargained. Neither the State or the Church can decide our place! The state has the duty to guarantee the respect of diversity, especially when it does not infringe upon the rights of other citizens.

For the freedom to sell or buy sex among consenting adults

Because in the total absence of violence, force, or exploitation, prostitution, when carried out under complete freedom of choice, is an expression of sexuality. First, to prohibit it is ridiculous; moreover, it is illegal.

For the fight against the trafficking of women and for authentic regard and concern for its victims

Because all the forces of investigative and judiciary machinery must be concentrated towards striking against and dismantling the networks of Mafiosi criminality which derive profit from the misery, the hunger, the poverty, and the pursuit of happiness of the women involved.

Beyond Tolerance and Compassion for the Recognition of Rights

Against arbitrary operations of the police towards prostitutes and their clients

Such operations are unfounded because the intent and the letter of the Merlin Law are distorted. In reality, these operations, which show the repressive face of the State, are an open aggression against the liberties of our Status of Rights.

Against the moralistic hypocrisies of Government representatives

Who sheepishly renounce the defence of the laity of our Republic State, while readily accepting nearly everything that is gratuitously inveighed against by the ecclesiastical hierarchy of the Vatican.

Against the false fight, against the exploiters of prostitution, which effectively strikes only against victimised prostitutes rather than against the criminal exploiters who are members of racketeer-influenced and corrupt organisations

Everyday the Minister of the Interior and the State Police authorities proudly announce the number of prostitutes that have been hauled-up, arrested and expelled from our country as well as the number of clients that have been fined and denounced. O that they might begin to tell us, even occasionally, how many exploiters that have been arrested, condemned, and expelled!

Against policies that produce stigmatisation and social exclusion of prostitutes

Such policies compound the unmotivated and irrational fears of public opinion, which is manipulated by political demagoguery from all sides for electoral results. These policies stir up racism and xenophobia and give greater substance to the generic, yet dangerous, "demand for law and order", which would concede wilfully trampling upon the rights of certain categories of citizens. We must realise that ignoring the rights of the least of our citizens or residents can and will eventually lead to erosion of the rights of all.

In 1984 students went on strike in support of us. Some high school students in Bologna decided to protest against censorship when prostitutes were prohibited from giving a lecture in their school. Thousands of students took the streets and we led a long march across the city.

During less hectic periods, the committee produced papers, studies on prostitution, and even a magazine, *la Lucciola*,[3] which was regularly distributed in bookstores for two years. When AIDS arrived in Europe we became preoccupied for much of the 1990s with organising self-help groups and other prevention strategies including, for the first time in Italy, mobile health service units for prostitutes.

It has not been easy to talk about condoms or safer sex in a Catholic country like Italy but we organised a campaign from our own resources, helped by a generous contribution from an advertising agency in 1995. The enormous posters of condoms that appeared on Italian city walls and in magazines were impossible to ignore.

The Vatican continues to influence the Italian government's policies on sexuality. There are, for example, close links between many MPs and Opus Dei, the personal prelate of the Catholic Church based in Rome and devoted to the promotion of traditionalist approaches to women and sexuality (Urquhart 1997).

In 1995, during the United Nations Fourth World Conference on Women, 41 nations announced reservations to approximately 20 parts of the Platform for Action[4] mostly in the areas of sexual and reproductive rights. These dissenting delegations included the Vatican and countries controlled by Catholic or Islamic religious forces.[5]

In 2000, *Comitato per i Diritti Civili delle Prostitute* had to make another public appeal for prostitutes' rights and the committee collected signatures from Italy and other European countries. Tadej Pogacar, a Slovenian artist, responded to the appeal and in June 2001 organised the 1st World Congress of Sex Workers and New Parasitism[6] (49th Biennale di Vinizia in Venice, Italy) which ended with the *March of Red Umbrellas*. Pogacar's project, entitled *CODE: RED, Sex Worker*, attracted great interest, while the media labelled it as a big provocation by the Biennale.[7]

During the Congress and through a metaphorical *tableau vivant* prostitutes from several northern, eastern, and southern countries raised the issue of the marginalisation of prostitution in front of the international public.

1st World Congress of Sex Workers and New Parasitism, *March of the Red Umbrellas*, June 2000

Changes in the organisation of business and work have affected the sex industry. Prostitutes' lives and working conditions have deteriorated in comparison with clients, who now have to pay less in real terms for sex. In addition, those who mediate the sale of sex such as the Mafia, have made enormous profits in Italy over the past ten years.

Immigration has led to increased competition and lower prices. We must denounce the inevitable, albeit unintentional, collaboration formed between police, criminals, and clients that has placed newly arrived immigrants in the hands of criminal networks where they are sometimes violently exploited.

Immigrant and Italian women work secretly so as to avoid police repression; clients take advantage of this situation to force women to lower their prices. Non-Europeans endure a particularly difficult double repression in both prostitution and immigration. Some prostitutes perceive foreigners as a threat who compete with them and cut prices. Our committee, however, is committed to solidarity and tries to help smooth both the process of immigration and of working as a prostitute.

On the eve of Christmas 2002, the cabinet announced that it would submit a new bill to parliament. The draft bill will radically change the current situation based on the 1958 Merlin law (see footnote 1). In an attempt to sweep prostitution off the streets and control illegal migrants, the lawmakers have come up with the idea of legalising brothels, a return to the pre -1958 situation.

Under this new proposal street work would be completely illegal (with harsh penalties for both sex workers and clients caught in the open air and public venues) and prostitutes allowed to sell sex in private only. This could be in a flat or house, with a maximum of three women and no children living on the premises.

The proposal also calls for the registration of all sex workers, an impossible move for those who have pimps (who would probably not view too favourably women's participation in a government scheme) and for the majority of sex workers in Italy who are illegal migrants.

Besides banning street prostitution and mandatory registration, the new law would lead to compulsory medical checkups for prostitutes who would receive a licence to sell services from private homes. Lastly the issue of taxation was raised in the bill, with all sex workers paying taxes on their income and future 'house managers' paying for social benefits. This may be another well-meaning reform that would in theory give sex workers more safety and comfort but in practice it will further the two-tier system of legal and illegal sex workers.

For *Comitato per i Diritti Civili delle Prostitute*, this law, soon to be approved by parliament, is ugly, repressive, cruel, and anti-constitutional. Prostitution is being submerged by reactionary tides and nineteenth century prescriptive attitudes that seek to repress poor women.

The future for prostitutes does not appear bright. Once again, this tendency affects several European countries. The evident incapacity to manage immigration and the fear of a menacing economic crisis lead governments to embrace very dubious policies.

For example, prostitution is criminalised in the name of the fight against illicit trafficking in people. Were we to apply the same criteria to the labour market, where clandestine workers abound, we would need to abolish work altogether. People do not take into consideration the will of people who become prostitutes, nor do they consider the complexity of the phenomenon.

Sex workers' associations are committed to a fierce struggle in the months and years ahead; we will rise to this challenge. We cannot remain indifferent in the face of war, famine and mass migration. We must push our political leaders to adopt more generous policies that help disadvantaged people to achieve social justice.

Notes

[1] Pia Covre is co-founder of Comitato per I Diritti Civilli Delle Prostitute, Italy.

[2] The Merlin law or Merlin's Act (so called as it was introduced by socialist reformer, Angela Merlin) decriminalised the crime of practicing private prostitution. This marked a profound change for prostitutes. Up to 1958, prostitution had only been allowed in brothels that were regulated as bars (i.e. under a strict regime with specific opening hours and closed to the public on Sundays). The Merlin Law abolished that system, led to the closure of brothels and women became free to work on the streets and in private houses.

[3] *La Lucciola* translates as the firefly, a popular Italian name for prostitute. It literally refers to a night insect yet it is a poetic image that evokes distant lights in the darkness.

[4] The Platform for Action included major advances for women in the areas of violence against women, health, economic equity, and the rights of girls.

[5] See, for example, writings from The Feminist Majority Foundation and New Media Publishing Inc. http://www.feminist.org/research/report/73_glob.htm (Accessed October 2003)

[6] The artist Tadej Pogacar makes in his work an analogy between a live organism in nature (hence parasitism) and an institution of society. This analogy is expressed by representing the fictional institution (the model of an institution as an artistic system-work) as a parasite that hangs onto (inhabits, consumes, uses, exhausts and brings death to) the "real" and "existential" social institutions (museums, archives, agencies, anti-institutions enacted by homeless people, as well as private institutions of everyday family life). For more details, see http://www.ljudmila.org/scca/parasite/notes2.htm

[7] *Code: Red Sex Worker* is an ongoing project that explores and discusses selected aspects of prostitution and sex work as a specific form of parallel economy. The project takes the form of an open dialogue between artists, sex workers, and the public. The partnership between the *Comitato* and Tadej Pogacar's P.A.R.A.S.I.T.E. Museum is based on a the following central them: " How to organise a marginal organisation and survive".

References

Urquhart, Gordon (1997). *Opus Dei: The Pope's Right Arm in Europe.* in Conservative Catholic Influence in Europe: An Investigative Series. Washington DC: Catholics for a Free Choice.

Websites

Comitato per i Diritti Civili delle Prostitute website http://www.luccioleonline.org/documentazione/press.htm (accessed January 2004)

Mobility and Migration

Chapter 6
Daring Border-Crossers: A different vision of migrant women
Laura Mª Agustín

This article was originally published with the title "Challenging Place: Leaving Home for Sex" in a slightly different form in Development *(Volume 45, No. 1, March 2002, pp 110-17). It is reproduced by kind permission of the Society for International Development (www.sidint.org).*

As soon as people migrate, the world tends to sentimentalise their home. Warm images are evoked of close families, simple household objects, rituals, songs, and foods.[1] Many religious and national holidays, across cultures, reify such concepts of 'home' and 'family', usually through images of a folkloric past. In this context, migration is constructed as a last-ditch or desperate move and migrants as 'deprived' of the place they 'belong' to. Yet for millions of people all over the world the place of their birth and childhood is not a feasible or desirable one in which to undertake more adult or ambitious projects, and moving to another place is a normal — not traumatic — solution.

How does this decision to move take place? Earthquakes, armed conflict, disease, lack of food give some people little element of choice or any time to process options: these people are sometimes called refugees. Single men's decisions to travel are generally understood to evolve over time, the product of their normal masculine ambition to get ahead through work: they are called migrants. Then there is the case of women who attempt to do the same.

Research in a marginal place: geographies of exclusion
For a long time I worked in *educación popular* in various countries of Latin America and the Caribbean and with Latino migrants in North America and Europe, in programmes dedicated to literacy, AIDS prevention, health promotion, preparation for migration and *concientización* (whose exact translation does not exist in English but combines an element of consciousness-raising with an element of empowerment). My concern about the vast difference between what first-world social agents (workers in government or NGOs, activists) say about women migrants and what women migrants say about themselves led me to study these questions and bear witness to what I found. I deliberately located myself on the border of both groups: migrants and the social sector in Europe, where the

only jobs generally available to non-European women are in the domestic, 'caring' and sex industries (Agustín 2003).

My work examines both social agents and migrants, so I spend time in brothels, bars, houses, offices, 'outreach' vehicles and 'the street'. Data come from my own research and that of others in many countries of the European Union, and include testimonies of women both before and after migrating from Latin America, Eastern Europe, Asia and Africa (Agustín 2001). Data on what social agents say come from my research with those who work on commercial-sex issues in those countries, including as evaluator of projects for the International Labour Organisation and the European Commission.

Although researchers and NGO personnel have been working with migrants who sell sexual services for nearly 20 years in Europe, publication of their findings rarely finds its way into mainstream press and journals. Most of the people who have met and talked with migrants are neither academics nor writers. 'Outreach' is regarded as distinct from 'research' and generally funded by HIV/AIDS prevention programmes. This means that the fruit of outreach research is generally limited to information on sexual health and practices, while the many other kinds of information collected remain unpublished.

Some of those who work in these projects have the chance to meet and exchange such information, but most do not. Recently, a new kind of researcher has entered the field, usually young academic women studying sociology or anthropology and working on migrations. These researchers want to do justice to the reality around them, which they recognise as consisting of as many migrant sex workers as migrant domestic or 'caring' workers. Most of these researchers do oral histories and some have begun to publish, but it will be some time before such findings are recognised. Stigma works in all kinds of ways, among them the silencing of results that do not fit hegemonic discourses.[2] The mainstream complaint is that 'the data is not systematised' or even 'there is no data'. In my research, I seek out such marginalised findings.

Discourses of leaving home

It is striking that in the year 2004 women should be so overwhelmingly seen as pushed, obligated, coerced or forced when they leave home for the same reason as men: to get ahead in life through work. But so entrenched is the idea of women as forming an essential part of home, if not actually *being* it themselves, that they are routinely denied the agency to undertake a migration. A pathetic image is so drawn of innocent women torn from their homes, coerced into migrating, if not actually shanghaied or sold into slavery. This is the imagery that accompanies those who migrate to places where the only paid occupations available to them are in domestic service or sex work.[3] The 'trafficking' discourse relies on the assumption that it is better for women to stay at home rather than leave and 'get into trouble' – trouble being seen as something that will irreparably damage women (who are grouped with children), but which men are routinely expected to overcome.

But if one of our goals is to find a vision of globalisation in which poorer people are not constructed solely as victims, we need to recognise that strategies that seem less gratifying to some people may be successfully utilised by others. Therefore, this chapter is not about whether domestic service can ever be pleasant or prostitution should be accepted as 'work'.[4]

The bad beginnings or sad, frightening or even tragic moments of people's migrations to find work need not forever mark them nor define their whole life experience. Relative powerlessness at one stage of migration need not be permanent; poor people also enjoy 'multiple identities' that change over a life-course composed of different stages, needs and projects. By insisting that people may decide, for instrumental reasons, to migrate under less than ideal conditions, the reality of the worst experiences are not negated. The abuses of agents who sell would-be migrants ways to enter the first world happens to those who work as domestic servants and in sweatshops, *maquiladoras*, mines, agriculture, sex and other industries, whether they are women, men or transgender people. But these most tragic stories are fortunately not the reality for most migrants.

Displacement or misplacement? Questions of will and 'choice'

Research among migrants selling sexual and domestic services reveals little essential difference in their migration projects and demonstrates that migrations that may have begun as a kind of *dis*placement (a feeling of being pushed out, of having no reasonable choices) are not doomed to be permanently sad stories.[5] Even the poorest and even the partially 'trafficked' or 'deceived' look for and find spaces to be themselves in, run away, change jobs, learn to use friends, clients, employers and petty criminals. In other words, they do the same as other migrants and in all but the worst cases tend to find their way eventually into situations more to their liking, whether that means finding a good family to clean for or a decent brothel owner or the right contacts to work freelance.

Neither are migrations totally economically motivated. Exposed to media images that depict world travel as essential to both education and pleasure, potential migrants learn that first-world countries are highly comfortable and sophisticated places in which to live. They are excited at the prospect of meeting people from other countries. All poor people do not decide to migrate; many that do are people interested in and capable of taking the risks involved in uprooting in order to 'find a place in the world'.

My example here is migrant women and transsexuals in Europe, but the discourses which construct them as 'trafficked' exist all over the world and are being addressed by international bodies.[6] At the time of writing, the majority of migrants selling sex in Europe come from the west of Africa, Latin America, eastern Europe and countries of the former Soviet Union. While domestic workers have begun to unite across ethnic borders to demand basic rights, sex workers have not, making them impossible to fit into classic migration frameworks. For a variety of legislative and social reasons, not least of which are the repressive policies of police and immigration all over Europe, migrants selling sex tend to keep moving, from city to city and from country to country.[7] This itinerant lifestyle prevents them doing the things migrants are 'supposed' to do, such as rooting themselves in their new society, forming associations and becoming good (if subaltern) citizens (the Roma suffer from the same impediment). While nomadism is considered romantic in people who live far away (such as the Bedouin) it tends to be seen as a social problem inside the West.

Writers on migrations and diaspora maintain a nearly complete silence about people who sell sex,[8] though they can be studied as daring border-crossers who typically (and repeatedly) arrive with little information, luggage or local language. But the only aspects of their lives discussed (by everyone, not only by lobbyists against prostitution) are their victimhood, marginalisation and presumed role in the transmission of HIV/AIDS, injustices that reproduce stigmatisation. Yet it is safe to surmise that if men were the predominant group using commercial sex as a means to get into Europe and earn good wages then it would be seen as a creative move – not routinely characterised as a tragedy.

Finding pleasure in the margins

A crucial element in this gendered reaction is the widespread assumption that a woman's body is above all a sexual 'place', where how women experience sex and use their sexual organs is essential to their self-respect. While this may be true for many, it is not universal, and the use of the body for economic gain is not considered so upsetting or important by many selling sex, who usually report that the first week on the job was difficult but that later they got used to it.[9]

Some theorists assume that something like the soul or real self is 'alienated' when sex occurs outside the context of 'love', and that women are fatally damaged by this experience. But these must remain moralising hypotheses, impossible to prove. Some women feel this way and some find pleasure in prostitution, which only means there is no single experience of the body shared by everyone. In any event, even sex workers who don't like what they do say it is better than a lot of other options they also don't like; learning to adapt to necessities and ignore unpleasant aspects of a job is a normal human strategy.

In the midst of the sentimental musings that surround the subject of 'uprooted migrants', the myriad possibilities for being miserable at home are forgotten. Many women, homosexuals and transsexuals are fleeing from small-town prejudices, dead-end jobs, dangerous streets, overbearing fathers and violent boyfriends. Home can also be a boring or suffocating place, as evidenced by the enormous variety of entertainment sites located outside of it. In many third-world cultures, only men are allowed to partake of these pleasures, occupy these spaces, while in Europe, everyone can. People who sell sex also have private lives, go to films, bars, discotheques, restaurants, concerts, festivals, church parties and parks. Their wish to leave work behind and be ordinary is no different from that of other people; in the context of urban spaces they become *flâneurs* and consumers like anyone else.

Social constructs of identity

Various NGO projects in Europe work with migrants selling sex and would like to promote their self-organisation to defend their basic rights.[10] Such projects inevitably require, however, that subjects 'identify' as prostitutes or sex workers, which few do; rather, they identify as migrant people from Cali or Benin City or Kherson who are selling sex temporarily as a means to an end. This means they are less interested in questions of identity than in being allowed to get on with earning money the way they are, without being harassed and subjected to violence on the one hand, or pitied and subjected to projects to 'save' them on the other.[11]

Those who want to help often set up a dichotomy about 'place' which consists of, in the first place, home (which you loved and were forced to leave) and, in the second place, Europe (which you don't want to be deported from). The complicated relationships migrants have to 'home' – which may or may not be a place they wish to visit or actually live in again – are excluded from discussions about them. And when migrants are referred to as 'trafficked' they are assumed to have been wrested away against their will, allowing immediate unsubtle deportation measures to appear benevolent (and to be characterised by some ironic activists as 're-trafficking'). [12]

Various theorists have pointed out how migrants' work of caring for children, the elderly and the sick creates 'chains' of love and affection which take in the families that migrants leave behind, the families they come to work for and new relationships started abroad (Hochschild 2000). This more nuanced vision of the role of 'place' in women migrants' lives is generally not extended to sex workers, however.

Milieux as workplaces . . .

All this theorising impinges little on women focused on getting ahead. A rural woman from a third-world country can arrive in Europe and, with the right contacts, soon be in a position to earn €5,000 or more a month. This figure does not refer to what are sometimes called 'high-class' prostitutes who work with 'elite' customers (and who can earn much more) but refers to an amount commonly earned in large or small clubs and brothels as well as flats, whose names and particular characteristics change from country to country.[13]

With this amount, a migrant may be able to pay back debts undertaken to migrate fairly soon, and to earn it she works in multicultural, multilingual clubs, brothels, apartments and bars. Here you find people from Equatorial Guinea working alongside people from Brazil and Russia and people from Nigeria alongside people from Peru and Bulgaria. For those selling sexual services, *milieux* are workplaces where many hours are spent socialising, talking and drinking, with each other, clientele and other workers like cooks, waiters, cashiers and bouncers. In the case of flats, some people live in them while others arrive to work shifts. The experience of spending most of their time in such environments, if people adapt to them at all, produces cosmopolitan subjects, who may consider the world their oyster, not their home. And there is nothing in the cosmopolitan concept which excludes poor people or prostitutes.

It is easy to find migrant sex workers who have lived in multiple European cities: Turin, Amsterdam, Lyon. They have met people from dozens of countries and can speak a little of several languages; they are proud of having learnt to be flexible and tolerant of people's differences. Whether they speak lovingly of their home country or not, they have overcome the kind of attachment to it that leads to nationalist fervour and have joined the group that may be the hope of the world, the one that judges people on their actions and thoughts and not on how they look or where they are from. This is the strength of the cosmopolitan.

Some doubt that ordinary work relations can exist in *milieux,* as though all other workplaces were less alienating: offices, hospitals, factories, mines, sweatshops, farms, academic institutions. But the sex industry is huge, taking in clubs, bars, discotheques and cabarets, erotic telephone lines, sex shops with private cabins, massage parlours and saunas, escort services, matrimonial agencies, flats, cinemas, restaurants, services of domination and submission and street prostitution. Much of this work is part-time, irregular or a second job, and working conditions for these millions of workplaces across the world vary enormously. Though frequent change of personnel is common, this is also true of work in the cinema and performing arts, as well as of 'temporary' office and computer workers (where no one doubts that normal relationships occur). Relationships with colleagues may cross ethnic lines or not, according to the individuals involved; the chance of this is increased where a great variety of people is found with no one type predominating. This is the situation in the *milieux,* now that migrants constitute the majority of those selling sex in Europe (Tampep 1999).

. . . and *milieux* as borderlands

Milieux are not only multi-ethnic, they are borderlands: places of mixing, confusion and ambiguity, where the defining 'lines' between one thing and another are blurred. Since so many of those selling sex in Europe are foreigners, languages spoken in the *milieux* include pidgins, creoles, signing and *lingua francas,* where Spaniards learn to communicate with Nigerians, Italians with Russians, French with Albanians. Similarly, many clubs would appear to be carnival sites, the world upside down, where the prostitute is like the *pícaro*, the half-outsider who substitutes trickery for dignified work, living the role of 'cosmopolitan and stranger . . . exploiting and making permanent the liminal state of being betwixt and between all fixed points in a status sequence' (Turner 1974: 232).

The *milieux* are sites of experimentation and show, where masculinity is performed by some and femininity by others. Investigations as far apart as Tokyo and Milan demonstrate that for many the sexual act carried out at the end of a night on the town or *puttan tour* is not at the centre of the experience, which rather resides in sharing with male friends an experience of talking, drinking, looking, driving, flirting, making remarks, taking drugs and, in general, being 'men' (Allison 1994, Leonini 1999). The person selling sex in a prostitute's 'uniform' is doing whatever will lead to making money; in the case of the transsexual, often a hyper-performance of womanliness. While any sexual service contracted usually occupies no more than fifteen minutes, not only workers but clients spend long hours having no sex at all.

In the sex industry it is men who are publicly 'permitted' to experiment with their sexuality (and masculinity) and relate to people they would not meet anywhere else. The availability of migrant women, homosexual men and transsexuals means that millions of relationships take place every day between people of different cultures. The reduction of these relationships to a series of undifferentiated 'acts' and their elimination from cultural consideration because they involve money cannot be justified.[14] For some who theorise sex as culture, sexual practices are seen as constructed, transmitted, changed, even globalised.[15] In this vision, migrant sex workers are bearers of cultural knowledge

Everyone agrees that the sex industry exists within patriarchal structures. Some critics will continue to lament migrants' loss of home and the near impossibility of their organising formally. But one must also give credit where credit is due, recognise the resourcefulness of most migrant women and allow them the possibility of overcoming feelings of victimhood and experiencing pleasure and satisfaction within difficult situations and in strange places.

Notes

[1] The word 'home' in English connotes much of this all by itself, but this is not true in all other languages.

[2] David Sibley (1995) contributed invaluable evidence of this in his chapter on W.E.B. DuBois' rigorous sociological research on 'The Philadelphia Negro', which never was accepted by the academy.

[3] Domestic service involves many of the same isolating characteristics as work in the sex industry, and the two are undertaken simultaneously by numerous women looking to acquire more money in a shorter amount of time.

[4] As one member of Babaylan, a migrant domestic workers' group, said: 'We look at migration as neither a degradation nor improvement . . . in women's position, but a restructuring of gender relations. *This restructuring need not necessarily be expressed through a satisfactory professional life.* It may take place through the assertion of autonomy in social life, through relations with family of origin, or through participating in networks and formal associations. The differential between earnings in the country of origin and the country of immigration may in itself create such an autonomy, even if the job in the receiving country is one of a live-in maid or prostitute.' (Hefti 1997) (*Author's emphasis*)

[5] Published findings by and personal communications with researchers in Spain, the U.K., Italy, France, Belgium, Germany, Holland and Switzerland. A recent example is Oso 2003.

[6] Important other current sites of discourse on the issues are India, the Mekong Delta, Nigeria and the Dominican Republic, as well as Canada and the U.S.

[7] Police and immigration efforts to 'clean up' sex work sites or pick up 'undocumented' workers vary from city to city across Europe, change from day to day and are targeted, according to the moment's policy, on street, bar or brothel workers. Few workers are completely exempt from fears of police attention.

[8] The most notable exception to this silence is negative and emblematic. Discussing Mira Nair's film *India Cabaret*, Arjun Appadurai begins by describing young women from Kerala who 'come to seek their fortunes as cabaret dancers and prostitutes in Bombay', a neutral enough treatment of the situation. Two sentences later, however, he refers to 'these tragedies of displacement', without providing any justification, and likewise criticises the men who frequent the cabarets as returnees from the Middle East, 'where their diasporic lives away from women distort their very sense of what the relations between men and women might be'. Appadurai provides no references and no theoretical backup for these typically moralistic opinions about how sex and relationships 'ought' to be (Appadurai 1996: 38-9).

[9] I am not referring here to particular people who actively enjoy their sex jobs and want their rights as workers recognised. Some of these are organised and lobby against the criminalisation of prostitution and for sex workers' rights.

[10] Note that these are solidarity projects *with* sex workers and not composed *of* sex workers.

[11] Many will note that being allowed to 'get on' in sex work relies on the prior social proposition.

[12] The late realisation that such arguments are convenient to conservative immigration policies - those basically intended to close borders and exclude migrants - has led to various national proposals to allow trafficked people to remain, whether they agree to denounce their exploiters or not.

[13] The surprise this figure may cause is related to the media's nearly exclusive coverage of either street prostitution or interior sites of worst exploitation. The ability to earn such an amount depends on being introduced or introducing oneself into this market, having the skills to operate there and learning to manage this kind of money (a frequent problem is large-scale consumption which tends to cancel out high earnings). Working fewer hours or days or taking breaks between contracts reduces income. For more on the 'skills' required, see Agustín 2000.

[14] The latest 'place' to be inhabited by migrant prostitutes is cyberspace, like cosmopolitan space borderless. The stigmatisation of prostitutes and the wish of many clients to hide their desires make cyberspace ideal for everyone, and, in a rapid proliferation of forms, sexual services are offered and/or completed in chat rooms, on bulletin boards, in pages with images and recorded sound, in direct advertisements with telephone numbers, and, via webcams, in both one-on-one and more 'public' shows. Here women are emerging as consumers, perhaps because of the dearth of 'places' where women may go to seek anonymous, public or commercial sex. Consider a study carried out in Europe which showed women to make up 26 per cent of visitors to pornographic websites. (Nielsen Netratings 1999)
[15] 'Contextualising sexuality within political economy has underscored how extensively prevailing notions about sexuality, gender, and desire are fueled by a colonialist mentality that presumes a crosscultural rigidity and consistency of sexual categories and the durability of geographic and cultural boundaries imposed by Western scholars.' (Parker, Barbosa, and Aggleton 2001: 9).

References

Agustín, Laura (2000). 'Trabajar en la industria del sexo.' *OFRIM Suplementos*, No. 6, June, Madrid. English translation, 'Working in the Sex Industry', on http://www.swimw.org/agustin.html.

Agustín, Laura (2001). 'Mujeres inmigrantes ocupadas en servicios sexuales.' In *Mujer, inmigración y trabajo*, Colectivo Ioé, ed., 647-716. Madrid: IMSERSO.

Agustín, Laura (2004). 'A Migrant World of Services.' *Social Politics*, 10, 3.

Allison, Anne (1994). *Nightwork: Sexuality, Pleasure and Corporate Masculinity in a Tokyo Hostess Club*. Chicago: University of Chicago Press.

Appadurai, Arjun (1996). *Modernity at Large*. Minneapolis: University of Minnesota Press.

Hefti, Anny Misa (1997). 'Globalization and Migration'. Presentation at conference *Responding to Globalization*, 19-21 September, Zurich.

Hochschild, Arlie Russell (2000). 'Global Care Chains and Emotional Surplus Value.' In *On the Edge: Living with Global Capitalism*, W. Hutton and A. Giddens, eds., 130-146. New York: Vintage.

Leonini, Luisa (ed) (1999). *Sesso in acquisto: Una ricerca sui clienti della prostituzione*. Milan: Edizioni Unicopli.

Nielsen Netratings, published in *Ciberpaís*, 9, March 2001, p. 13, Barcelona.

Oso, Laura (2003). 'Estrategias migratorias de las mujeres ecuatorianas y colombianas en situación irregular.' *Mugak*, 23, 25-37.

Parker, Richard, Barbosa, Regina Maria and Aggleton, Peter (2000). *Framing the Sexual Subject: The Politics of Gender, Sexuality and Power*. Berkeley: University of California Press.

Sibley, David (1995). *Geographies of Exclusion*. London: Routledge.

Tampep (Transnational AIDS/STD Prevention Among Migrant Prostitutes in Europe Project) (1999). *Health, Migration and SexWork: The Experience of Tampep*. Amsterdam: Mr A de Graaf Stichting.

Turner, Victor (1974). *Dramas, Fields and Metaphors*. Ithaca: Cornell University Press.

Chapter 7
About sex, vaginas and passports
MAIZ [1]

Migration. A piece of land behind us, a piece of land under our feet. Under the fingernails the remnants of the country, the earth of our gardens, our memories and passions. In the vagina your sperm. Below the feet, earth, below the feet, earth, land.

All around borders, exclusions, prohibitions, allocations, delimited inhuman degrading roles. And locked doors. Forward only through the ways that the lords of the land permit: prostitution, brothels, baths, pelvises, penises, men, also in the proper middle class living rooms, kitchens, beds and sofas as obedient wives. Helpless before violence, in pain and rage.

Helpless before violence, in pain and rage.
Yes: rage. Pride and resistance: thus: no pity, please.

It is not about a moral complaint: it is not about shifting the whole weight of the situation on to the moral plane: it is about justice, about the recognition of our rights. How long will it continue, passive and uncaring?

How long? we asked and we continue to ask. Emigration means to refuse to waste time with crossed arms. And here, in the old world, we waste time with folded arms.

Mobilised by our outrage, through our shared experience of having European sperm in our vaginas for centuries, six years ago we started the work of MAIZ. The principles are: the development of political consciousness instead of charity work. The recognition of prostitution and sexual choice instead of double morality. Thus in recognition of the legitimacy of our role as protagonists we attempt, through work in several areas, to find answers to the problems of women's working migration, to develop strategies and to carry them out in order to allow ourselves a proper life. One of these areas is health and street work: MAIZ works on health programs for sex workers: cultural mediators (i.e. women from the same culture) communicate through street work, visits to bars, direct contact with sex workers as well as consultations in the health services: information and awareness about AIDS, venereal diseases and protecting health. *Infomaterial* exists in 10 different languages. An important part of this work is the education of disseminators of information. We have also produced an information brochure, Cupiditas, published in 4 languages.

Some of the problems with which we are confronted during street work are:

- Migrants are even more stigmatised than other sex workers (they are not only whores, but also poor, foreign and sometimes black).

- For various reasons migrants in the sex industry are very mobile, changing bars, cities and even regions throughout the EU.

- The majority of women do not know much about the sex industry. Many women were not active in the sex industry before they migrated and did not want to become active in this trade. Most do not see themselves as sex workers and see their activity as short term.

- We repeatedly find women who are victims of the trade in women. This illegal status means that the women, among other things, live under extremely bad conditions and can easily be abused. They cannot go to the police or protect their rights in any other way. Exploitation through reduced pay, long hours, unprotected and unhealthy work conditions, isolation through cultural difference, language problems and the lack of access to, or lack of information about, their rights and the law are the results.

- The number of children and minors involved in the sex industry is growing. Many have drug problems.

- In street work we are often confronted with opposition and annoyance from pimps and club owners, primarily in the illegal brothel area. Several forbid entrance to their clubs or any contact with the women.

- Around half the punters / customers want unsafe sex (without a condom) and are prepared to pay double or triple price for it.

In conjunction with our activities in MAIZ, in the course of ongoing work through cultural mediation, which enabled us to reach migrant women, we were able to gain the confidence of these women, especially the migrant women who work as sex workers in Austria. In this context, it has been possible for us to appear in public with these women. Aware of the risks this involves, we attempt to use existing forms of mediation and communication or develop new ones together, which enable all of us to be protagonists, yet without being perceived as exotic victims.

In the following interviews, we attempt to convey to the readers an insight into the situation of migrant women trying to improve their living situation here through sex work. These are women who refused to resign themselves to poverty in their countries of origin and set out on the path of migration. Opportunities for migrant women in European countries, however, are reduced almost exclusively to sex work or marriage, and prostitution is usually regarded as a necessary phase in their lives, in the hopes of attaining their desired goals.

In this context, "attaining" is a key term. Prostitution is not the wish of these women, but rather a means to an end. However, sex work cannot be called an opportunity, because it would be cynical to speak of opportunities where there is no choice. Seeking to attain desired goals has its price because sex work in migration is very often linked with exploitation, isolation, racism and violence.

Before you begin to read these interviews, we think it is important to explain two things. First of all, depending on the situation (framework, recipients, contact person), the women articulate their statements in different ways. Secondly, it is not a question of formulating a moral complaint, but rather we seek to 'attain' a removal of the taboos surrounding sex work, so that we can formulate and address the changes needed, in order to truly improve the living and working conditions of migrant women in sex work.

"We are all actually psychology professors"

Interview with a Hungarian

Why did you come to Austria?

Because of money. Simply the money. The situation in Hungary is heavy, it is very sad. I had no possibilities there.

Have you been able to fulfil your wishes, your plans, your expectations here?

No, not really. It is not my strongest desire to work in the sex industry. It is more due to necessity.

How do you feel in Austria? Is this home?

In general I have it good here. The city is pretty and clean, the people are nice, but it is not my home.

Do you feel integrated?

No, I do not feel integrated. Often I suffer jealousy from other women. It happens quite often that I am looked down upon, or receive strange looks from Austrian women on the street or in shops. Often I can feel racism on my skin. I think it is a problem for most Austrians that we are here. I mean as a person, an individual. At work it is a bit different. There it doesn't really matter where you come from. Naturally, some guests do not want me when I say that I am from Hungary. But that happens very rarely. I tend to have positive reactions to my roots. Many Austrian men appreciate Hungarian women. They find us attractive and nice. But I imagine living here as a foreigner, outside the milieu, is hard. Thus, at work I am not really confronted with racism, but on the street, in my normal life, I feel it strongly. And it upsets me a lot, because I do not believe that there is any reason at all that justifies racism.

How does one learn the basics for working in the sex industry?

Ah, that is hard, there are no two identical men. Every person who comes in is different. This is a very tough job.

What do you need for sex work? Are there special characteristics that are important? What are you good at?

You are good when you do not show your tiredness. You always have to be in a good mood, happy. The people who come to such bars are psychologically damaged. All, or almost all of them, have problems. Many problems: with themselves, with the world, with other people. They expect that they can unload their problems on you, or that you can charge them up with energy. Thus you must be open and communicative, you must have a lot of understanding, pay attention when listening. Often it doesn't matter how the girl looks. It is much more important to listen. The most important thing is that you have two open ears and that you are nice to them. Then they are spellbound. We are all actually psychology professors.

What do you like about your job?

Yes, sometimes I really like it. The best thing for me is when I see that the guest leaves and he is happy and satisfied. When I see a man all sunk within himself and I can make him feel better, give him something positive, then I am happy. The second thing that I like about my work is of course the money. But it is vital that you have some fun in the work other than the money, otherwise you go mad quickly.

What good things have happened in your work?

Actually there are two great things that happened, that I gladly think about and talk about. One was when I got to know an old man at work. It was very comfortable and amusing to be with him. It was nice and even revitalising to be with him, we had good chats. In this case he charged my batteries, he gave me something. Sadly it lasted only a few hours. I would have liked to have remained in contact. This is impossible in this line of work. The other was a really nice sexual experience. The punter stimulated me unbelievably. He found just the spot for me that turns me on. It was unique! It is still wonderful to think about it.

Are there threats in your work? Are you afraid of sickness?

Naturally there are dangers. Every day I am afraid of disease. We all live with the fear. The other thing that scares me are the perversions. But primarily disease. And I do not experience it just as a fear, but as a danger, a threat. I know a lot about AIDS and venereal diseases and continue to learn, but there are so many diseases, such as skin diseases and suchlike, that I do not know very much about. There are always guests who pull my hair or who hit my back during the act, some kind of perverts. That is naturally always uncomfortable, one does not get used to such things. I do not let it continue. A daily experience is the fight: with or without a condom. Many punters do not believe that AIDS exists and that it is very dangerous. This fight often exhausts me. I cannot understand how these people can be so simple, they have no fear, they do not want to perceive the danger. Naturally there are also those who try to talk us into it, none gets past me. I patiently explain why I do it. And when he then says "no thank you", then that is his problem and I do not worry about the money. The money that I can earn like that, I don't need. My health is more important!

Are there any special practices in your work?

Yes, there are always little tricks, but my biggest "weapon" is that I am nice. I am not particularly pretty, do not have a wonderful face, I cannot dance very well, I earn my money with attentiveness. I care for my guests, I talk with them a lot, I listen to them attentively, I hold eye contact. And that works for them. They feel safe with me. I know it because they say so, but I also realise this because of my regulars, who always come back to me. I am, thank God, very patient. It is interesting for me that many men are afraid of pretty, attractive women. I haven't worked out why, yet. I think that being nice is the best way for me.

How does your future look?

Well, I reckon that in a year, or at most two years, I will leave the sex business. If I continue to earn like I am now earning, then I will be ready in at most two years. I have a thirteen year old daughter in Hungary, I want to be able to do everything for her. My goal is to set myself up in Hungary. It is possible that I will remain in Austria, because I have a good relationship with a man here. How my future really will be, I still don't know.

...Yes, I determined what and how...

"At the start I just danced. Now I do something else."

Interview with a woman from the Dominican Republic

Why did you come to Austria?
It is hard to say... Do you know? All the people in Santo Domingo are poor, unemployed. It is a poor country. I wanted an improvement in my life.

And did you know what you would do?
I knew what I would do here.

From friends?
Yes.

Has it met your expectations and hopes?
I haven't done everything. I must do a job that I have never done before.

Do you like your work?
No, it is not good, but I have to work. And I do not have any other work, I do not understand much German. I cannot get any other job here.

Do you like it here?
No, I don't like the work, but what should I do?

Would you like to return home?
Yes, totally.

Are you afraid of diseases?
Yes, totally.

Are there positive experiences?
Yes, sort of...sometimes...you know

Can you give us an example of a positive experience?
(Laughter...)
I have gotten to know some interesting people...sometimes men come in, they are nice, I can talk with them, they are prepared to give support, they respect us...

How do you live otherwise? Do you try to separate work and private life?
Yes, one has to have fun...sometimes I go to the disco...I usually work until 10 pm, then I go home, sometimes on Sundays I go out...not always.

Do you feel safe? Are you insured in Austria? Are you integrated in society?
Yes, I feel safe. I am registered to work and I work in a licensed brothel. Thus I have health insurance, but no social [unemployment or pension] insurance.

Do you also have Austrian friends?
Friends yes, but no relationships.

Do you need any special skills in your work? What is important in your work?
Learning the language.

The language? German or body language?
Both. (laughter)

Isn't it important, how you look at someone? The erotic game, to attract a client, isn't it important?
You have to always be happy. You may never be sad!

Do you have to do everything that the men say?
No, I do what I want. They pay, but I only do what I want.

Do you have the power?
Yes, I determine what and how.

How does your future look?
I want to do so much! I want a car, I want to buy a house...I want to do much more...everything!

In Austria?
No, in Santo Domingo! I do not want to stay here much longer! I will stay perhaps another five years here.

Don't you want to marry here?
For legal reasons I want to marry. Maybe I will find a good man, then I will marry him on the spot.

What do you tell your parents that you do here?
They think that I work here in a restaurant. Hmm, I don't tell them what I really do here. Most of the people that do this here, do not do it in Santo Domingo. Only here we do work like this. I never did this before.

Did you come here through an agent?

No, through a girlfriend. She has always helped me. She knew that my family is poor, she helped me get my papers. She asked me if I wanted to come here to dance.

Did you dance?

Yes, at the start I just danced. Now I do something else.

You have an artist's visa as a dancer...did you believe that you were just a dancer?

Hmm, they already told me in Santo Domingo, you can dance, but if you want more money, then you must do something else.

That means it was your decision? There was no pressure?

No, it was my decision. I have to send money to my family every month, there are many children, many sick relatives, my mother is old, my father...

That means, you send the money...

Yes, I also pay rent here, pay the taxes, life here is expensive...

...I respect my partner and expect that he respects me...

"In the peepshow I am a living photo."

Interview with a Brazilian

You have worked in a peepshow - how is it?

There are various sorts of peepshow. There are those that are all closed in, and there are those that are partly open. The man can touch the woman and the woman can touch the man, if he wants that. There are many possibilities. For instance, when a man goes into an open booth, then he knows that he can touch the woman and he can also demand that the woman gives him a blowjob, for instance. But there are men, who do not want to use condoms, and they try it again and again and offer more money. I will not cooperate.

What are you doing at the moment?

At the moment I am table dancing. I am doing alright where I am. I do my show and have no troubles with it. If I was a prostitute, I wouldn't be so happy.

Why?

Not because of the sex, I like sex, but you know, all sorts of people come to a brothel. When I do my show, when I dance naked in front of men, I can choose who touches me and when. In a brothel the woman cannot choose the men. When a customer wants you, you must go with him.

What is the work like in a table dancing club?

In the peepshow I am a living photo. I stimulate the man and he masturbates. Table dancing I make my show, I dance then I chat with the men. There is no contact, it is all psychological. For instance there are men who are not attractive and wouldn't normally have the chance to spend time with a beautiful and erotic woman. There are men who pay between 5,000 and 30,000 Austrian Schillings an evening, only to talk with me. That's mad! Normal customers pay between 1,000 and 5,000 Austrian Schillings. I am there, I talk to them...I am attractive and sexily dressed.

Here we motivate the customer to drink, but for me there is the option to drink alcohol-free drinks. Usually I throw the drinks away. If I were to drink all the drinks that I am given I would be an alcoholic. My job is to extract money from the men. I must give him the feeling that he is attractive, good and wonderful. Other men want an intellectual chat, like we are having now. With other men I need to use other capacities, I must moan....move erotically and show that I find him attractive. There is no sex involved, I dance naked, then chat with the men. From the bar I get a fixed wage and a commission of 30% on the consumption of my customer at the bar.

There are men, very uncouth men, they are frustrated and want to release their frustration at me. But I am a professional, I do this for money and do not let such things upset me. I am never unfriendly to a customer, so that they always come back to me.

What is decisive for a good show?

It depends upon the customer. For example, I am small, pretty, like "Lolita". Not all men like such women. A good show is when the man is all hot and bothered.

How do you perform? What do you do?

He sees me and finds me interesting. Sometimes I wear very fine clothes, like I was going to the theatre or the opera, sometimes I dress like a classical whore. There are various expectations and imaginations and I have to meet them. There are men who like vulgar looking women, there are other men who like women to be well-dressed and behave appropriately. You find all sorts of women; pretty, fine, vulgar, fat, Rubinesque, etc. Some owners go to lengths to have every taste in women, others only want pretty women.

Don't you have to touch or masturbate your customers?

Not with table dancing. Most table dance clubs have no *separees*. Where I work at the moment, there is a small room, somewhat separated from the bar. There the customer can touch me, but he has to pay extra for it. But I decide whether and how and what he may do. First he must order a bottle of Champagne. That costs 5,000 Schillings - such a bottle will be drunk in half an hour! Then we go into the little room, but before he can touch me, he must pay again. Often they ask me how the *separee* is, and I say, "Cuddly." He asks, "How cuddly?" And I answer, "It depends. When you give me a small tip, then I am a bit cuddly, when you give me more, then it is more cuddly."

What sort of peepshow have you worked in?

One with a closed booth.

Does a woman earn more in a peepshow with an open booth?

Yes, in an open booth you can earn more, because you have contact with the person. The more contact, the more you can earn. Nevertheless I prefer the closed booth. After a day of work I do not want the feeling that I have to wash myself...because of those horrible guys...

Is this work a choice?

Yes, I chose this. I am there and do my job. When a man comes into the booth, then I ask over the "telephone" what he wants, a pussy show, a strip, whatever. I do what he wants, him on one side, me on the other. And there are rules. I do what I want. Here I have the power to decide on borders and rules. Then I do my show. He gets excited, beats off. End, *Finito. Ciao.* These men, who come to a peepshow or in a table dance club are mostly men who have girlfriends or family but who want another sexual life than they have with their women. Many cannot or will not go to a brothel, because they do not have enough money or do not really want contact. They want to watch a woman and masturbate. We, the man and I, are at no risk of infection. I do my show without any contact. A pussy show...

What is a pussy show?

It's like, I get undressed while dancing, sexy, sexy looks so that the man gets all exited, like on the internet, only here there is no monitor. I am really there in front of him, and I ask him what he wants, I spread my legs, I stick my finger in...there is also the vibrator show. That costs more. I get undressed, a strip, I caress my breasts, I should excite him. For health reasons I always use the vibrator with a condom, we also have a disinfectant for our hands. You know, I take money with my hands, I need to take care.

104

Doesn't it work with coins, that get fed in a slot?

The coins are usually for the business. That is the case, when he is there and I am in the booth. But what I do for him, he must pay me for. From the business I am paid a basic wage, but I really earn with the extras in the booth. For instance, a strip costs 200 schillings, but when he wants a show with anal and vaginal vibrators, then that costs 2,000 schillings.

Can you see the man?

In some cabins you can see the man, in others all I see is the mirror in front of me, then I have to imagine that I see the man, I have to act the whole erotic show as if I were able to see him, the tongue, the facial expressions, stroking my breasts, pretend to lick and suck...I am paid to excite the man. When I do that well, he comes back to me. My show isn't any better or worse than the show from other women. It is simply my show and certain men like my show. I cannot excite or stimulate them all.

Do you feel safe?

Yes. Also, I am officially employed. I have health insurance, I have to pay tax. The negative thing is the fact that I do not work here. I live here, I am happily married here, but I work in another town. I live there in a room with other women who work at the same place. I earn well, but I also pay a lot. I am also always tired.

How many hours a day do you work?

Between 12 and 14 hours.

How did you begin to work in this area? What capabilities do you need?

I searched a long time for a job and found nothing that was interesting and well paid. I had no problem working as a cleaning woman. I clean my flat, I do everything...but I know that I am attractive and intelligent and decided to use my beauty to earn money. In the beginning I was told how the business in a peepshow works, the rules, the prices, but nobody taught me how you should move, what you should do, to excite a man. I receive affirmation for my work through the return of my customers. Beauty is important, but it is not the main thing.

In the beginning I did not know how to seduce a man. Now I know. I sit there and it is often enough to give him a particular look, he is fascinated and comes to me. It is important to control this magic, this charisma. A "tchan" as we say in Portuguese, charm, magic...like a seller...I sell something, I do not sell myself, but my words, my style, my company.

Eye contact is important when dancing. The men want the feeling, that you look at them specially, that you dance for him. Mimicry is very important. It is also important to be able to speak the language.

What are you planning for your future?

When I was younger, I wanted to marry a man who would offer me security. With time I noticed that I cannot live with a man who controls my life. I want to have my money, to be able to do what I want when I want to do it. I respect my partner and expect that he respects me. As to my future I want to have a house, to be loved, be [financially] secure, but not dependent upon a man, I want to be independent. I work in this field for the money.

Do you want to remain in Austria, or do you want to return home?

I like Europe a lot and will live here for many years, because the structures are better here than in my country. I love my country, I enjoy holidays there, but I like living here. I want to have children here, that they grow up here and go to school here. One has more security here... ..but I find the people here are very cold and egoistic...problems are everywhere...I like Brazil, but I like it better here. I am happy and like my life. I earn a lot, but I do not just think about the money, I always try to support my family in Brazil. The people here are not really supportive of one another. The infrastructure is good, the state supports the people, but between the people, it is not good. I have the impression that we are happier than the people here.

Notes

[1] MAIZ - Autonomous Center for and from Migrant Women. MAIZ is an independent organisation active in Linz and Upper Austria that has been working with the problems of female work migration and the situation of sex workers in Austria since its founding in 1994. MAIZ is an organisation from and for migrant women from many continents who are simultaneously protagonists and victims. MAIZ is active in the following fields: social, legal and employment advice and assistance, health protection for sex workers, education and public work, culture work, working with the second generation (children and youth).

Chapter 8
Mobility in prostitution, the impact of policy and the implications for health: A case study from the Netherlands
Thérèse van der Helm

Introduction

During my 28 years as a public health nurse, prostitution has changed dramatically. Western European countries opened their borders to individuals who had previously needed a visa, and a large number of foreign prostitutes arrived in the Netherlands in the 1990s. Many were brought up surrounded by poverty in a society where no help could be expected from their governments. This internationalisation of the sex industry in The Netherlands had meant that our educational materials has had to be presented in different languages and adjusted for the varying backgrounds of the sex workers. Co-operation with cultural mediators –support workers who can speak the languages of migrant sex workers and have insight into their culture – has become integral to our fieldwork, helping us to contact and communicate with a diverse and multicultural population. Then, in October 2000, the law in the Netherlands changed. Brothels were legalised and sex workers employed by them registered. It was unclear, however, whether this law would simply improve 'public order' or whether it would also improve working conditions for all prostitutes.

Mobility in prostitution

In the 1960s Dutch women dominated prostitution in The Netherlands. At the beginning of the 1970s, migrants, mostly Southeast Asian women from Thailand, appeared in Amsterdam and other cities. In the 1980s we began to see prostitutes from Latin America and Africa. Since the fall of the Berlin Wall in 1989 the numbers from Central and Eastern Europe have increased dramatically. The numbers rise and fall according to developments in Europe as a whole; for example, Bulgarians have not needed a visa to travel to Western Europe since 2001 and the numbers working in prostitution have increased noticeably. Although Bulgarians can travel without a visa, they still need a work permit to work legally, and many have been arrested and deported as a result of regular police raids. Some return to The Netherlands within a few weeks to work illegally once more.

Most Dutch prostitution is operated through legal businesses. About 60 per cent of sex workers are based in clubs, windows and private houses, with 30 per cent in escort services or working at home. Only 10 per cent of prostitutes, male and female, work on the streets. Women perform the vast majority of sex work.[1] There are increasing numbers of transgender prostitutes, most of whom are migrants from countries outside the European Union.

It is hard to estimate the numbers involved. There are perhaps 20,000 sex work jobs in The Netherlands, including around 8,000 in Amsterdam, but the numbers of individuals involved is much higher because of a rapid turnover and extensive mobility. In Dutch cities the majority come from outside The Netherlands – from Latin America, West Africa, South-East Asia and Central and Eastern Europe. Many stay a short while and move on to other European countries, presumably because their visas expire or they have no resident status. The table presents results of a Europap survey in 1999, showing that more than two-thirds of prostitutes in The Netherlands were migrants in 1999.

The origin and gender of estimated number of prostitutes in The Netherlands

	Women	Men	Transgender	Total	%
The Netherlands	6,054	265	1	6,320	32
Other EU countries	1,112	125	10	1,247	6
Central and Eastern Europe	3,277	375	35	3,687	18
Asia	635	-	45	680	3
Latin America and the Caribbean	3,208	160	912	4,280	22
North Africa	899	50	-	949	5
Sub-Saharan Africa	2,480	25	-	2,505	13
Unknown	-	15	-	15	1
Total	17,665	1,015	1,003	19,683	100

Source: EUROPAP survey undertaken in 1999 in The Netherlands.

Until the 1990s there had been a national policy of toleration towards foreign prostitutes, which meant that prostitutes who worked in The Netherlands did not fear arrest if they asked for help. Good relations existed between sex workers, non-governmental organisations and health workers, and long and stable associations could be built up. However, as the sex industry grew and diversified, political pressure mounted to introduce more controls.

A new law came into effect in October 2000 that imposed regulations on owners of brothels. In this new 'brothel law', owners were prohibited from employing women outside the EU who did not have a residence permit. These rules had an immediate effect on the numbers of arrests and deportations, and on the numbers entering the country.

New prostitution law in The Netherlands

During the French domination of The Netherlands at the end of the 18th century, prostitution was regulated in Holland, similar to the situation in France. Every prostitute had to register with the police and was checked for venereal disease every two weeks by a doctor. Most prostitutes paid little heed to the regulation, including its enforced medical examination. At the beginning of the 19th century, there were an estimated 3,000 prostitutes in Amsterdam, of whom only 800 were registered. In the second half of the nineteenth century, there were calls throughout Europe to abolish prostitution both on the grounds of morality and in support of the emancipation of women. This led to a law in 1897 which outlawed brothels in Amsterdam. This legislation, Article 250, was adopted nationally in 1911. As a result clandestine prostitution increased, brothels were called hotels, and prostitutes were called domestic help. (Coutinho, 1989).

Despite this law remaining in place, over the twentieth century the Dutch developed a pragmatic approach to prostitution. While the personal exchange of sex for money was not considered to be a criminal offence, organised prostitution was forbidden even though, in practice, commercial brothels were allowed to operate in freedom. This semi-legal status of brothels allowed employers to do their business without fear of government sanctions even if they seemed to be abusing employees either mentally or physically, or failing to provide hygienic working conditions.

It proved difficult to control the excesses of this large and varied semi-legal prostitution, and some people considered that the toleration of brothels was hypocritical and also illegal. Many attempts to solve the discrepancy between the official law and actual practice by rewriting Article 250, including attempts to legalise organised prostitution, failed.

In the 1980s and 1990s, there was a major debate over the regulation and legalisation of prostitution, culminating in the major legal change that came into effect in October 2000. The 'brothel law' meant that brothel owners who meet the requirements of this new legislation could obtain a licence; those who did not would have their brothels closed. Requirements of the law include that:

- brothels have to be clean, hygienic and free of fire risk
- prostitutes who work in brothels may not be forced to drink alcohol nor may they be forced to have unsafe sex with their clients
- minors (under the age of 18) are forbidden to work in prostitution
- women from outside the EU without residence permits are not allowed to work in prostitution

The new law offers advantages for those who can work legally since they enjoy better occupational health and safety conditions. Moreover, prostitutes may be covered more adequately by the wider social security system through labour laws that will turn prostitution into a legal profession. The re-organisation of brothels also make it easier for health and social services personnel to contact prostitutes, provide education and medical care and, where relevant, referral to social services.

Despite these potential advantages, the new system of registration has driven some prostitutes who could work legally into hiding. Working for a short period, many oppose the new legislation because they are concerned about being registered as a prostitute long after they have ceased to be one, and also because they do not want to pay taxes. Prostitutes from outside the European Union have fewer rights and are indeed prohibited from working in The Netherlands. Many have disappeared into escort work or private circles of contacts that are difficult to reach. These women in particular are vulnerable to violence and intimidation.

As there is no system in The Netherlands for registering prostitutes individually, it is difficult to provide numbers on different categories of sex workers but we estimate that the number of 'legal' as compared to 'illegal' prostitutes is very small.

In 2000, as a response to the change in the law, the de Graaf Foundation[2] set up a National Platform for organisations working with prostitutes, especially in health and social services, to improve contact with prostitutes driven underground by the new policy and to improve working conditions generally.

Prostitution and the trade in women

Another major topic of debate related to the sex industry concerns the issue of 'trafficking'. In 1987, women's lobby groups against sex tourism and trafficking in people founded the Stichting Tegen Vrouwenhandel (STV, Foundation against Traffic in Women). It now has extensive global experience of the effect trafficking has on victims. According to the STV, about 2,000-3,000 thousand women in The Netherlands are trafficked every year. They report that individuals are forced into prostitution through deception, intimidation and violence. Most are women from other countries, especially Eastern Europe. Currently, the Dutch government recognises such trade in prostitution but it will soon extend the relevant laws to cover other trafficked individuals who may be forced to work in other industries and businesses, as domestic servants or 'mail order brides'.

Since 1995 more and more 'victims' of trafficking have been reported. This may reflect greater political sensitivity and STV have certainly noted more calls about this issue from the clients of prostitutes. It may also reflect better cooperation between STV, prostitution outreach workers and the Dutch police. The police report most victims to STV (STV 1997-2000).

Certainly, the increase in Eastern Europeans working in The Netherlands has been accompanied by an increase in reported trafficking. Victims have some legal rights but lose any right to stay in The Netherlands after their case is resolved, and so many are reluctant to report abuse to the authorities, a reluctance that is aggravated by fear of retaliation from traffickers. Approximately 350 women a year report trafficking to the police (ibid).

This is only the tip of the iceberg. Most of the victims are very young, naive and dependent on others. They experience great difficulties in coping with these traumas. It may therefore be important to guarantee some basic security in the form of a home, an income and plans for the future. Indeed, follow-up care in some form of shelter seems critical in preventing similar exploitation of these women in the future.

STV has developed a program to train professionals in this work throughout The Netherlands. In addition, it has initiated prevention activities in the countries from which women migrate, in co-operation with the La Strada project and other non-governmental organisations in relevant East European countries. Prevention is a key aspect of good policy, and women in these countries will now be informed about the activities of criminal organisations as well as shelters that have been set up for their protection.

However, abuse depends on perspective and what some perceive as trafficking or slavery is seen by others as just another cost associated with working. The following two accounts, the first from the perspective of a social worker (more precisely, a cultural mediator – see below) and the other from a prostitute, illustrate the difference.

> I know the red-light district very well; I have lived there for some years. I never expected that after my study of Russian and Bulgarian at university, I would be asked to work in the Intermediary project.[3] I also work in the Living Room[4] one evening per week. The contacts with the women there are very different from those in the red-light district. The encounters I have in the red-light district are usually short, 15 minutes only. In the Living Room there is more time to build up relationships. I cannot imagine that these very young Eastern European women knew the circumstances they would have to work in. The stories of their lives are often abominable. They have to pay their pimp €500 every week. He has them believing that he has to pay for the medical check-ups in the Living Room. We told the women this was a lie because all check-ups are free of charge. Still, they don't dare to stand up to the pimp because they are very frightened. I think they are part of a large network of human trafficking. I give information about the special facilities for victims when they report trafficking: during investigations of, and trials against, perpetrators, they have the right to stay in The Netherlands. But this is not what they want; in many cases they have children and most of the women want to go home as soon as possible.

Sara, cultural mediator. (van der Helm 1989)

Lisa is a 22 year-old woman from Belarus. She came to Amsterdam via Greece and Germany, together with six other women from her village. They all have Greek passports, arranged by an 'agency'.

They have to work in prostitution to pay their debts. They have worked in brothels in different places. In Amsterdam, they all worked illegally. "None of us will go to the police", Lisa said.

> Of course the men of that agency are taking advantage of us; we have to pay a lot of money, but we knew what the contract was about. ... We will be happy to stop working in this job once our debts have been paid, but we will not go back to Belarus. Although we are well-educated, there is no employment for us at home. ... The men in my village are also unemployed; they drink too much and abuse their wives and children. ... We will find a nice man here, so that we can stay; we are survivors.

Lisa's comments could be construed in terms of the 'trade in humans' criminalised by Dutch legislation. But they also show that some women, at least, do not consider themselves as 'victims' but rather 'survivors', earning a living as best they can in difficult circumstances, made worse by restructuring in Eastern Europe.

In 2001, a survey of 124 prostitutes using the Living Room in Amsterdam showed that many East European prostitutes considered it normal to pay pimps or agencies through contractual agreements and therefore had no reason to report any offence to the police. Moreover, since police in their own countries were often corrupt, they had little confidence in the police system elsewhere (Heleen Driessen 2002).

Health issues in prostitution

The Dutch Foundation for STD Control serves as the national coordinating body for STI/HIV prevention in prostitution. It supports activities at a regional and local level, primarily supported by the municipalities. Municipal Health Services usually take the leading role in coordinating and implementing local prevention activities. In larger cities, drug treatment organisations, including methadone and needle-exchange programmes, Living Room projects, and social work organizations also play a role. The Foundation has developed a national campaign focused on prostitutes, their clients and the brothel owners, aimed in particular at small intervention projects for those who run the highest risk of contracting HIV – prostitutes who inject drugs, migrants (both prostitutes and clients), and male prostitutes.

The programme includes educational materials primarily aimed at

- increasing the amount of contact with target groups
- increasing knowledge about STI and HIV transmission and prevention
- reinforcing and promoting safer sex as a social norm.

Most prostitutes are aware of the risk of contracting STI/HIV in their work if they practise unsafe sex. All over the world it is commonly known that there is a difference between knowledge and practice, however. Money, alcohol or drugs are often important reasons for not consistently using condoms. In a number of cases, women considered their clients to be gentlemen, married men, and therefore they felt there was 'no need for safe sex'. Still, the percentage of sexually transmitted infections and HIV among prostitutes is low. Since 1992, six-monthly cross sectional studies at the Municipal Health Services' STI clinic in Amsterdam have shown that HIV prevalence is below 1 per cent among heterosexual clinic attendees, including non-IV drug using prostitutes and their clients. Sexually transmitted infections were found in about 36 per cent of the clinic attendees and 20 per cent of prostitutes. (Fennema et al 2002)

Nevertheless, these figures leave out of account a large number of migrant prostitutes who have no health insurance and therefore buy medicines, such as antibiotics, on the black market or at home via intermediaries. Only a small percentage of migrant women use contraceptives in addition to condoms. Despite regular accidents with condoms and subsequent unintended pregnancies, many migrant sex workers distrust other methods of contraception. Some women have had two or three abortions while they were in The Netherlands. (van der Helm and van Heusden 2001)

Cultural mediators

I have been working in the Intermediary project since 1994. I used to work in a Turkish restaurant in the red-light district. In Santo Domingo [Dominican Republic], I worked in a hospital; I like to work with people. In 1994 there were many prostitutes from Latin America in the red-light district – about 80 per cent of all prostitutes. Some were a bit jealous of me because of my job in the project and I was afraid that they would not want to talk to me. But that changed after they noticed that I offered support if they got into trouble. I helped them if they needed medical help or needed to go to a social work agency. Since 1996, there has not been so much work for me to do in the red-light district. Because of the strict Amsterdam policy,[5] many women have left the legal arenas. I feel sorry about this because we were always very close. However, some women from the Dominican Republic still come to The Netherlands via Curacao. I also work in the Living Room, during the clinic consultation hours, one evening a week. Compared to working with women in the windows, there is more time to talk because prostitutes come to rest in the Living Room. Contact with prostitutes in the windows can be very rushed if women are under pressure to earn money. As a woman, I sometimes find it difficult to talk with transgenders about intimate subjects; they are in fact men, and some of them feel sort of ashamed to talk to me.

Luz, cultural mediator (van der Helm 1999)

The Dutch Foundation for STD Control, together with the Municipal Health Service, has set up a project in the larger cities to offer sex workers support from cultural mediators. (van den Berg, 2001) Cultural mediators from Eastern Europe, Africa, Asia and Latin America work with prostitutes who share their culture and/or speak the same language. They receive training as reproductive health messengers, and so sexually transmitted disease prevention is only one element of their work. In Amsterdam they work with staff from the Intermediary project at the Municipal Health Service. The most important objectives for cultural mediator's outreach work are:

- making contact with foreign prostitutes
- providing education on reproductive health
- improving techniques for negotiating safe sex
- informing prostitutes of health and social services available and improving their access to them
- support in reporting exploitation, abuse and rape to the police.

Although a full evaluation has not been completed, preliminary results show that cultural mediation can improve the effectiveness of fieldwork. For example, when prostitutes have not talked to outreach workers and when communication is difficult, cultural mediators establish how to proceed. In isolated cases, it seems that these contacts with cultural mediators were difficult for prostitutes;

one, for example, said she was "ashamed, meeting a fellow countrywoman while she was working".

Given the high mobility of sex workers, relevant information has to be provided at the first meeting since they have often disappeared, to be replaced by others, by the time of a second visit. Therefore, conversations during the first contact focus on safer sex, HIV, tuberculosis and other infections, condoms, lubricants, and birth control and, where relevant, condom use is demonstrated on a dildo.

Women are provided with educational material in the appropriate language and with contact information on how to obtain free assistance in The Netherlands. Flyers are distributed in nine languages with information about the work of the Vice Squads' 'human trade and prostitution' units. This may encourage women to notify the authorities if they consider themselves to be victims of exploitation or abused in other ways.

> I have worked for the Intermediary project since 1995. A large number of Ukrainian, Russian and Polish women were working in Amsterdam at that time. The attractive part of my work was that I had something to offer these women, especially the ones from my own country. Most of them were very young, and they seemed lost. This work has completely met my expectations and I have met very nice women. I think women in windows work more safely than women in the brothels. In brothels the men are often drunk and expect more services from prostitutes because the prices are higher than in windows. The clients should be better informed. They think that prostitutes in a classy brothel are "clean" and therefore they can have sex without a condom. Most of the Eastern European prostitutes I have met will never admit to working without a condom. When they were fearful of being infected or becoming pregnant, it was because of a "condom failure". Sometimes it was hard to talk positively about contraception because I knew they did not like contraception, in particular, the pill. Initially, they would reject information but, in the end, some asked doctors for contraception.
>
> Daria, cultural mediator (van der Helm 1999)

It may seem obvious that these prevention projects can only succeed when meetings are held in relatively safe, stable environments. The Living Rooms for street sex work in those districts where the police tolerate prostitution offer such conditions. Here, prostitutes can rest and drink, chat with their colleagues, have a check-up and, if they want, talk to cultural mediators. When national and local policies are pursued to deport prostitutes working illegally, prevention activities become far more difficult. In this situation, prostitutes avoid contact with any 'officials' for fear of deportation. Ignorance of local services, insecurity about work and the fact that many women are constantly being moved from place to place makes it difficult to prioritise health in general and sexually transmitted disease prevention in particular.

Conclusions and recommendations

Since 1990 prostitution in The Netherlands has become a profession practiced largely by migrants from countries experiencing a great deal of economic or political instability. Because of the high level of turnover of these workers, there is little knowledge of the social and health services available to them. Moreover, migrants have responded to the new Dutch legislation by avoiding all contact with officials and the 'outside world' for fear of deportation. The new regulations and laws make it very difficult to contact illegal migrants in particular, and prostitutes in general.

It is too early to assess the overall effects of the new brothel law of October 2000. Fear of registration has driven 'legal' prostitutes into illegal arenas and fear of arrest and deportation has driven 'illegal' prostitutes into the same arenas. Municipalities have developed different local policies but not necessarily coordinated them so that working conditions can improve alongside public order. A number have not yet implemented the new brothel law and some have attempted to ignore the legalisation of the sex industry altogether.

Under these conditions, easy access facilities for uninsured migrant prostitutes must be provided. Education and information would then be available for illegal migrants. Information in various languages and co-operation with cultural mediators would extend support for sexually transmitted disease and HIV prevention to vulnerable prostitutes.

A coordinated national policy must be promoted. This must include prostitution projects working on reproductive health and social care, despite local government opposition. Specific policies to avoid discrimination and racism and to foster the integration of (migrant) prostitutes in Dutch society will require a culturally sensitive approach.

Policy towards prostitution differs across Europe and the results of this Dutch experiment will not be clear until all municipalities implement the new policy. Yet prostitutes continue to migrate and move; EUROPAP exchange programmes since 1993 have consistently pointed to the international scope of prostitution. Exchange programmes on policy differences and innovative prevention programmes will remain important planks of any European programme. It is strongly recommended that individual European countries co-operate on this issue.

Notes

[1] Because women perform the vast majority of the sex work, I use the pronoun, she, in this chapter.
[2] The Mr A. de Graaf Foundation is the Dutch national centre for research, documentation, public information, policy development and advice on the issue of prostitution and related phenomena. See www.mrgraaf.nl
[3] The Intermediary Project is a governmental organisation working with migrant and Dutch sex workers.
[4] The Living Room projects provide a meeting place and services, including health care, for street-based sex workers close to their place of work. At the end of 2003, the Living Room project in Amsterdam was closed as part of a move by police to clamp down on 'illegal' workers.
[5] In Amsterdam the new law on brothels was effectively enacted for several years before the national legal change.

References

van den Berg R (2001). Annual report, Dutch Foundation for STD Control. Amsterdam.
Coutinho RA (1989). Van Pokken, Syfilis en AIDS. , Amsterdam: Drukkerij De Bij.
Driessen H (2002). van Oost naar West, Een onderzoek naar potentiele slachtoffers van mensenhandel uit Centraal-en Oost Europa op de tippelzone, Amsterdam.
Fennema Johan SA (2002). Annual reports 1992-2002. , Municipal Health Service., Amsterdam.
van der Helm T, van Mens L (1999). Mobility in prostitution in the Netherlands 1998-1999. Europap, Amsterdam (www.europap.net.).
van der Helm T (1999). The Amsterdam Intermediary Report: Ten years health and social care in prostitution, Amsterdam on (www.opvang.nl).
van der Helm T, van Heusden B (2001). *Health risks in prostitution, A survey among 100 prostitutes in Amsterdam* report to Europap, Amsterdam.
STV (1997 – 2001). *Annual reports STV Foundation against trafficking in women* La Strada, Utrecht.

Health

Chapter 9
Health care for sex workers in Europe
Rudolf Mak

Introduction

The relation between sex work and health has always received a great deal of attention, especially regarding the role sex workers are considered to play in spreading sexually transmitted diseases. The emergence of the AIDS epidemic renewed interest in sex workers, not necessarily because of their own risk of infection, but often because of the perceived risk that sex workers would pose to others in the population.

In textbooks on sexually transmitted disease, sex workers are generally mentioned as a risk group, and recommended as targets, along with health care workers and childcare personnel, for preventive activities such as hepatitis B vaccination. (Viral Hepatitis Prevention Board 1996, CDC 1999). However, for sex workers, health is more than a simple absence of infection, and includes issues related to reproductive health, safe alcohol and drug use, the impact of irregular working hours, street work, and personal safety. Many sex workers have health problems linked to the psychological pressure of having to hide their occupation from relatives and friends. This broad range of issues is relevant to the provision of health care and health promotion services for sex workers.

If a broader definition of health is widely accepted, has this been translated into appropriate health care that is easily accessible to sex workers in Europe? Unfortunately the answer is no. Health care varies widely across Europe. The objective of the first Europap programme in 1993 was to learn from practical experiences of projects for sex workers. The network was named: 'European intervention projects AIDS prevention for prostitutes' (see Note 1, Introduction), and the focus of attention was on AIDS as the project was financed by the European Commission through the Europe Against AIDS Programme. In the first years, information was gathered from all participating countries on health, health care and sex work, and one of the first conclusions of our early discussions was that AIDS prevention could not be considered separately from other health and social issues (Mak ed. 1996). The organisation of health and social services plays an important role, particularly in determining access to health care, but at least as important is the legal framework in which sex work operates.

Another important factor is the legal position of sex workers themselves, as people without formal rights of residency or work permits find it difficult to gain access to health and social services. In most European countries, basic screening and treatment for sexually transmitted infections are available to all, regardless of legal status, but few people will be aware of, and confident enough to make use of them.

Major changes in society, including rising levels of inequality within and between countries, increasing numbers of people who live in cultures where they were not born, an increased proportion of the world population living in post-conflict societies, and a declining demand for low-skilled labour (Aral 2002) all increase the numbers of people moving between countries to find work, often sex work.

In this chapter I describe the health care services that should be available for sex workers[1], then look at some examples of what actually exists in Europe.

Health and sex work

We must approach health in a holistic way. Before organising practical health services for sex workers, or upgrading existing health services, it is important to consider how the local conditions under which sex workers operate will influence their health. Health care workers need a good knowledge of the local sex industry in order to give realistic recommendations.

Sexually transmitted infections, including HIV, can be considered as occupational risks for people who sell sex. The actual risk of infections varies widely (Day and Ward 1994) and many sex workers manage to minimise these risks through, for example, use of condoms and avoiding risky practices (Ward et al. 1999). Other sex workers are not able, for a number of reasons, to protect themselves so well. It is therefore essential that prevention and treatment of sexually transmitted infections and HIV are considered basic elements of health care for sex workers. Even those who use condoms are not completely protected; while condom use reduces the risk of transmission, condom breakage is not uncommon in sex worker/client contacts (De Graaf et al. 1993). Various factors may influence whether a condom will be used, including violence or threats by the client, management rules, financial   pressure and the influence of alcohol or other drugs before or during the transaction.

Health workers should recognise this variation in risk, even in their locality, and discuss the individual risk of each sex worker. These discussions should be open and non-judgemental, avoiding 'lecturing' about safer sex. The aim must be to support sex workers to reduce risks. Decisions about testing for sexually transmitted infections need to be negotiated so that the sex worker understands what is being suggested and why, and is able to provide informed consent.

Health care workers often ask us to recommend the best interval between screening tests for sex workers. They are inclined to apply the same strategy to all sex workers, irrespective of the real risk profile. This approach takes away the power of the individual to decide what is best for him or her.

We believe there is no place for mandatory testing for HIV. Mandatory testing is an abuse of human rights and, incidentally, leaves clients unscreened. Crucially, it also obstructs the delivery of effective health care. Mandatory testing, which still exists in Greece and Austria, is linked to a system of registration that generally covers only a small minority of sex workers. The rest are either ineligible for registration or, in many cases, refuse to be labelled and controlled in this way. The resulting two-tier system means that those who are not registered will avoid contact with health services. For those who are registered, the need for a certificate quickly leads to an administrative struggle, including the circulation of false certificates, bribing of doctors, and determined efforts by sex workers to conceal infection through, for example, harmful douching or self-treatment with antibiotics.

With mandatory testing many sex workers will be tested for no reason, draining health resources. In Greece, for example, until 1999 registered sex workers were required to be screened twice a week (Roumeliotou et al. 1996). If sex workers are found to have a treatable infection, they are temporarily banned from working and not given compensation. This will drive sex workers underground. Crucially, mandatory testing takes responsibility away from the individual in deciding what is best for his or her health, and suggests that the 'state' will keep the sex worker healthy, thereby also absolving clients from any responsibility.

Developing a system of voluntary screening and health care is not easy. Considerable efforts need to be put into developing communication at all levels. In areas where sex workers use many different languages this will pose problems, but it is essential to invest in overcoming these problems, and optimise communication with all sex workers. Prevention is a key issue in sexually transmitted infection management; sex workers need to be informed about signs and symptoms, about triggers for seeking professional help. Without communication this is impossible.

Similarly, when treating a sex worker for a sexually transmitted infection, communication is important, and all messages need to be tailored to the needs of the individual. Simple, standard instructions such as, 'no sex for two weeks', should be avoided as they may be inappropriate. Health care workers need to personalise the advice given, negotiate with the patient and come to an agreement which is understood and agreed by the sex worker, based on his or her real working conditions.

There are no vaccines for most sexually transmitted infections but, where they do exist, it is important that they are available to sex workers. Vaccination against hepatitis B should be offered to all sex workers, irrespective of nationality or workplace. Vaccination coverage of sex workers in most European countries, however, is far from complete. Results from Belgium indicate that about 80 per cent of the sex worker population is not protected against hepatitis B. The same holds for The Netherlands, UK, and all European countries where there is no universal vaccination for hepatitis B, or where it has only recently been introduced (Mak et al. 2003).

Another important health risk linked to sexually transmitted infection is cervical cancer. This is closely linked to infection with some sexually transmitted strains of Human Papilloma Virus, the wart virus (Walboomers et al. 1999). Women sex workers may therefore be at increased risk of cervical cancer, and cervical cancer screening should be part of their basic health care.

The risk for transmission of disease differs for the various sexual techniques, and health care workers can discuss these with sex workers, enabling them to make informed choices as to whether or not to accept, for example, unprotected oral sex.

The use of condoms is basic to preventing the spread of sexually transmitted infections, and health workers should not assume that all sex workers have the skill and the knowledge to use them properly. Many sex workers have recently entered the trade and health workers should check whether they are familiar with the use of condoms. The same holds for the application of lubricants with the condom. Oil-based lubricants can damage latex condoms and result in breakage (Alary et al 1993).

It is important that sex workers know what to do in case of condom failure and check for sexually transmitted infection one week later, and HIV three months later. Sometimes it is easier for a sex worker to admit to the problem of a broken condom than non-use. Low use of condoms with private partners may place some sex workers at increased risk of sexually transmitted infection (Warr and Pyett 1999) and health workers need to provide practical advice on how to reduce risks from private partners as well as clients.

Education and information targeted at the clients of sex workers should lower the demand for unsafe sex, and support sex workers. Using appropriate methods, clients are willing to speak about some aspects of their sex life (Gomes do Espirito Santo and Etheredge 2002).

Psychosocial factors

Sexually transmitted infections have been considered an occupational risk for sex workers, but they are not the only relevant health issue. Many report psychosocial problems. As with infection, we should not assume that all sex workers have the same risks. Indeed many men and women in sex work report no psychological problems at all. It is likely that the degree of self-determination and control at work will be important elements in the generation of stress for sex workers, just as they are for other workers (Karasek 1979).

The more someone is able to decide for themselves how to organise their work, the less stress is generated, even in the case of a high workload. For sex workers, it is very important to be able to refuse clients who misbehave, are drunk, and show no respect. Where managers require sex workers to drink alcohol with clients and to work long hours, workers have a low degree of self-determination. Another problem is the social stigma of sex work that can lead to a double life, with a strong separation between professional and private life. This double life and the lack of respect from their clients were among the worst aspects of the job noted by sex workers in the 2001 Europap health survey in Belgium (Claeyssens 2002)

Other health issues

There are many more general health issues directly or indirectly linked to working in the sex industry. The use of alcohol and other drugs, apart from their risks as such, may lower a sex worker's ability to make sensible decisions, such as avoiding risky sex, or risky clients. Since condoms break, it is also important for women to use reliable contraception.

There are specific problems related to reproduction for women sex workers. For example, women who want to get pregnant will have to balance the need for contraception with clients with the unprotected sex they will have with their partner. In this situation, if a condom breaks with a client, there may be doubt about the paternity of any child, and a woman may be in the difficult position of having to terminate a pregnancy that she wanted. It is essential that health workers are able to offer appropriate advice for such specific problems, and to provide emergency contraception and termination referrals in some cases, as well as antenatal advice and referrals in others.

Other specific health problems mentioned by sex workers in different situations include infectious diseases, such as tuberculosis, injuries following violence, complications after plastic surgery and, for transgenders, hormone treatment.

Advice relating to general hygiene at work should also be discussed, including the use of sponges during menstruation, vaginal rinsing or douching and the use of disinfectants. In general, a fair knowledge of her own anatomy will help a woman make a better estimate of when a doctor is needed.[2]

This description of possible healthcare needs could of course be expanded, but it is important to remember that the most basic principles of delivering health care are good contact and communication. A relationship of trust must be built up, and this brings us back to the influence of the organisation of sex work in the local and national area. If health services are to reach all sex workers, as many barriers as possible must be torn down. Despite what many people believe, sex workers often have no money to spend on health, and the services should therefore be free of charge.

As long as sex work is a taboo in society, services need to be confidential or anonymous. For illegal sex workers, it is also important to be able to attend health centres without fear of identification. When a sex worker comes to a clinic, it is not easy for her or him to explain exactly what working conditions are like, or to say in words how she works in the streets, in a brothel or a massage parlour.

Often sex workers have no opportunity to leave their workplace. Working hours may be irregular, and they may not fit with the opening hours of a clinic. Pressing daily problems may mean that the motivation to seek health care, especially prevention, will be low. In these conditions, outreach work may well be an answer. In brothels, hotels, private houses and massage parlours, health consultations can easily be organised on the spot. Premises can also be rented close to areas of street prostitution, where outreach workers can provide accessible consultations.

Another important keyword is continuity. It takes a long time to build trust with sex workers. In fact, words are not enough; a health initiative will only gain the trust of those it is aimed at through the actual delivery of appropriate, accessible and effective services. Collaboration and consultation with local sex workers will help establish services of this kind. Moreover, measures have to be adopted to train and keep staff. Otherwise, staff will quit and take with them their experience and skills and sex workers will have to relate once again to people they do not know.

The organisation of health services for sex workers in Europe

These broad recommendations on health care are not new, but few countries in Europe can boast that they deliver services of this kind to all sex workers. Indeed, there are no reliable data on the extent of sex work or services other than those collated by projects such as Europap. In 1996 we produced an overview of the situation in eleven European countries (Mak ed 1996). Belgium, France, Germany, Greece, Ireland, Italy, Portugal, Spain, Sweden, The Netherlands and UK all reported some form of sex worker specific health initiative, although none of them claimed comprehensive coverage.

Most published data, although very useful, only show part of the overall picture. In a survey of sexually transmitted infection policies and programmes in Europe conducted in 1998-9 (Dehne et al. 2002), only eight of 18 western European countries reported the existence of projects or special public sexually transmitted infection services for vulnerable populations such as sex workers, with five of 12 central and south eastern European countries, and nine of 15 newly independent states. Belgium was reported to have no such services, even though specific NGO's can be found in both the French-speaking communities and in Flanders (Prévost et al. 2000, Wouters 2002, Mak 2003). Similarly, The Netherlands was reported as having no services, while in Amsterdam and other major cities municipal health services have a long tradition of delivering specific services to sex workers.

The validity of data provided by official governmental institutions and ministries of health should therefore be questioned

(Bingham 2002). However, what is clear from all sources of data is that existing health care services are not reaching sex workers with preventive measures that are internationally recommended.

The poor availability of the hepatitis B vaccination to sex workers is an indication of the lack of attention to health issues in sex work. To evaluate whether health services are approaching sex workers with a broad view on health, we need more research about individual perceptions of health and health care. We need better statistics on the health problems of sex workers. However, in most of Europe we do not even know how many sex workers there are, given the criminalised and hidden nature of the population.

There are some estimates of the numbers of sex workers and the people involved but these are very crude. Many sex workers are not accessible to those who undertake such research and, often, sex workers only work intermittently, making enumeration very difficult. The legal framework in which sex work is organised in Europe mostly criminalises the people around sex workers, but the way the laws are applied not only differs between countries, it differs within countries as well, and over time, so that sex workers are unclear about their status and often hide their work.

Over the last fifteen years, a large number of projects have emerged, including many non-governmental organisations, that are trying to bridge the gap between existing health services and sex work. A major problem faced by many of these organisations is the lack of structural funding. The moral issues surrounding prostitution are still very influential in the discussion for, if sex work is morally rejected by society, how can the same society finance initiatives that are seen to support sex workers?

There is no substantial evidence supporting the idea that organising health and social services for sex workers will attract young people into prostitution, but this is still a common perception by many people. Recognising the need for public toleration of sex work is not incompatible with a personal view that prostitution is morally wrong (Marshall 1999).

Some services are being established by governmental agencies. This is the case in The Netherlands and Germany, where the legislation has changed recently and sex work is recognised as a form of labour. However, in most of Europe, sex work has no legal status and the state does not take any responsibility for providing occupational health care. This situation also applies to many sex workers in The Netherlands and Germany who are not part of the regulated sector, particularly those from non European Union countries. For them, barriers to health care have not been lifted, despite legal reforms decriminalising sex work. The debate about whether illegal persons should have access to health care (and to the education of their children) is a general issue, extending far beyond the sex worker community.

Some examples of health services for sex workers in Europe

Early in 2003, local coordinators of Europap were asked to assess the proportion of sex workers in their country reached by existing services, and to specify whether these were provided exclusively for sex workers. They were asked to evaluate whether these health services were appropriate, whether they included prevention, and if they provided hepatitis B vaccination.

A brief report from Finland, Norway, The Netherlands, Portugal, Luxembourg and France is presented.

Finland

Sex workers can visit private doctors as they wish.[3] They have to pay for everything themselves if they do not have a Finnish health insurance card. Sex workers are covered by insurance if they stay permanently and legally in Finland, but those who do not have legal status cannot get an insurance card. Sexually transmitted infection services, including treatment, are free for everybody including migrants without papers. Hospitals make a small daily charge for bed and food, but outpatient departments are free for sexually transmitted infection treatment. For all other medical problems, non-insured sex workers have to pay. For acute problems, they are charged a small fee but no treatment is provided for non-acute problems.

The government provides services with the exception of one non-governmental organisation, the Prostitute Counselling Centre in Helsinki. Very few sex workers from outside Helsinki come to the counselling centre. Hepatitis B vaccination is free for all sex workers and available in the Vaccination Centre in Helsinki and in the Prostitute Counselling Centre. It is also available free in all health centres to those who identify themselves either as injection drug users or prostitutes; for almost all sex workers, this is a deterrent. If they are willing to pay, they can also get treatment from private practitioners without any identification.

Needles and syringes are available in many cities in Finland. There are condoms and hepatitis B vaccinations for injection drug users. These services are free of charge and available for migrants and other people without papers.

Norway

It is estimated that there are about 2500-3000 sex workers in Norway every year.[4] All Norwegian citizens have a general practitioner. As a rule, individuals attend this general practitioner for most services. By law, local medical services provide information, prevention, examinations and treatment for contagious diseases, and they also monitor patterns of infection. These services are free and do not need referral from a general practitioner. However, most sex workers use neither general practitioners nor sexually transmitted disease services, the main reasons being:

- injection drug using sex workers do not relate very well to the general health care system.
- The social stigma makes it difficult for sex workers to consult a general practitioner, and there is a general lack of information among these doctors about the special needs of prostitutes.
- About 40-50 per cent of sex workers are of foreign origin. Even if they have obtained Norwegian citizenship, they do not usually tell the medical services about their sex work. We also know that many prefer to use medical services from their home countries (e.g. the Thai community). Those that are in Norway on a tourist visa or illegally are most hesitant to use the Norwegian medical system for various reasons, among others, language barriers and lack of knowledge of their rights or how to approach the services.

Local authorities run sexually transmitted disease clinics but the services established specifically for sex workers are non governmental. Some provide medical services as well, ranging from prevention, counselling, vaccination for hepatitis A and B, first aid and outpatient treatment for drug users. One project in Oslo, Pro Sentret, also offers full gynaecological examinations. Outreach services are used by a considerable number of sex workers (especially drug users), and are free.

It is estimated that 25 to 30 per cent of sex workers are injecting drug users. Among these, the rate of testing for HIV and hepatitis is thought to be high. In Oslo, this may be related to outreach medical services that offer screening.

Sex workers are considered to be a risk group for sexually transmitted infection, and vaccination for hepatitis B is free of charge. It is not possible to estimate precisely what proportion are vaccinated, but it is assumed that the figure is less than 30 per cent as this service only began in 2002. Being very popular, however, quite a demand is expected in 2003-2004.

There is no mandatory testing for either drug users or sex workers. However, any doctor who detects a sexually transmitted infection is obliged to trace the source of contamination, and to report incidents to the central authorities.

The Netherlands

The number of sex workers in the Netherlands is estimated at around 20,000.[5] Municipal health authorities in most cities maintain regular contact in the field to offer sex workers information and education about STD and safer sex. In three cities, Amsterdam, Rotterdam and The Hague, social workers have practically daily contact with sex workers.

Information on health is widely distributed. During fieldwork, subjects such as general health care are raised with the sex workers. Fieldworkers and educators often function as intermediaries who refer sex workers to other services.

Illegal status is the most frequent reason for not seeking health care. The cost of health care and lack of medical insurance are other common problems. Moreover, not all migrant sex workers are aware of the healthcare system in The Netherlands and do not know how or where to seek help. The owners of brothels and pimps sometimes maintain this lack of awareness, as they want to keep sex workers hidden from health and social work agencies.

Not every sex worker makes use of the health care system or social services in the region in which they work. Some prefer to visit, if necessary, their GPs where they live. Others go for sexually transmitted infection screening or medical help to the 'big city' (for example, Amsterdam, Rotterdam or Utrecht) because they can be tested anonymously and free of charge.

In Amsterdam and the other main cities an active hepatitis B vaccination campaign is targeted at sex workers.

Portugal

Sex workers have the same right as all other residents.[6] They regularly use primary care services; yet, they rarely disclose their work to health care providers. Others may even avoid health services for a variety of reasons :

- General health care services may not be adequate to sex workers' needs
- They report inadequate confidentiality and a fear of being denounced to the police
- Opening hours of health services may not be compatible with their work time
- They fear health care workers' negative attitude towards prostitution
- Most health care workers ignore specific problems faced by sex workers.

Being aware of these constraints, some projects working in this area felt a need to provide health promotion and care to their users. In Lisbon, the *Centro de Aconselhamento* drop-in, established in 1994, is part of a programme aimed at HIV/AIDS and other sexually transmitted infection prevention among street sex workers. Since 1995, the project has provided care and treatment once a week, free of charge. Pre- and post-test counselling are available. A programme of hepatitis B vaccination has been implemented.

In the north of Portugal, the project *Auto-Estima* started in 1998 in Porto, for female street sex workers. Now four counselling centres (at Porto, Braga, Viana, Guimarães) provide free check-up and treatment of sexually transmitted infections along with gynaecological care, including contraception, maternal care and breast/cervical cancer screening. Other available services are psychological and social support, and consultation with nurses and psychiatrists.

Luxembourg

Street sex workers are mainly from neighbouring countries such as Belgium and France but most who use drugs are from Luxembourg.[7] In cabarets, where officially no prostitution is provided, most sex workers are non-European and come from as far away as the Ukraine and Dominican Republic. There is a system of state and private health insurance in the country, and sex workers' access to care will depend on their status and on what they can afford.

A few non-governmental organisations provide sexual health screening and health care, most include, but are not specifically for, sex workers. They include *Planning Familial, Jugend und Drogenhilfe* (Youth & Drug help), and *DropIn Croix-Rouge*, where screening and sexual health care are provided free, whether or not sex workers have health insurance. When a customer of the DropIn needs to consult other doctors, the project covers the costs if the sex worker is unable to pay. Unfortunately, a lot of sex workers under 30 and those without residence permits do not use any sexual health services.

Street workers are often hepatitis B vaccinated, but many drug users do not complete the schedule and may not be fully covered. Many part-time sex workers and those working in another job do not consider themselves at risk and certain groups such as those working in flats and artists have proved hard to reach and remained unknown to projects.

France

In France there are around a dozen community-based projects,[8] and they came together in 1996 as the *collectif Olympio*, an informal working group promoting the exchange of practical experience and ideas for activism. Sex work is forbidden indoors and pimping is prosecuted. There are no bars or Eros centres and most sex work is based on the streets, although individuals also work via the internet. In some large cities (Paris, Marseille), *salons de massage* or bars exist, but they are illegal and clandestine. We have no information on the organisation of health care in cities where there is no outreach program. Currently, outreach programmes exist in Paris, Lyon, Marseille, Avignon, Toulouse, Metz, Lille and Montpellier. In general, the majority of street sex workers in these cities have information and support on access to care.

Community based non-governmental organisations provide support and information, and help sex workers access social security, to which they are entitled, and private or public services. These community organisations do not directly provide health services themselves because there are extensive and well-organised public health services in France and also because they consider it important that sex workers receive the same services as any other citizen or resident. There is no mandatory testing or control for sex workers.

French nationals or foreign people with official permission to stay in France are entitled to the universal insurance, the *Couverture Maladie Universelle* (CMU), which is free of charge under a certain salary. However, in order to have access to this insurance, individuals must show several official documents which they generally do not have, such as a tax declaration or a current address. Foreign people without documents or with a temporary document (less than a year), were until recently covered by *Aide Médicale d'Etat* (AME), under certain conditions - if they are going to be in the country for more than 3 months, and have a regular address. This AME provided free access to the main public services, in a public not a private hospital. But, the law has now changed: AME access has been restricted and health services are no longer free for these people. Non-governmental organisations in France, such as *Médecins du Monde* and *Act-up!* have protested helplessly. Apart from the network of community-based organisations in France, there is no information, support or service dedicated to sex workers. Sex workers are marginalised and strongly stigmatised.

A new bill passed in January 2003 (*loi LOPSI*) criminalises sex workers, especially foreigners, including victims of trafficking. They risk two months jail and a fine of €3,500 for 'passive soliciting' (which means being on the street). Foreign people will be expelled for soliciting. This will probably increase the exclusion of sex workers from health services, prevention and access to care.

Conclusion

These examples give an idea of the diversity of health initiatives in Europe. In some countries, like The Netherlands, governmental services are more and more shaped to the health needs of local sex workers, although predominantly in urban areas. In other countries, like France, where abolitionist laws exist, it is left to non-governmental community organisations to try to organise services for sex workers, but many cities have nothing at all. In order to arrive at the kind of health services that we believe should be available to sex workers all over Europe, a lot of work still needs to be done.

We need more research on the relation between health and sex work, including economic studies of the cost-effectiveness of different interventions. Most European countries have a well established occupational health system, which is basically preventive. Is it time to bypass the moral debate, to be practical, and see sex work as a professional activity at least in relation to health?

Notes

[1] The information and recommendations contained in this chapter are based on ten years of work by the Europap network, plus my own experience as a medical doctor in an outreach project in Ghent, Belgium, which is now seeing 650 different sex workers each year. Some of the recommendations on the organisation of health services are based on a Europap working group that has developed guidelines on health services for sex workers (see www.europap.net)
[2] For detailed advice on all these topics see the guidelines on health services for sex workers and Hustling for Health, both on www.europap.net.
[3] Personal communication from Raija Laisi, Prostitute Counselling Centre, Helsinki
[4] Personal communication from Arne Randers-Pehrson, Pro Sentret, Oslo.
[5] Personal communication from Thérèse van der Helm, Municipal Health Service, Amsterdam.
[6] Azevedo J, Santo I. Health care for prostitutes in Portugal. Poster presented at Sex Work and Health in a changing Europe, Milton Keynes, UK, 2002.
[7] Personal Communication from Carmen Kronshagen, DropIn Croix-Rouge, Luxembourg
[8] Personal communication from Françoise Guillemaut, CABIRIA, Lyon.

References

Alary M, Peeters M, Laga M, Piot P, Van den Hoek A, Van der Helm T, Fennema H, Roumeliotou A, Papaevangelou G, Komarou H, Worm A-M, Cardos J, Azevedo J, Brazao M, Day S, Ward H, Mezzone J, Farrar S, De Andres Medina R (1993). HIV infection in European female sex workers: Epidemiological link with use of petroleum-based lubricants, *AIDS*;7(3):401-408.

Aral S (2002). Determinants of STD epidemics: implications for phase appropriate intervention strategies. *Sex Transm Infect*;78(suppl I):i3-i13.

Bingham J (2002). Services for sexually transmitted infections in Europe and central Asia. Editorial. *Sex Transm Infect* ;78:320-321.

CDC (1999). Update: recommendations to prevent hepatitis B virus transmission – United States. *Morbidity and Mortality Weekly Report* ;48:33-34.

Claeyssens M (2002). Sex work in Belgium in 2001: social and behavioural aspects. Abstract 4th *European AIDS Conference, Vilnius, Lithuania, September 19-21, 2002.*

Day S and Ward H (1994). Female prostitution and sexually transmitted disease. In Lankinen KS, Bergstrom S, Makela PH, Peltomaa M (eds) *Health and disease in developing countries.* London: Macmillan Press: 95-104.

De Graaf R, Vanwesenbeeck I, van Zessen G, Straver CJ, Visser JH (1993). The effectiveness of condom use in heterosexual prostitution in The Netherlands. *AIDS*;7(2):265-269.

Dehne KL, Riedner G, Neckermann C, Mykyev O, Ndowa FJ, Laukamm-Josten U (2002). A survey of STI policies and programmes in Europe: preliminary results. *Sex Transm Infect*;78(5):380-384.

Gomes do Espirito Santo ME, Etheredge GD (2002). How to reach clients of female sex workers: a survey "by surprise" in brothels in Dakar, Senegal. *Bulletin of the World Health Organisation*;80(9):709-713.

Karasek RA Jr (1979). Job Demands, Job Decision Latitude, and Mental Strain: Implications for Job Redesign. *Administrative Science Quarterly*;24:285-308.

Mak R (ed) (1996). *EUROPAP: European intervention projects AIDS prevention prostitutes*, Gent: Academia Press.

Mak R, Traen A, Claeyssens M, Van Renterghem L, Leroux-Roels G, Van Damme P (2003). Hepatitis B vaccination for sex workers: do outreach programmes perform better? *Sexually Transmitted Infections*;79(2):157-159.

Marshall S (1999). Bodyshopping: the case of prostitution. *J of Applied Philosophy*;16(2):139-150.

Prévost C, Cheront C, Bertrand F, Tonglet R (2000). Pertinence et faisabilité d'un programme de vaccination contre l'hépatite B proposé à une groupe de prostituées à Bruxelles, Belgique. (in French) *Arch. Public Health*, 58(1):37-48.

Roumeliotou A, Kornarou H (1996). Country Report Greece. In Mak R (ed) *EUROPAP: European Intervention Projects - AIDS Prevention for Prostitutes.* Gent: Academia Press.

Viral Hepatitis Prevention Board (1996). Consensus statement on universal hepatitis B vaccination programmes. *Viral Hepatitis*;4(2):9.

Walboomers JM, Jacobs MV, Manos MM, Bosch FX, Kummer JA, Shah KV et al (1999). Human papillomavirus is a necessary cause of invasive cervical cancer worldwide. *J Pathol*;189(1):12-19.

Ward H, Day S, Weber J (1999). Risky business: health and safety in the sex industry over a 9 year period. *Sex. Transm. Inf*; 75(4):340-343.

Warr D, Pyett P (1999). Difficult relations: sex work, love and intimacy. *Sociology of Health & Illness*;21(3):290-309.

Wouters K, Van Damme P, Vercauteren A, Verheyen J, Castermans S, Meheus A (2002). Sexually Transmitted Infections (STI) among prostitutes in Antwerp, Belgium. Importance and feasibility of a Hepatitis B vaccination programme. *Arch. Public Health*;60(1):27-38.

Chapter 10
Approaching health through the prism of stigma: research in seven European countries

Sophie Day and Helen Ward for the health research group in Europap[1]

Introduction

The 'prostitute's' body is inscribed as a site of disease and a source of contagion; these webs of signification affect the research and interventions designed as well as the interpretation of results. Yet, stereotypes about sex work also change and we describe shifts in the imagery since the 1980s, when an AIDS panic was projected on to sex workers who, it was feared, would infect everyone else. This fear was soon dispelled through a lack of corroborative evidence.

Nevertheless, AIDS has been linked more recently with specific types of sex workers, who silently cross borders and bring diseases with them. This figure of the 'migrant' is blamed for many of the problems of globalisation and considered a threat to national identity and cohesion. Migration raises questions about trafficking, inequality and the morality of commerce that have been compared to earlier concerns about a white slave trade (Doezema 1999).

Shifting representations of disease and sex work are described in this, the first of two chapters on stigma, with reference to a twenty-year history of AIDS. At one level, this short summary simply shows that the more things change, the more they stay the same. European sex workers will most likely acquire and then transmit the virus that causes AIDS (1980s); in fact, they do not (1990s); then perhaps it is only foreigners or some other sex workers that will both suffer and cause this problem (2000s). If the story is already written, what alternatives can be produced and considered? Our short account demonstrates the historical specificity of the stigma attached to prostitution as well as its remarkably uniform contours. We ask whether research on health and disease in a European network for HIV prevention in prostitution (Europap) can do more than reproduce this stigma. In the second of these two chapters, we look at the relationships between stigma and health over time, related to women's careers in the sex industry and their life course more generally, so as to tease apart the many senses of the term stigma and their multiple relationships to health. Such an approach may help specify the scope for change and the effectiveness of interventions.

AIDS and sex work in Europe: the "core"

In the 1980s, it was thought that sex workers in Europe might be at increased risk of HIV/AIDS, which could lead to inappropriate political responses such as forced regulation and testing. Epidemiological research has focused on transmission from prostitutes to their partners and a notional general population. It was suggested that a small number of people having high numbers of sexual partners could be seen as a core group who would play a disproportionate role in transmission (Yorke et al 1978; Thomas and Tucker 1996). The degree to which those with a high rate of partner change, such as prostitutes, mix with those with a relatively low rate of partner change can have an important impact on the pattern of spread.

Concepts of core groups are linked to older images of reservoirs and pools of infection which were important in attempts to control disease in many countries, including most of Europe at various times (Harsin 1985, Walkowitz 1980). However, for much of the twentieth century prior to the AIDS epidemic and excluding periods of war, prostitutes in many European countries were considered less central to the transmission of infection. General programmes addressed 'professionals' and 'amateurs' alike (Wigfield 1972). Towards the end of the twentieth century, explosive epidemics of HIV among prostitutes in some non-western countries, together with epidemics of poverty and drug use in the west, led to a renewed interest in the transmission of infection from prostitutes.

Appeals to core groups in this environment have been contradictory. Images of core transmission re-established 'the prostitute' as a timeless unitary 'transmitter' of infection – in Rwanda and London alike. At the same time, they promoted extensive empirical investigation demonstrating, to the contrary, that the role of prostitutes varied from one place and time to another and could not be understood independently of the social context.

Contemporary investigations and interventions are also linked to broader political approaches to prostitution. For example, sex workers are still subject to compulsory registration in some European countries for the purposes of screening and treatment and many other sex workers have no access to health care. Such policies have been considered at best irrelevant to disease control and, at worst, to exacerbate public health problems (Rosenberg and Weiner 1988). New approaches have been developed over the past decade within the European Union and are in the process of implementation and evaluation, as discussed by other contributors to this book.

Perversely, the prejudice that labelled prostitutes core transmitters of disease also led to financial support for hundreds of projects, most of which work on the basis of harm minimisation and promote safer working environments in prostitution. Many project workers in Europe came to see the 'core' image as part of the problem for sex workers: it equated prostitution with disease in a way that justified discriminatory policies and stigmatisation. As project workers developed close links with sex workers over a number of years they found that this discrimination was related to a variety of health problems. In this way, images of prostitutes as transmitters of disease both stigmatised sex workers and led to projects that were keen to counter this stigma because it had detrimental effects on health.

In the 1990s it became clear that sex workers in Europe were not playing a key role in spreading disease, and the AIDS panic about prostitution abated. Yet, stigma persists and new panics emerge that lead to policies attempting once more to control disease through policing categories of people: we hear of potential pockets of infection in immigrant prostitutes alongside news of traffic in people, and concerns about protecting the borders around 'Fortress Europe'. At the same time, support for HIV prevention projects is threatened.

European collaborative research

In the late 1980s a research project in nine European centres was established to look at HIV risk in prostitution.[2] The results were hard to interpret. Criminal and other sanctions make it impossible to enumerate the relevant population and so samples are inevitably biased. Data are commonly drawn from captive or highly visible groups such as prostitutes who work in poor neighbourhoods or those in contact with state institutions such as police, prisons and health services. It is not even easy to agree upon a common definition of prostitute (Day and Ward 1994).

These problems make it difficult to generalise or compare results, and estimates of prevalence cannot be considered representative of a wider population of sex workers. Nonetheless, at the time, the results of this research were important in suggesting a relatively low risk of HIV among sex workers in Europe. They counteracted widespread prejudice and also showed that infection in sex workers reflected rates in other population groups as well as specific risk factors such as injecting drug use.

The policy consequences of these and other findings were historically contingent. Around 1990 the virtual absence of HIV in sex workers did not lead to funds being withdrawn; on the contrary, HIV prevention programmes were set up nationally and at the European level. The most widespread public health approach across Europe advocated harm minimisation to maintain the low levels of HIV and other sexually transmitted infections; this platform was based on a social definition of health encompassing notions of well-being, human rights and, in particular, safer working conditions.

Europap

Europap began in this climate and was formally established in 1993. Rather than pursue larger epidemiological studies, which could never overcome biases because of the legal penalties attached to sex work, we established a network for health promotion with sex workers (see Introduction). We developed and shared models of good practice, including manuals for appropriate health services and staff training. Within the network, the focus was as much on barriers to health care as levels of HIV or other infections. During the decade, Europap as a whole attempted to promote accessible and appropriate holistic services based on principles of harm minimisation. That, in turn, meant understanding the issues faced in different sectors of work and different countries by women (largely) who came themselves from all over the world and from highly diverse social circumstances. The majority were poor and disqualified from many forms of work for a variety of reasons including family obligations, lack of education and lack of documentation.

By 2000 much had changed in Europe. Further integration of the European Union and imminent enlargement had been accompanied by devastating economic crises, especially in the ex-Warsaw Pact countries of Eastern Europe and the newly independent states of the former Soviet Union.

Many, but not all, of these countries privatised state assets, withdrew industrial and social subsidies and deregulated trade and the labour market (see Chapter 1). As a result both capital and certain types of labour became highly mobile. Increasing inequalities within and between nation states along with high unemployment in some countries and increasing job insecurity promoted migration as people searched for work. Yet, restrictions on mobility limited migration into 'Fortress Europe' and also some forms of movement within the European Union so that the informal sector grew to incorporate those who could not migrate or work legally in the formal economy.

These changes prompted us to ask whether health issues had altered for sex workers and whether our health promotion programmes were still appropriate to the circumstances. By the second half of the 1990s stateless migrants were increasingly stigmatised as carriers of HIV because, it was thought, they came from areas of high HIV prevalence. But what was the evidence?

Further Research

We designed a survey to look at the prevalence of different health problems among sex workers, which we piloted between 1999 and 2000. This caused extensive debate within the Europap network, which included different views both about prostitution itself and about appropriate health interventions.

Harm minimisation had provided the middle ground for pragmatic interventions on the part of Europap that gradually broadened over the decade, from a focus on sexual health and known individual risk behaviours to a study of risk environments, especially at work, where multiple forms of violence and exploitation intersected to the detriment of workers.

This health care focus was the major concern of the programme. Yet, for some participants in the network, harm minimisation also meant an end to prostitution, understood as a form of violence against women. For others, any research on sexually transmitted infections among sex workers, especially HIV, was stigmatising per se. They were concerned that the survey might be detrimental to health insofar as it would merely reconstruct negative stereotypes about sex work and disease. Many argued that the programme should focus on the particular vulnerability of migrant sex workers and develop services to meet their needs.

The majority agreed about the importance of a rights-based approach to service provision for sex workers arguing for occupational, civil and human rights more broadly. But we disagreed about the inevitably stigmatising nature of research on health. Failure to monitor the results of screening, we argued, could be as damaging as, or more damaging than, the stigma of disease. Moreover, the exclusive focus on migrants proposed by some participants could equally feed into pre-existing prejudices and exacerbate divisions among sex workers by linking a type of sex worker with AIDS control.

In what follows, we argue our case in relation to a Europe that changed significantly during the 1990s. By 2000, the new paradigm that considered migrants to be particularly at risk and of risk to others already existed and circulated widely, at least in the popular press. It should, we thought, be evaluated along with our programmes designed on the basis of research into conditions the previous decade.

Between 2001 and 2002, we conducted a survey of over 500 sex workers in contact with projects in seven cities.[3] Sampling varied by centre, but was opportunistic, based on sequential clinic attendees or outreach contacts. Participants were asked for basic information on background, sex work, migration and health, and this was linked, with consent, to results of health screening. As stigma is so difficult to define, especially across such a wide range of social and cultural settings, we explored participants' ideas through a number of direct and indirect questions.

We asked participants to describe the worst and best things about prostitution, and also what advice they would give to a sister or daughter who was considering sex work, a question we have previously found to reveal something of their own attitudes. In the survey we measured the prevalence of HIV and other sexually transmitted infections; access to health care (as indicated by rates of hepatitis B vaccination, HIV and cervical smear screening); drug and alcohol use; and violence. All these questions were placed in the context of demographic and background information such as age and family, along with a description of individual experiences of sex work. All information was confidential and anonymity guaranteed.

After describing the setting for this survey, we present results that show no evidence for any association between HIV infection and migration. We also explore concerns about HIV infection in relation to other health problems and then return to the impact of these findings on debates within the Europap network.

Settings

Helsinki, Finland

The survey was carried out by the Pro-Tukipiste prostitute counselling centre in Helsinki who work with migrant and street sex workers. The centre distributes drugs paraphernalia to street workers, and has a mobile health unit and a pilot vaccination project. There are an estimated 4,000 sex workers in Finland, including 1,700-1,800 non-Finnish women. Since the late 1990s, prostitution has been subjected to increasing state control and more restrictions have been applied to non-EU citizens. Most survey participants were older Russian women (median age 34) who had been working for about two years. In the past they had other jobs but high levels of unemployment led them to commute to and from Finland, where they were mostly based in bars.

Ghent, Belgium

Local recruitment took place through PASOP outreach to workplaces and included health screening and services. In Belgium, there are between one and two sex workers per 1,000 population. Most participants were women in their twenties from Belgium and Western Europe (77 per cent) working in bars and private houses, but they were a diverse group including some who had worked for twenty years and some who had worked for less than one.

Dublin, Ireland

The research was carried out through the Baggot Street Health clinic, a specialist service for female sex workers, with a small number of women (38). In the early 1990s, there were between 100 and 600 known sex workers in the country but a booming economy has attracted increasing numbers of non-Irish women to Dublin. At the same time, repressive measures have driven sex work underground and, in particular, off the streets. Most participants were Irish women in their late twenties who worked as escorts or on the streets. They reported relatively low levels of education and cited financial reasons and having friends who were sex workers as reasons for entering the industry.

Lisbon, Portugal

The survey was conducted in the Lisbon drop-in counselling centre and clinic for sex workers. Prostitution is more or less tolerated in Portugal, with legal restrictions only on exploitation, aiding and abetting. Sex workers and clients are not directly criminalised. During the 1990s there was an increase in migrants from Africa (primarily Portuguese speaking parts and West Africa), Spain and the United Kingdom and, more recently, there has been a small increase in migration from East Europe (Romania, Russia, Hungary and Bulgaria). There are close links between the sex and drug trades: 50-60 per cent of the street sex workers contacted by the local projects used heroin and cocaine.

Most participants in the research were African (51 per cent) or Portuguese (44 per cent) in their late twenties, working on the streets. Most of the migrants had arrived very recently (median, 1 month) and nearly half had previously worked in the sex industry in Spain or Italy. Participants had low levels of education.

Madrid, Spain

The survey was conducted by the Medicos del Mundo mobile outreach unit, which provides health promotion, supplies and support for sex workers on the streets and working in local premises such as bars and saunas. Sex work in Spain is criminalised in much the same way as other European countries, with particular sanctions against management, trafficking, and under-age sex work. However, street workers are visible in many cities and tolerated to varying degrees. Participants (46) were mostly South American women in their thirties working in brothels (44 per cent) and bars (33 per cent). Most had arrived in Spain within the past year, and several combined prostitution with other work.

London, UK

The survey was conducted by the Europap Coordinating Centre with the Praed Street Project, which runs a clinic for sex workers. Data for a hundred consecutive new patients were collated for 2001-2. There is increased control of prostitution in the UK as a result of various legal reforms, including the criminalisation of advertising cards used by many sex workers, police offensives, and the growing repression and stigmatisation of migrants and asylum seekers.

At the same time there has been an increase in the numbers of migrants working in the industry, particularly but not exclusively, in London. Most participants were migrants (79 per cent) in their twenties who worked in flats or escort agencies. Many were from Eastern Europe and had arrived in the UK a few months earlier.

Amsterdam, The Netherlands

The survey was conducted by the Intermediary Project (Municipal Health Service, Amsterdam) in English, Spanish and Dutch with a hundred prostitutes working in brothels, windows and a drop-in centre for street workers. Sex work has been informally tolerated in The Netherlands to a much greater degree than other European countries and recently regulated to allow citizens of the European Union to work legally.

However, over the last two decades, prostitution has become a profession mostly practised by migrants working illegally. In the last decade numbers from Eastern and Central Europe have increased steeply, while numbers from Latin America have declined. Participants were mostly born outside Holland (78 per cent); one in five came from Eastern Europe or the former Soviet Union and one in three from South America. They had been in The Netherlands for an average of three years and, in contrast to other centres, a significant minority were transgender (15 per cent).

Results

This survey suffers the problems associated with the earlier study. Moreover, comparison of results cannot show what has changed even within the limits of such studies since the survey was conducted with fewer people and in some different centres. Nonetheless, the results are in line with broad trends in Europe and permit a few cautious generalisations to be made.

First of all, the workforce differed. Over half (56 per cent) of the 2001 participants were migrants, by comparison with less than a quarter (24 per cent) a decade earlier. Migrants also came from different countries. In 1991, most migrants came from other Western European countries but, in 2001, they came in roughly equal numbers from Africa, Eastern and Western Europe and, in smaller numbers, from a greater variety of countries in other parts of the world. There was a wide variation between sites in 2001 in the proportion, turnover and origin of migrants. In some centres, migrants had arrived very recently: the median time in the country prior to interview was only one month in Lisbon, and four months in London. At the other extreme, migrants reported a median stay of five years in Ghent.

Secondly, we have not detected any overall increase in HIV infection, and injecting drug use remains the major risk factor.[4] In 1991, 5% of 866 sex workers had HIV-1 and, in 2001, 4% of 493. However, there was an increase from 1% (9/756) to 3% (12/375) among non-injecting drug users. Variation by site was evident in both surveys. In the 1991 study, no HIV-1 was found in participants working in Antwerp, London, Copenhagen or Athens while 32 cases of infection were found in Madrid (29 among injecting drug users). In the 2001 survey, no infection was found in Helsinki or Madrid, one case was found in Dublin, two in Amsterdam and in London and thirteen in Lisbon; infection thus ranged from zero to 13.5 per cent across the seven sites.

In 2001, HIV-1 infection was significantly associated with being based in Portugal, a history of injecting drug use, working on the streets, and other infections (HIV-2, past hepatitis B and C, and syphilis infection), but not with being a migrant or originating in any particular part of the world.

Many of these factors are linked, with almost all the sex workers in the Lisbon sample working on the streets for example. In a multivariate analysis, putting all these variables together, the only factors significantly associated with HIV-1 were being recruited in Lisbon, and previous injecting drug use.

HIV and other health risks

HIV was not the only, or even most serious, health problem for women. Many participants were concerned primarily about violence at work; physical assaults were reported by between 20 per cent (in Ghent) and 50 per cent (in Helsinki) of women, attributed mostly to clients but also to managers, police and colleagues and included serious assaults involving the use of weapons and drugging.

Problems with alcohol and other drugs were widely reported: injecting drug use by 2 – 19 per cent of participants (by site), cigarette smoking by 43 – 77 per cent and problem alcohol use by 2 – 15 per cent.[5] Sexually transmitted infections were an occupational health issue. Collating information about acute infections from those who were screened revealed a wide variation, for example, the lowest rate of chlamydia was in Helsinki (2 per cent) and the highest in Dublin (18 per cent), but again these results are based on small numbers and varied recruitment methods.

We assessed access to health care in various ways including coverage with vaccination and screening programmes, and access to a family doctor, defined by having a consultation within the past year. These are relatively crude indicators since recent entrants into sex work may not have had time to complete a vaccination course, and screening programmes vary widely across Europe. In some countries, access to a family doctor depends on social insurance schemes, which commonly exclude sex workers and migrants.

Nevertheless, results indicate that health care remained a problem in 2001. Hepatitis B vaccination had been completed by 2 per cent of participants in Helsinki and, at the other extreme, 44 per cent in Ghent. One in three women overall had never had a cervical smear. The numbers reporting a previous HIV screen ranged from a little more than half in Helsinki and Madrid, to almost all in Ghent and Dublin. Use of and access to a family doctor varied from 17 per cent in Lisbon to 95 per cent in Ghent.

Reported condom use remained very high; indeed, it was higher than in the 1991 study. However, seven participants (in Amsterdam, Lisbon and Madrid) reported the use of oil-based lubricants that may cause condom failure, a practice that was identified as a risk for HIV in the earlier study (Alary et al 1993). This suggests continuing difficulties with health promotion.

We asked women about the worst aspects of their work, which we subsequently categorised. Most often, women complained about dirty, abusive, drunk and exploitative clients. Comments referred as much to stigma ("clients who treat you like a dog", "lack of respect from clients") as to health problems caused by clients ("a lot of men use you; the clients are aggressive", "men asking for sex without condoms", "fear of disease").

The next most common response concerned work conditions. Women spoke of financial exploitation in brothels and windows (Amsterdam, Ghent); they spoke of insults, humiliation and a lack of respect from managers (across all centres). They spoke of the cold outdoors and of requirements indoors to drink alcohol and work long hours, staying awake day and night. Some spoke of the drug culture at work, and some of the lack of money. Many said they had to be alert constantly to attempts to rob, assault or otherwise exploit them.

A third focus was the emotional and psychological parameters of the job. A sex worker in Amsterdam said: "you need a smiling face and you need to be polite to keep your clients. It is difficult to get used to the job; it is difficult to get out of the job". Women spoke of "the psychological effects", "the lack of respect", "the degradation" and "'the humiliation" of the work. Across centres, women also spoke of their own distaste for the job: "I do not have much feeling left", "it is a heavy job for the mind", "it is dirty", "it is still a taboo" and "you feel less pure, less proud. We have to play games. Sometimes we are paid to be misused". Seven women from Dublin talked of "self-hatred". In addition, respondents spoke of the difficulties of keeping secrets and leading double lives which they said affected their personal relationships in particular: for example, a woman working in Ghent said, "people who know what you are doing look differently at you". These references to prejudice, discrimination, humiliation and distaste merged with the fourth and last set of comments about the content of the work itself, where some respondents expressed discomfort with their status as a commodity, with particular types of sexual services or sex with strangers and the effects this had on relationships with other men outside work.

The negative aspects of working were emphasised more than the positive in all centres and especially with reference to possible advice for a sister or daughter contemplating sex work. When women spoke of changes that they would like to see, suggestions included compulsory condom use, health cards and other forms of health care, cleanliness in men, rooms and bedding. Women also spoke of the need for equity and an end to exploitation in relation to physical safety (for example, more alarm systems, putting an end to police and client mistreatment) or social justice (the need for documentation, social security and pensions; the need for employment protection at the workplace).

Participants in Lisbon were somewhat more troubled by their work than those from other centres. Among forty responses about the worst and best aspects of work, twenty women explicitly claimed that there were no good things about prostitution and several explained that the money was the only compensation. One said: "I don't know any good things, not even the money is good. I only do it because I don't have [legal] papers". When they were asked what they would like to change, women in Lisbon more commonly reiterated the difficulties of sex work: "I would like just to have another job, not to change anything in this one"; "[I would like to] stop working. I would like to go to Spain, and work in a factory".

Most reacted against the possibility of their sisters or daughters working, to the extent that some refused to entertain the idea of offering any advice at all. The vehemence of respondents was striking in the south generally. In Lisbon and Madrid, the vast majority said they would actively prevent their sisters or daughters from working and expressed horror at the thought. Thus, "I would tell her to quit because this life does not dignify a woman"; "I would not allow her to be a prostitute, because prostitution is not good"; "I would not let her, because prostitution disrupts your whole life". This majority narrowed to the north, in Helsinki, Amsterdam and Ghent.

Participants also spoke of positive aspects to the job. In particular, individuals referred to sociability, wealth, autonomy and independence. Respondents remarked on the confidence they had acquired in dealing with people and, occasionally, they spoke of enjoying their work. They pointed to their freedom outside work, with hobbies, leisure, money and enough time to spend with their children. A woman from Amsterdam explained: "I feel myself more grown-up. You meet different people. With some of them, I have very good sex, excitement, and I learn a lot about myself. You can earn a lot of money ..."

Occasionally, sex workers commented on collaboration more generally, with police who protected them, colleagues and (other) professionals in counselling and allied work. At times, a particular value was placed on internationalism where women spoke of their far-flung networks and the languages they had learned. Thus one woman, working in Ghent, said, "I have learned many languages and cultures, made many social contacts, and I value my role in society in providing psychological help for men".

Most participants considered themselves to be in good health in response to pre-coded questions, ranging from 63 per cent in Lisbon to 79 per cent in Ghent.[6] It is unclear how stable these codes are over different settings and it seems likely that participants downplayed acute problems that had been resolved and ailments so prevalent in sex work as to be thought not worthy of mention.

Trends from Lisbon and London

To explore HIV and other health risks, we looked in more detail at trends in the data, focusing on Lisbon and London between 1991 and 2001. The Lisbon group participated in the first and second surveys, and recorded the highest level of HIV in our 2001 survey. Although the numbers are small, the trend towards increased HIV risk for sex workers fits with national data. Portugal has the highest AIDS incidence in Europe with 103 cases per million population compared with 60 or less in all other countries. There has also been an increase in syphilis, including vertical transmission. Surveillance is incomplete but the epidemic appears to be primarily heterosexual (European Centre for the Epidemiological Monitoring of AIDS 2002). High rates of HIV and heterosexual transmission have been associated with migration from sub-Saharan Africa and yet, among sex workers at least, HIV is found less in migrants than in Portuguese women even though sex work is increasingly practiced by non-nationals. In 2001, for example, 9 out of 42 Portuguese women (21 per cent) and 4 out of 54 migrants (7 per cent) were found to have HIV-1 (see table). Of the 10 women who reported ever injecting drugs, four had HIV, all of whom were Portuguese.

Prevalence of HIV-1 infection in a sample of sex workers in Lisbon, comparing results from 1991 and 2001 by self reported injecting drug use and country of birth

		Prevalence of HIV	
		1991	2001
Injection drug use	Ever	0/4 (0%)	4/10 (40%)
	Never	3/77 (4%)	9/86 (10%)
Country of birth	Portugal	2/15 (13%)	9/42 (21%)
	Elsewhere	1/66 (2%)	4/54 (7%)
All		3/81 (4%)	13/96 (14%)

The higher prevalence of HIV infection in Lisbon workers is most likely to reflect risks of acquisition locally, given the overall prevalence in Portugal. It is not possible to provide definitive answers from our data about any increase of risk in sex work specifically or in particular types of sex worker. Local Portuguese women had been working much longer than migrants when interviewed in Lisbon (median year of starting 1993, as compared to 2000) and those with HIV had started work earlier (median year 1995 compared to 2000), but these differences were not significant. Length of time in prostitution might increase HIV risk in accordance with the 'common-sense' approach to prostitution that suggests the more partners you have, the more likely you are to be exposed to infection (see Day and Ward 1994 for a critique of this argument). But it is also plausible to suggest that this risk reflects historical associations with a time when there was less HIV related health promotion. It is possible too that these associations might reflect pre-existing vulnerabilities that lead both to HIV infection and to a relatively long career in sex work, such as poverty or drug use. The free text responses reported above suggest particular vulnerabilities in sex work, which interact to produce a risky environment. It may be recalled that women working in Lisbon were less likely to consider themselves to be in good health (above) by comparison with other sites. They also reported less education, a proxy measure we employed to assess poverty or social class in crude terms. It has been found consistently that educational status is a strong predictor of self-rated health (Kelleher et al 2003) and so these two measures may reflect simply a general sense of disadvantage. The Lisbon workers were poor women with few work options. It is well established that poor people suffer worse health than the wealthy, and this applies at a general level to HIV illnesses as much as others. Despite the importance of these issues, trends from Lisbon can only demonstrate a lack of direct association between HIV infection and migrant status.

In London, as in other Europap centres, political and economic developments have promoted migration and heterogeneity in the work force. On the whole, this has been associated with growing repression, apparently targeted at illegal migrants but affecting all sex workers. Intense policing has led women to work in flats more often than on the streets. Baseline data on over 1,200 new patients at St Mary's Hospital between 1985 and 2000 indicate that these changes have not been associated with increased STI risk. This finding is all the more surprising given increasing migration from higher prevalence areas and increasing STI in the UK (Ward et al 2004). In this way, data from London provide further confirmation of the picture in Lisbon and the other centres participating in the 2001 survey: we found no evidence that migrants are at increased risk for HIV infection or other STIs. Injecting drug use remains the most important risk factor for HIV in European sex workers, whether in the West or East. Other findings from Europe support these conclusions (Rodriquez et al 2002, Clavo et al 2002).[7]

The Europap Story

Returning to the story of our network, we can now summarise the debate over health promotion in terms of the relationships between words and things. We were arguing about the way that labels constructed the world. Sex workers' comments from the seven sites show that a sense of vulnerability is derived from the labels attached to prostitutes. The power of these labels is reinforced by an interest in infection and assumptions about a sex worker 'core group'.

Yet, we were also arguing about the extent to which the world is constructed through labels. The results of our research challenge conventional wisdom because they provide no evidence that 'migrant' sex workers are repositories of infection. In this way, results from Europap parallel the earlier 1991 study, which found no evidence that sex workers in general were diseased. Such evidence rebuts prevailing assumptions and they are also important to sex workers' assessments of the situation.

Participants in Europap, particularly sex workers but also project workers, constantly found themselves having to assess the risk of disease 'against the grain' of common prejudice, sorting 'real' risks from blame and stereotyping. They also talked of a range of occupational hazards. Without exception, risks of HIV or other infections were associated with problems of safety that might lead to assault, abuse, loss of earnings and criminal records. What then was the overall relevance of HIV risk by comparison with other health problems and what then was the relevance of health in general by comparison with social repression?

Some participants in Europap had argued for an approach focusing exclusively on repression and rights. It is possible that such an approach would have avoided reconstructing stigma because it does not feed into the prevalent discourse on disease and dishonour. Certainly, accounts in the last thirty years have attempted to guide discussion into the realm of labour relations, displacing the emphasis on aberrant sexual relations (or non-relations) that created 'sewers' out of prostitute's bodies or reservoirs of 'contagion'.

Yet, these activities too can contribute to the reproduction of stigma, as indicated in Chapter 4, where the German reforms of labour conditions are considered to have marginalised sex workers once more through creating 'special' employment conditions and contracts. Similarly, reports from The Netherlands indicate that legal workers from within the EU are unhappy about the potential of labour reforms to simply increase surveillance of the workforce.

These different approaches all operate in an environment where labels are associated with stigma, and stigma with a range of health problems. Any work on migration, for example, can reinforce a sense of difference between 'migrants' and 'others' in which the migrant will be stigmatised. However, it is also possible to challenge these associations through investigating the phenomena to which labels refer. In this chapter we have shown that there is no empirical evidence to support contemporary readings of the 'migrant sex worker' as a source of disease. Such evidence makes it more difficult to justify discrimination against migrant sex workers and indeed prompts a more nuanced political reading of the very category.

The most visible change in European sex industries over the past ten years has been increased geographical mobility. This has occurred unevenly, but follows the broad patterns of migration, for example source countries include those experiencing major social upheaval. Sex workers are a diverse group, and many have education and previous work experience but are unable or unwilling to work in very low paid and insecure alternatives. Others have few alternative ways of earning a living given restrictions on the rights of migrants to formal employment.

At the moment of writing, HIV control programmes in Europe are increasingly aimed at migrants in particular rather than sex workers in general. The reasons are to be found in part in the troubles encountered in finding the 'core' associating all sex workers with the transmission of disease. But they may also be located in broader concerns about the territorial integrity of Europe, the effects of globalisation and the reshaping of health and other services for new and diverse national populations. The equation of trafficking and sex work has led to support for, and repression of, migrant sex workers just as the earlier core imagery supported and stigmatised sex workers more generally.

The equation of sex work and trafficking has affected campaigns for rights in recent years since a large proportion of workers are illegal migrants. Even liberalisation in countries such as The Netherlands has therefore failed to speak to the majority of the workforce, and may have exacerbated their problems through constructing a legal and an illegal sector in place of previous shades of grey. It appears more legitimate to deport poor women when they are seen as victims of trafficking than when they are seen as victims of neo-liberal economic policies in search of jobs, following the capital that has recently been rendered so mobile.

The equation between trafficking and sex work legitimises restrictions on the movement of people by assuming, once more, that sex workers are victims who have no choice over what they do, who are bought and sold by criminals or slave traders and who need to be rescued. In line with past legislation, the ostensible focus of this new wave of repression is the agent and often the client rather than the sex worker, but the practical effect is to distract attention away from work conditions, occupational and other rights (Butcher 2003). Clearly, there is little point in arguing about working conditions if you are trying to abolish slavery (prostitution).

The protean imagery of prostitution does not disappear but it has shifted to new sites of danger. The United States Leadership Against HIV/AIDS, Tuberculosis, and Malaria Act of 2003 set aside $15bn in aid in May 2003 (House of Representatives 2003) but only to those that had a policy explicitly opposing prostitution and sex trafficking (as though they were synonymous, see Sec. 301). No funds, it is written, may be used to promote or advocate the legalisation or practice of prostitution or sex trafficking.[8] Comments in the news by Colin Powell even censored entire countries along with NGOs for not putting an end to "trafficking come prostitution".[9] Similar policies and views can be found in Europe. For example, at the end of 2002, a press release from Stockholm claimed, "Sex Industry receives EU funding: This is shown in a preliminary study of the financial support from EU to projects and organisations that are advocating legalisation of prostitution..." (Marianne Eriksson, Vansterpartiet, referring to Europap along with other networks for AIDS prevention).[10] This reporting threatens to undermine European Commission funding for projects that look broadly at health and have concluded that HIV prevention can be tackled as much by advocating workers' and migrants' rights as through leaflets on condom use.

The Europap debate had asked how to address stigma. As we have shown, views changed over time in the AIDS epidemic and, as we show in the next chapter, they also changed during the course of individual careers. However, much also stayed the same. It seems that the major risk for HIV in sex work continues to be injecting drug use. Even though migration is not a risk, it has provided a new rationale for continuing repression of all sex work together with appropriate service provision. Concerns about migration provide new grounds for continuing to ignore sex worker claims to occupational, civil and human rights.

It will be hard to combat discrimination specific to sex workers along with the inseparable, multiple, overlapping attacks on expendable, mobile and disadvantaged populations. Immigration laws across Europe arguably affect more sex workers than prostitution-specific legislation and, of course, there are very many more poor migrants who work outside the sex industry. In this environment, the reconstruction of a 'dangerous' core of the most different or deviant others, migrant sex workers, overlaps with restrictions on migration in general and concerns about the shape of the world today. So it is that the more things change, the more they stay the same: sex work continues to provide potent images of danger and anxiety.

Notes

[1] Europap health research group (2000-2001): Jacinta Azevedo, Sophie Day, Pippa Greer, Raija Laisi, Ruud Mak, Paula McDonnell, Angeles Rodriguez, Irene Santo, Thérèse van der Helm, Bettina van Heusden, Helen Ward.
[2] A sociological and epidemiological study of female sex workers, co-ordinated by Peter Piot, Antwerp (1989-1991; supported by DGXII, European Commission).
[3] Participating projects: PASOP (Ghent, Belgium), Protukipiste Prostitute Counselling Centre (Helsinki, Finland), Baggot Street Health Clinic (Dublin, Ireland), Counselling Centre (Lisbon, Portugal), Medicos del Mundo (Madrid, Spain), The Intermediary Project, Municipal Health Service (Amsterdam, The Netherlands), Praed Street Project (London, UK). See further below.
[4] There were few injecting drug users in the 2001 survey (22) and data on injecting history was not linked to HIV results in one centre.
[5] We used the CAGE scale based on four questions about alcohol use. (Mayfield et al 1974)
[6] The question was, "For your age would you describe your state of health as: very good (1), fairly good (2), average (3), rather poor (4), very poor (5)", and we grouped the categories of very good and fairly good for analysis. On average just over 62% of women in the European Union report their health as good or very good according to one study (EUROPA 2003).
[7] There are exceptions. For example, a study in Moscow found a prevalence of around 15%, with no significant differences by reported use of drugs: 15.1% of 86 non IDU tested positive for HIV (Salamov and Detkova 2001).
[8] Included are "organizations advocating prostitution as an employment choice or which advocate or support the legalization of prostitution."
[9] BBC News, 11 June 2003: "Fifteen countries have been named by the United States for not making any significant efforts to stop human trafficking, which it describes as a form of modern-day slavery." Notably, the report also warned that problems could develop in post-war Iraq: "In many conflict situations criminal elements have exploited the breakdown of [the] rule of law and the desperation of

vulnerable families, and abducted, forced, or tricked individuals into prostitution." The news item concluded, "For the first time, countries that do not take actions to stop human trafficking face the loss of US assistance" (BBC 2003). [10] See also Eriksson 2004.

References

Alary M. Peeters M. Laga M. Piot P. Van den Hoek A. Van der Helm T. Fennema H. Roumeliotou A. Papaevangelou G. Komarou H. Worm A-M. Cardos J. Azevedo J. Brazao M. Day S. Ward H. Mezzone J. Farrar S. De Andres Medina R (1993). HIV infection in European female sex workers: Epidemiological link with use of petroleum-based lubricants, *AIDS*;7(3):401-408.

Butcher K (2003). Confusion between prostitution and sex trafficking", *The Lancet*; 361:1983.

Clavo P, Belza MJ, Sanchez F, Rodriguez C, Menendez B, Moral G, Jeref N, Sanz S, Ballesteros J (2002). Prevalence of STD, HIV and Hepatitis markers and risk behaviour in immigrant female sex workers in Madrid (MoPe C3489), in *Abstract Book of 14th International AIDS Conference, Barcelona, July 2002 volume I*, Barcelona: 132.

Day S, Ward H (1994). Female prostitution and sexually transmitted disease, In Lankinen KS, Bergstrom S, Makela PH, Peltomaa M (eds) *Health and disease in developing countries*. London: Macmillan Press: 95-104.

Doezema J (1999). Loose women or lost women? The re-emergence of the myth of 'white slavery' in contemporary discourses of 'trafficking in women'. *Gender Issues*;18 (1)23-50.

Harsin J (1985). *Policing Prostitution in Nineteenth Century Paris*. Princeton: Princeton University Press.

Kelleher C, Friel S, Nic Gabhainn S, Tay J (2003). Socio-demographic predictors of self-rated health in the Republic of Ireland: findings from the National Survey on Lifestyle, Attitudes and Nutrition, SLAN. *Social Science and Medicine*;57(3):477-486.

Mayfield D, Mcleod G, Hall P (1974). The CAGE questionnaire: validation of a new alcoholism screening instrument. *Am J Psychiatry*;131:1121-1123.

Rodriguez C, del Romero J, Clavo P, Ballesteros J, Lillo A, Sanabria A, Castilla J (2002). Decline in prevalence of HBV and HIV serologic markers and co-infection among voluntary testers. Madrid 1988-2000 (ThPe C7522), in *Abstract Book of 14th International AIDS Conference, Barcelona, July 2002 volume I*, Barcelona: 466.

Rosenberg MJ, Weiner JM (1988). "Prostitutes and AIDS: A Health Department Priority?" *American Journal of Public Health* 78 (4): 418-423.

Thomas J C;Tucker M J (1996). The development and use of the concept of a sexually transmitted disease core. *Journal of Infectious Diseases*;174 (Suppl 2):S134-43.

Walkowitz J (1980). *Prostitution and Victorian Society: Women, Class and the State*. Cambridge: Cambridge University Press.

Ward H, Day S, Green A, Cooper K, Weber J (2004). Declining prevalence of STI in the London Sex Industry, 1985 to 2002. *Sex Transm Inf* (in press).

Wigfield S. (1972) 27 years of uninterrupted contact tracing: The `Tyneside Scheme'. *Brit. J. Vener. Dis.* 48, 37-50.

Yorke JA, Hethcote HW, Nold A (1978). Dynamics and control of the transmission of gonorrhea, *Sex Transm Dis* 1978;(5):51-56.

Websites and unpublished reports

BBC (2003) *US names human trafficking offenders*. Published Thursday, 12 June, 2003. http://news.bbc.co.uk/go/pr/fr/-1/hi/world/americas/2983222.stm (accessed November 2003)

Eriksson M (2004). European Parliament Committee on Women's Rights and Equal Opportunities. Draft Report on the consequences of the sex industry in the European Union, 9 January (Rapporteur Marianne Eriksson). http://www.europarl.eu.int/meetdocs/committees/femm/20040119/519398en.pdf (accessed Jan 2004).

Europa (2003). Activities of the European Union: summaries of legislation; Public health: women's health. http://europa.eu.int/scadplus/leg/en/cha/c11558.htm (accessed November 2003).

Europap (2003). http://www.europap.net/ (accessed November 2003).

European Centre for the Epidemiological Monitoring of AIDS. (2002) *HIV/AIDS Surveillance in Europe*: Mid-year report 2002: No 67. http://www.eurohiv.org/AidsSurv/Rapport_67/contentsGB.htm (accessed November 2003).

House of Representatives (2003). *US leadership against HIV/AIDS, tuberculosis and malaria act, 2003* Resolution HR 1298 http://thomas.loc.gov/cgi-bin/query/D?c108:2:./temp/~c108CVxqg5 (accessed November 2003.).

Salamov GG, Detkova NV (2001). HIV infection, viral hepatitis and syphilis in prostitutes, *Epidemiology and Infectious Diseases* (in Russian) 1:20-22, cited in European Centre for the Epidemiological Monitoring of AIDS. *HIV/AIDS Surveillance in Europe*: End of year report 2002: No 68. http://www.eurohiv.org/AidsSurv/ (accessed November 2003).

Chapter 11
Approaching health through the prism of stigma: a longer term perspective
Sophie Day and Helen Ward

Introduction

Stigma in sex work tends to be so taken for granted that it becomes either mere platitude or monolithic cause, making change unnecessary or impossible. Perhaps because it is so difficult even to conceive of sex work independently of stigma, and because the interactions between stigma and health are so complex, it seems critical to disentangle the various effects at both a conceptual and empirical level. In this chapter, we argue that problems noted in the literature can, in fact, be turned to advantage.

Stigma has been criticised extensively for being too broad, glossing very different kinds of disadvantage, and also too narrow, focusing on individuals and their psychological reactions to discrimination. Some have suggested that the term is unhelpful; for example, stigma "is creaking under the burden of explaining a series of disparate, complex and unrelated processes to such an extent that use of the term is in danger of obscuring as much as it enlightens." (Prior et al 2003:2192) Yet, this very 'vagueness' also conveys a potentially useful holism, reflecting crucial links between a sense of dishonour, the institutional machinery which puts sex workers at risk of poor health, and the attraction between one form of stigma and another such that those from poorer backgrounds, without documents, with the wrong colour skin and, perhaps, enjoying disapproved sexual or recreational activities are disproportionately disadvantaged. It will be easier to change stigma if the links between these different forms of inequality can be specified. We offer a preliminary attempt to relate individual 'psychologies' and social 'structures'.

As we have seen in the previous chapter, the stigma of sex work is compounded by additional prejudices that wax and wane, including the association with HIV infection and migration. In addition to this historical dimension, we argue that the effects that stigma may have on health can only be measured over time. A life course approach may allow us to explore these varied forms of inequality as they interact and unfold through experiences of, in this case, ill health.

We have been documenting changes in the London sex industry from 1985 to 2000, one aspect of which involves analysing the careers and life course of sex workers we initially met in the 1980s.[1] We propose a developmental model of stigma on the basis of these data so as to emphasise its long as well as short term effects, and the necessary relationships between psychological and sociological approaches. Stigma and reactions to stigma shape sex workers' lives in different ways over time.

Link and Phelan propose a definition of stigma encompassing "elements of labelling, stereotyping, separation, status loss and discrimination" (Link and Phelan 2001:367), implicitly acknowledging a necessary temporality in which the components of stigma "unfold" (ibid). They pay particular attention to the consequences of discrimination that are not immediately obvious in the process of labelling:

> First, stigma involves status loss – a downward placement in the status hierarchy. To the extent that this occurs, we can expect members of stigmatised groups to accrue all manner of untoward outcomes associated with lower placement in a status hierarchy... Second, structural discrimination can produce negative outcomes that have little to do with the stereotyped beliefs that initially motivated the structural discrimination. For example, the Not in My Back Yard (NIMBY) phenomenon resulted in treatment facilities for people with mental illness being located in relatively poor and powerless areas of the city that were also crime ridden and dangerous (Dear & Lewis 1986). As a consequence, people with mental illness are much more likely to be victimised than other people. Third, people's efforts to cope with stigma may have untoward consequences that are seemingly unrelated to the stereotype (James et al 1984, Smart & Wenger 1999). Social epidemiologist Sherman James put forward the concept of what he calls 'John Henryism' – the tendency for some African Americans to work extremely hard and with great pressure to disprove the stereotype of laziness and inability. (Link and Phelan 2001: 379)

African Americans then became ill; the attempt to combat stigma had led to ill health. As Link and Phelan suggest, stigma involves many outcomes which often occur together such that "members of stigmatised groups are disadvantaged in a broad range of life domains (e.g. employment, social relationships, housing, and psychological well-being)" (ibid), including life itself. The long extract suggests that stigma is relevant to a great many life chances.

162

Differing reactions to stigma

We followed individual women from 1986 to 2000 through the early AIDS panic, including concerns about drug use, and into the new divisions between local and migrant sex workers. We look first at varying reactions to the links made between sex work and 'disease' over time, and then to the life course perspective more generally.

Our work was funded initially through concern for AIDS prevention; HIV was a major issue for sex workers in the 1980s when AIDS was recognised as a new disease. While HIV and other STI remain important occupational health issues today, widespread safer sex practices have led prostitutes to consider them no more important than other health issues such as violence, exploitation and stress.

One woman we met in 1986 was still working in the year 2000, but in much worse conditions. She had stressed financial and social advantages to her work in the 1980s but gradually came to dislike her work, as she lost most of her money, but was unable to change her job. She had mentioned a history of herpes when we first met, acquired she thought when she began work in the earlier 1980s. As time passed, this woman came to attach all that she disliked in prostitution to the blemishes caused by herpes, which had 'spoiled' her identity in a permanent way (Goffman 1963). Her comments were not so much about the infection itself, or the possibility of transmission, but the disgrace of permanently embodying and carrying the stigma of an STI, made worse many times by the indelible link with sex work.

In our interpretation, we felt that this woman would have expressed similar concerns had she never been a sex worker – after all, herpes is a very common infection. Moreover, we felt that the sense of dishonour, linked to the stigma of sex work, only became an overriding concern once this woman had experienced a range of mishaps, including downward social mobility and difficulties in her personal life. She faced occupational problems including links with the drugs trade, police repression and difficulties in acquiring a legitimate identity so as to use and invest earnings. The dishonour of herpes gradually came to stand as an explanation for all these misfortunes.

Concerns that greeted AIDS were similar, albeit more acute, than earlier anxieties about herpes. Women used our clinical services extensively to assess what the high risk attached to sex work meant. They gradually turned the common stereotypes on their head as they came to see clinical screening in terms of their own professionalism and concerns with safety. In this way, the negative connotations of health checks that served only to confirm the link between prostitution and disease were challenged. Through frequent visits to the clinic, sex workers constructed and confirmed a contrasting image of hygiene and cleanliness (Day 2000). Safer sex remains a high priority today, reflected in almost universal condom use and low levels of infection (Ward et al 1999).

Stereotypes about disease relate closely to concerns about fertility. Many women using our clinic wanted to know whether they could have children, as they were worried that they might be infertile, perhaps through previous infections (Day 2001). One woman we knew in the 1980s was referred to an infertility clinic for investigations. When the gynaecologist realised that she was a sex worker, he sent his colleagues out of the room and berated her for using his service. He implied, as far as she understood, that she had only herself to blame if she were infertile and that he could not possibly assist a sex worker to become a mother.

She was subsequently referred to another specialist and, following tubal surgery, had a child some years later. This woman had been devastated not only by the prejudice of her doctor but also the possibility of permanent damage from sex work. Unlike the woman with herpes, she did not find herself permanently 'spoiled' in practice but rather temporarily subjected to an extraordinary prejudice that she later resolved through circumventing structural disadvantages in the use of health services.

Concerns about diseases and their sequelae were difficult to negotiate as sex workers needed experience, skill and luck to distinguish effectively between prejudices and other occupational risks. The beliefs and attitudes of more powerful people affect the ways that the sick and stigmatised see themselves (Sontag 1989, Gilman 1988). It took time and effort for sex workers to distinguish metaphorical assaults from biological disease; time that often entailed further medical investigations.

It proved impossible to predict how individuals would react to the stigma of disease and risk. One woman we knew throughout this period of fifteen years had enjoyed her work and rejected mainstream prejudice along with other conventions. She acquired a number of sexually transmitted infections including four episodes of gonorrhoea, which she attributed to her private life, and she also fell pregnant repeatedly. After several abortions she decided that she did not want children at all and she was sterilised. Throughout this period, she considered that infections were an occupational hazard and assumed control by insisting on condom use at work. However, this clearly did not protect her from acquiring gonorrhoea in her private life when she did not use condoms. This woman understood that her own control over safer sex was limited both by her potential to enforce safety at work and by her own wishes and desires outside work, where she found that she did not want to insist on condom use.

By 2000, she worked as a maid rather than a prostitute and she worked part-time since she had saved enough for her everyday needs. She expressed few regrets and no sense of dishonour or shame. To the contrary, she was proud of the way she had managed her money and dealt with the violence, exploitation and disease that accompanied her work. The stigma attached to prostitution had fuelled what might be called a counter-argument on her part about independence, strength of character and a sense of freedom. She eventually left sex work because she found herself so much older than her colleagues: she had enjoyed herself more with real peers and now found that she could only make her money by taking it off these younger women. In addition, she said, work conditions were worse. In our interpretation, she also enjoyed an income sufficient to meet her needs without working at all, at least for the time being.

These three brief vignettes indicate some of the variation we encountered. The first woman had felt the stigma of sex work in her experience of herpes before we knew her but, over time, she felt this discredit more and more acutely until it came to represent all that was wrong in her life. The second experienced a similar stigma in relation to potential infertility but came to associate it especially with the prejudice of other people who had power over her health. The third approached infections as an occupational risk largely within her own control and bypassed the stigma of sex work through living her life in an alternative social space among people who likewise expressed little regard for mainstream attitudes, customs and prejudices.

A three-stage model of stigma

Such variation makes it difficult to generalise. Nonetheless, we have discerned broad patterns and themes in our data, including the life course data on which this chapter is based, comprising a fifteen-year prospective study of 130 women.[2] In brief, sex workers came into the industry concerned about a blemish on their characters; they shared views that were common inside and outside prostitution about this 'whore stigma'. After a short time, however, women represented stigma in largely social and structural terms, emphasising how this 'whore stigma' was produced and reproduced through policy, law, gender relations and the organisation of work. The 'whore stigma' was thereby credited largely to the external world. Later still, women were often concerned once more about a blemish on their own characters, albeit one caused by social repression. More specifically, they felt that the stigma had affected their lives and they spoke especially about their mental well-being and life chances.

Early in their careers, many women were uneasy about their jobs. One woman, for example, noted how, "Your body is your temple, [I'm] abusing it as a prostitute..." as she described various mechanisms for distancing herself from street work in West London. Others also alluded to a sense of sin but, more commonly, they referred to dirt and pollution especially in conversations about the risk of acquiring and transmitting infection. However, women soon learned to ensure effective condom use, scrutinise dangerous strangers, negotiate with management, evade state officials and move to safer sectors of the industry. As they acquired these skills, they talked of their inexperience and vulnerability and often made use of support from colleagues, project staff and sometimes agents or clients. As the months passed by, many women continued to express concerns about the morality of their job. Commonly, they emphasised how they planned to work for a strictly limited period before embarking on a new life with another job and a family. However, after a few months, they also insisted that they were simply working, stressing the legitimacy of what they did despite their doubts, and in opposition to conventional prejudices. In this way, they opposed as well as shared common views of the 'whore stigma'.

After even limited experience – as little as six months – women spoke more and more about their structural position and the social relationships in which they were marginalised. They spoke of the multiple risks that we described in the last chapter and they spoke even more about restrictions on their lives outside work in which they were penalised for having partners and/or children, making money that they could not then use, and prevented from moving to other countries (see also Pheterson ed. 1989). For example, one woman had invested her savings abroad on the advice of a client and then found she could not bring her money back to the UK easily when she wanted to buy a house. Another refused to have a boyfriend while she worked as he would be penalised and possibly criminalised as a pimp for sharing her money. Certainly, with experience in the industry, women spoke less of disease risks than social dimensions to their health. They spoke less of dishonour and prejudice than the structural inequalities they suffered.

Many of these issues are covered in the literature. In the UK, for example, a 'common prostitute', prosecuted for loitering or soliciting in public, is treated differently from other offenders: it is the only offence that applies purely to women and can be cited in court by the prosecution as evidence. Women identified as 'common prostitutes' are also concerned about carrying condoms in case police officers should use these as further 'evidence' of soliciting or loitering (Edwards 1996). Women who work indoors face different problems. In the UK, they have to work alone in order to operate legally and find themselves exposed to violence from strangers but are then unwilling to make a report to police, for fear of further problems. Others adopt a front by working for saunas or escort agencies; they complain about high overheads and serious restrictions on their work. For example, a woman might have to live within a certain distance of the business where rents are high. She might have to agree to pay for private medical check-ups with the doctor chosen by that business. She would expect to pay 20 to 25 per cent of any booking to the agent. She might not be allowed to turn down a client, or refuse a particular service. These and related issues led women to talk less and less about dishonour and more and more about injustice.

By the year 2000, we found the same women speaking in another register. On interview, they stressed the ill effects of social marginalisation in a way that resonated with the more psychological readings of many new recruits. They used much the same terms that they had used themselves ten or fifteen years earlier, and spoke of the personal cost of sex work. They were still aware of the wide range of structural constraints and they still spoke of the profits that other people made, the exploitation and the violence but they presented these inequalities in terms of the long-term effects on their own lives. This shift back towards a more individualised reading of stigma applied both to women who were still working as prostitutes and those who had left the industry. We met roughly equal numbers in these two categories.

A discussion among four sex workers who had been working for many years in a range of different sectors including streets, flats, agencies and privately will indicate how some women at least came to these conclusions. They were relatively well off and considered themselves successful. The conversation, explicitly established as a research discussion, shows that the stigma of sex work continued to take a toll once these women had managed to secure significant advantages at work and enjoy the benefits outside.

The most animated conversation and the most prominent theme in this discussion concerned clients, a focus that resonates with the results of the 2001 survey reported in the previous chapter. It was hard to minimise exposure to violent or difficult men; as one participant said, "one of the reasons I am careful about saying what type of work I do, is that, you know, like prostitute, there are some people who think that gives them a license to murder you, or to stalk you or to treat you badly."[3] She objected to the term, whore, because it encouraged abuse, enabling men "to… treat [you] as less than a human being." Another woman explained how the stress caused by this lack of respect had led her to stop working by telephone and move to the internet, where men checked what they wrote before they sent their messages. The first responded, "the more you feel in control and, – because control for me relates to safety –, the more safe you feel. To me the stress is about safety. It's not about the stress of working hard. I don't really consider it hard work. For me, it's not the stress of doing something I don't want to do. The thing always is the safety." A third woman explained how her concerns about safety had led her to work from a car where she was more in control. All four emphasised that their experience, which allowed them to assess potential clients quickly and make clients observe their rules, had enabled them to work successfully and safely.

Regular clients, who visit the same sex worker more than once, were as troublesome as new clients. One woman talked of their narcissism, "That's one of the worst parts of the mental health in this work … their incredible self-involvement. It's one of most wearing things about this job." Men fell in love with you and treated you as though you were a girlfriend; they became obsessed and stalked you; they might hit you when they could not have an erection; they treated you as a friend and told you all the intricate and tedious details of their daily lives.

Once the four women had agreed that stress was the major problem in their work, they moved on to attribute it to popular prejudice just as much as state sanctions. One said how appalled she had been by a television programme about the legalisation of prostitution, in which it was implied that a woman who had worked as a prostitute, saved her money and gone back to college had moved on in life, "This guy is saying you know, the cliché, well now we've heard from a working girl who's gone on to better things, … I choose to do this work and I see it as a profession and I see it as something I continue to do." All four talked about their work with pride.

No one seemed to think that the stress of working with clients got worse or better over time but the stigma and enforced isolation had taken a heavy toll. For example, one said, "When I am 60 or 70 I don't want to have mental scars from doing the job I liked. I have to keep it at a distance all the time and I have to make sure day to day and client by client that my mental health is in good order."

But she still had to deal with a general prejudice towards her occupation, which meant that she had to lie about what she did and institute a series of different identities that were hard to remember and sustain. Another participant explained how she had worked secretly for the first seven years of her career and more openly thereafter. The double life had proved intolerable but now, she said, "it is so much easier than having to lie and remember what you lied about". Another woman agreed, "I used to have recurring nightmares about being found out. And they stopped when I came out to people". These two women described the confidence they had gained on finding friends who acknowledged their work. The other two women were more concerned about the effects of disclosure. In the short term, it had made sense to keep secrets so as to avoid the prejudice of other people. Although this led to social isolation, it also enabled them to work and accumulate for their futures. However, in the long term, this isolation had proved damaging to their life chances and, particularly, their mental health.

While the conversation ranged over many dimensions of stigma, it was the long-term effects of prejudice that troubled these women most. This prejudice does not necessarily disappear on stopping sex work. Another women we knew throughout the research period no longer works as a prostitute; she has a reasonably well-paid and high status job in administration, which she nevertheless dislikes. She is married, owns her home and hopes to have children one day. Fifteen years ago, when we first met her at the age of sixteen, she painted a picture of exploitation and misery, associated with a man she later described as a pimp, working on streets, and periodically homeless.

She first came to our Project (the Praed Street Project) suffering from herpes, gonorrhoea and chlamydia. She talked constantly of leaving sex work and resorted now and again to badly paid work in hotels and restaurants. She had no other resources or qualifications to fall back on. After two or three years, she spoke differently. She had more control over her business and more money. Indeed, once she stopped sex work in the early 1990s, she came to look back on this period with some nostalgia, regretting the loss of independence she had enjoyed when she could choose her own hours of work, and earn enough to live well.

Her experiences of discrimination seemed to preclude any return to the business. However, the stigma continued to affect her life, outlasting the occupation she had left behind. She had trouble "reintegrating" into "normal life", in her own words, dwelling in particular on the claustrophobia she suffered as a housewife and the rejection she endured from her in-laws (the family of the man she later married). She also found that she could not negotiate the career she wanted for fear of police checks that would have revealed her past, checks that are mandatory in the UK for the career she wanted. She had no 'meaningful' job.

In 2000 she reflected on how she had overcome poverty in the past when, as a teenager, she was more or less homeless on the streets. She remembered with pride how she had recovered from health problems that included violence as well as infections. After three years' counselling and a degree in social science, she had come to feel that it was best not to talk about her past work, as the stigma was too heavy. She would remain forever outside "normal" or "straight" life and would have to reinvent herself accordingly in a job that was less closely scrutinised by the state. At the same time, she recognised the positive effects of this stigma; she associated her strength of character closely with the way in which she had ensured, bit by bit, that the benefits of sex work outweighed the disadvantages, including prejudice and abuse. She saw herself as a free spirit.

Other women we contacted had left the industry and kept their secrets. They placed sex work within an epoch of their lives that was definitively at an end and they associated their previous prostitution with a different personal identity and commonly a different geographical location. For example, we contacted one woman at the end of the 1990s who we had known well in the 1980s by telephone, as she lived in another city. She was as friendly as she had always been but made it abundantly clear within thirty seconds that we were not to refer to her past at all. She spoke from her current workplace, and managed to demonstrate that she had achieved her earlier dreams for this particular job, and for a meaningful private life, for she lived with a friend in her own home.

The stigma of sex work made it hard for these women to achieve what many have analysed in terms of "biographical integration". [4] This notion of biography implies that the future is built, little by little, in a progressive way. Whether or not women spoke of their past prostitution and whether or not they continued to see the same friends, they rarely achieved this sense of continuity.

None of the outcomes that we have briefly noted are straightforward. Some women we contacted had jettisoned the past, when they worked as prostitutes. It is likely that many women who we were unable to re-interview had taken this option and remained generally silent about their previous sex work. Some women acknowledged sex work, now or in the past, with some people and not others. They found that they did not fully belong in some places such as their families where they kept their work secret, and were unable to move into others for fear of sanction, which prevented them, for example, from pursuing the jobs they wanted. Some were relatively open about sex work. However, they found that they could only celebrate, value or share this work in an alternative social space with a small and highly select group of like-minded friends.

Those we managed to follow up to 2000 reported a range of psychological problems including stress and depression, insomnia, flash backs, panic attacks and fears of disclosure, problem alcohol and drug use, nervous breakdowns, anorexia, bulimia, manic depression and severe personality disorder. We had not intended to research psychological problems and did not therefore define these issues closely but noted rather the linkage between mental health problems and a sense of stigma and injury in sex work, which persisted on changing jobs. [5]

"John Henryism" can be applied in this context: the very success of individuals in managing a difficult environment led to problems that confirmed mainstream prejudices about sex work (namely, sex workers were all unbalanced). Many sex workers

171

stressed that they had learned to manage occupational risks through controlling encounters with clients and instituting safety measures at work. Negotiating their material environment with care, they bypassed or minimised institutional forms of discrimination including legal repression, gender inequities and exploitative work conditions. However, over time, their successes were associated with a morbidity expressed primarily in psychological terms. At times, women hid their work identity and coped with the consequent isolation; at times, they 'came out' to a chosen few with whom they more or less successfully established new relationships. Some women expressed a sense of loss for the work and families they might have had; others took pleasure in the special societies they had chosen and created for themselves. By and large, they spoke less of institutional discrimination as they reflected on their careers as a whole, and less about physical damage in the form of diseases and assaults. They spoke more about identity and the effects of stigma on their psychological well being.

Stigma in the life course: implications

These few illustrations indicate how the effects of stigma change over time. Stigma had not disappeared. Certainly, the four women in the research discussion had found methods of avoiding the worst exploitation in the industry and felt they worked in better conditions than most. They are a small, select group and this bias may explain why they focused more on the personal dimensions of stigma than structural disadvantages. However, other women spoke in similar terms.

We find a life course approach suggestive for it points to changes in the understanding of stigma in which an initial psychological reading meshes with subsequent interpretations of the social structures that reproduce stigmatising environments. This is a suggestion based on our interpretation of what women said at different stages of their career, and how they revised their opinions over time. Our reference to a developmental model implies a progressive understanding; in other words, women learned with experience.

There is no reason to imagine that sex workers bring very different assumptions, attitudes or beliefs to the job than those who do not take it up. Despite investigations claiming that sex workers form a particular type, our data show that they come from all walks of life with widely differing experiences and backgrounds.

172

Therefore, the initial psychological reading of sex work that we presented is most likely very common in the UK among sex workers and non-sex workers alike. New recruits saw sex work in terms of stigma, and they saw stigma as a badge of disgrace or a dishonorable identity, albeit one that was probably foisted upon them and had to be rejected. They were concerned about stereotypes whether these concerned morality, earning power, disease, freedom or pleasure.

Few spoke of the structural organisation of stigma at first but, with even limited experience, they began to qualify their earlier statements by reference to the organisation of everyday life and social interactions at work and outside. Sex workers re-presented stigma in terms of social processes that actually created 'the prostitute' and discriminated against sex workers in many ways that they had not even anticipated.

After a decade or more, women pointed especially to the long-term effects on their lives of a prejudice that led to extreme segregation and marginalisation. In the research discussion cited, women spoke of unanticipated effects, which occurred despite their successes and which persisted over time. All had gained significant advantages from their work and many espoused a 'sex worker identity' associated more or less closely with the values attached to freedom, alternative ways of life and financial security. Ultimately, however, they embodied the stigma of sex work in a way that other people did not. In contrast to new recruits, these more experienced women attributed the 'psychological' burden directly to structural inequalities and they reflected an abiding sense of injustice in their comments about 'mental health'.

Sex workers learn about the social dimensions of stigma in their work; experience demonstrates clearly how psychologies of dishonour, discredit and prejudice are socially constructed and structurally imposed. This is a lesson that can be shared with non-prostitutes, including powerful people and groups who make these labels 'stick'. As Link and Phelan concluded their review, cited above, policies need to address "the fundamental cause of stigma" in the "deeply held attitudes and beliefs of powerful groups" (ibid: 381). These must either be changed themselves or neutralised by limiting the power of dominant groups. Failure to locate stigma in social inequalities of a broad structural kind clearly limits psychological perspectives, particularly when the focus is on change and reform.

Parker and Aggleton claimed of HIV and AIDS-related stigma, "the resistance of stigmatised individuals and communities [can be] utilized as a resource for social change." (Parker and Aggleton 2003:13).[6] Sex worker organisations can mobilise their communities in unions and other ways to organise for change and also to inform dominant groups of their experiences, in the expectation that they will modify their preconceptions, which legitimise even if they do not directly create abuses of sex workers' human, civil and occupational rights.

The few illustrations we have offered from sex workers after leaving the industry or after many years in the industry suggest extensive knowledge and understanding of the social conditions of prejudice. They show how the sense of stigma unfolds over time, partly in the embodiment of health and disease and partly too in unique personal histories that are of course constituted in relation to changing historical circumstances such as those indicated in the preceding chapter.

Cohort effect?

This model of stigma relates to a particular historical context. Over the period of research, AIDS figured alongside a sex worker rights movement rooted in the politics of civil rights, other social movements and feminism. These politics also affected the group of women that we followed up and we often reflected on the similarities and differences in our lives. How did changes in sex work relate to the changing position of women more generally, and at home as well as work?

Many of us grew up in the second half of the 20th century thinking that we could live outside disabling and constraining social groups such as families and small communities. Sex workers had often escaped their natal and marital homes, so too had they fled poorly paid and boring jobs. Some had explicitly rejected normative and coercive relationships in the wider society; more had simply imagined that they would build better and more satisfying families and careers than their parents and neighbours. However, in mid-life, in their late thirties and older, some wondered what was left. Having never had that child, it was now too late. Lack of social recognition for working skills in prostitution meant that it was difficult to deploy achievements and experiences in other jobs and activities. Migration and the pleasures of travelling sometimes dissolved the sense of a place back home. These older women wondered whether they were left with nothing, with no replacement for the home, that "haven in a heartless world" and no significant attachments. Of course, many of the women we re-interviewed were in a much better position than they had been and many considered that sex work had enabled them, by and large, to build the lives they wanted. Even the abiding sense of stigma had a positive outcome in goading women into a constructive oppositional politics of affirming the freedom, autonomy and even identity that sex work provided.

Yet, these reflections were also coloured by a sense of loss and disenchantment. Women acknowledged ruefully the naivety of the young; they wondered why they had ever thought they could build the good life when no one else had. Some also felt betrayed by politics of the 1960s that had led them to feel so suspicious of normal and normative relationships but not to consider what would replace them. Many of the women we knew by 2000 suffered serious social isolation. They were not simply more experienced in sex work by the year 2000; they were older too and, in conversation and interview, reflected on a particular historical epoch of uncertainty and change, in which women had been both emancipated and individualised.

Conclusion

While our illustrations are not sufficient to make a general argument, our developmental schema from a life course perspective raises important issues in three different areas. First, we have attempted to elaborate the sheer burden of stigma over the life course, following the argument of Link and Phelan. It should be appreciated that the effects of stigma are long term, probably permanent, and difficult to address. Women's comments later on in sex work alongside their efforts to deal with stigma may usefully be made available to younger women who are newer to sex work and to those designing specific interventions to address the immediate consequences of a range of issues such as legal exclusion, gender inequalities or exploitation at work. It is only within this general encompassing whore stigma, which sets sex workers radically apart from other people, that all the other facets of stigma take hold and the interventions designed to reduce stigma may take effect.

Secondly, we argue that sex workers themselves, the ones most directly affected by stigma, will play a fundamental role in challenging, and thereby changing, the prejudices of dominant groups. Stigma depends fundamentally on social inequalities such that dominant groups can institute labels that discriminate against subordinate groups as 'different' or 'deviant'. As sex workers unravel and examine the threads of stigma through their everyday activities over time, so too can these be held up for examination and change. This entails close analysis of the interrelationship between, for example, a social cause and its psychological effect. As it is used, stigma sometimes seems to gloss over the many levels of discrimination and to distance one form of inequality from another. However, this weakness can be turned to advantage from our perspective, for stigma can be used to characterise a complex whole, in which inequalities that appear to be disparate are in fact related.

Finally, as implied in this commentary, it is important to link psychological and sociological studies. Drawing on the insights of sex workers over time, we suggest that the firm distinction between psychological and sociological perspectives in the literature on stigma is part of the problem. These perspectives can only be separated from specific and limited perspectives; from other positions, they appear inseparably intertwined.

Ultimately, it was the consequences of the socially constructed identity that preoccupied women, namely their own personal and permanent embodiment of stigma. This stigma, experienced many years after first working in the industry and often many years after leaving sex work, will still be rejected; indeed, most sex workers refute prejudice and discrimination effectively. But it continues to isolate sex workers and former sex workers in a counter culture and/or in seclusion, in denial and silence. These social restrictions troubled the women we knew and were often associated with health problems.

In the literature on sex work, it often seems that stigma is of one piece and so pervasive that it becomes almost meaningless, and impossible to change. We suggest that closer attention to the historical moment as well as the stage of life and career will allow us to specify better the full range of processes that women actually experience in their lives. These include both social and psychological parameters, causes and effects. The term stigma can then be used with more precision but still within a holistic framework. With some optimism, we have outlined a developmental model in the hope that sex workers' experiences can guide interventions to reduce ill health in the short term and also provide a platform through which to change the behaviour of other people who sustain policies and laws discriminating against sex workers in particular and poor, increasingly migrant, often independent, women in general.

Notes

[1] We are grateful to the Wellcome Trust for their support (project grant, 053592/Z/98). We met sex workers in different settings, mostly related to the Praed Street Project, which has a sex worker clinic and a drop in. The Project also offers advice and counselling in one-to-one meetings, and conducts fieldwork/outreach in the area (see previous chapter).

[2] These women were primarily white and British; the majority began sex work in the 1980s. Although they seemed to be representative of sex workers at the time, those we followed up to 2000 are likely to differ from those we could not contact. Half of them were working in the sex industry at the end of the 1990s.

[3] Thanks to Kate Cooper and Anna Green for facilitating the discussion. See Day 2004 for further analysis.

[4] For example, Williams described patients' interpretations of chronic sickness in terms of the creation of meaning, which he analysed largely in terms of a biography with some sense of continuity (Williams 1984).

[5] The findings immediately raise questions about another set of stereotypes, namely, that women must already be 'mad' to start working as prostitutes. However, the majority of participants considered their mental health problems to have begun while they were prostitutes. Some considered that their problems began on stopping sex work and only a small minority dated these issues to an earlier period, before they had begun sex work.

[6] This comment is part of the abstract to the review addressing, "the manner in which stigma feeds upon, strengthens and reproduces existing inequalities of class, race, gender and sexuality. [This review] highlights the limitations of individualistic modes of stigma alleviation and calls instead for new programmatic approaches in which the resistance of stigmatized individuals and communities is utilized as a resource for social change." (Parker and Aggleton 2003:13).

References

Day S (2000). The politics of risk among London prostitutes, In Caplan P (ed) *Risk Revisited*. London: Pluto Press, 29-58.

Day S (2001). Biological Symptoms of Social Unease: the Stigma of Infertility in London Sex Workers, In Tremayne S. (ed) *Managing Reproductive Life: Cross-Cultural Themes in Fertility and Sexuality.* New York and Oxford: Berghahn Books, 85-103.

Day S (2004). Secret enterprise: market activities in London sex workers, in Procoli A (ed) *Workers and narratives of survival in Europe: The management of precariousness at the end of the XXth century.* SUNY Press (in press).

Edwards S (1996). *Sex and Gender in the Legal Process.* London: Blackstone Press, Ltd.

Gilman S (1988). *Disease and Representation: Images of Illness from Madness to AIDS.* Cornell: Cornell University Press.

Goffman E (1963). *Stigma: Notes on the management of spoiled identity.* New Jersey: Prentice Hall, Englewood Cliffs.

Link, Bruce G, Phelan, Jo C (2001). Conceptualizing stigma, *Annual Review of Sociology*; 27: 363-385.

Parker R, Aggleton P (2003). HIV and AIDS-related stigma and discrimination: a conceptual framework and implications for action, *Social Science & Medicine*; 57(1):13-24.

Pheterson G (1989). *A vindication of the rights of whores.* Seattle, Wa.: The Seal Press.

Prior L, Wood F, Lewis G, Pill R (2003). Stigma revisited, disclosure of emotional problems in primary care consultations in Wales, *Social Science & Medicine;* 56 (10): 2191-2200.

Sontag S (1989). *AIDS and Its Metaphors* New York: Farrar, Straus & Giroux.

Ward H, Day S, Weber S (1999). Risky business: health and safety in the sex industry over a 9 year period. *Sex Transm. Inf.* 75 (5):340-343.

Williams G (1984). The genesis of chronic illness: narrative re-construction, *Sociology of Health and Illness;* 6:175-200.

Chapter 12
Violence and sex work in Britain
Hilary Kinnell

Introduction

This chapter examines sex workers' vulnerability to violence, in the context of current debates about commercial sex, and rapidly changing public policy towards it in Britain. Evidence from analysis of attacks on sex workers, and from reports on the deaths of 73 sex workers murdered or unlawfully killed since 1990, suggests that the context of sex work – whether it takes place on the street or indoors – has a strong influence on the vulnerability of the sex worker. Information about attackers suggests that many are serial offenders, with implications for how the criminal justice system deals with such offenders. Further, this chapter seeks to demonstrate that current policing strategies and much public policy towards commercial sex exacerbates sex workers' vulnerability to violence, to the extent that it is possible to conceptualise violence against sex workers as an aspect of public policy, providing both deterrence and punishment for involvement in sex work.

Many studies which report on sex workers' vulnerability to violence attribute this vulnerability to their personal characteristics, such as criminal histories, family background and drug use. Much less attention has been paid to questions explored by Benson (1998) of who commits such violence, what forms it takes, what strategies sex workers adopt to avoid violence, how police and courts treat crimes against sex workers, the role of press, policy makers and general public, and why some sex workers experience violence but others do not.

The dearth of literature examining violence against sex workers from this perspective may be an effect of the way sex work has been conceptualised in recent years, by commentators who accept the assertion that prostitution is "in and of itself, violence against women" (Jeffreys 1997). Within this discourse no woman is deemed capable of consenting to commercial sex, and even lap-dancers are regarded as victims of violence, 'forced' to commodify their own bodies. Where no qualitative difference is made between the 'violence' of society which 'forces' a woman to become a lap dancer, and the violence that expresses itself in beatings, rape and murder, there is no incentive to understand, or reduce the latter sort of violence.

Also worrying is the ease with which these beliefs about prostitution elide with repressive state policies toward sex workers, and with punitive religious views on sexual morality. Proposals to improve sex workers' safety by legitimising their working situations are rejected as legitimising violence against women, since sex work itself is deemed violence. Alternatively, such measures are rejected lest they 'encourage' women to enter or remain in prostitution, by making it safer and therefore more attractive.

The logical corollary of such arguments is that violence against sex workers should not be prevented, because it acts as a control on the numbers of women involved in prostitution.

But violence against sex workers is not inevitable and can and should be prevented, whether or not it acts as a deterrent to women being involved in the business.

The focus here is on violence against female sex workers,[1] since women are the subject of the discourse referred to above about how violence in the sex industry should be understood.[2] Violence is understood to mean acts which cause physical harm or fear of physical harm, the circumstances in which it happens and does not happen, and the characteristics of those who commit such violence. I will also examine the role of the judiciary, police, policy makers, media and public in reducing or exacerbating violence against sex workers.

British law criminalises trafficking, procuring, controlling, aiding, abetting and living off the earnings of sex workers, thus placing many kinds of relationship between sex workers and others outside the law.[3] Abuse and violence occur within these criminalised relationships – a substantial minority of murders of sex workers are attributed to people in these categories – but this chapter concentrates on violence committed while the victim is at work, whether engaged in street or indoor work, since it is principally concerned with the interaction between violence and state policies towards public manifestations of sex work, i.e. the location of sex work activity.

Information about violence against sex workers has been drawn from a variety of sources:

- Newspapers, media, internet

- Reports of attacks collected by agencies working with sex workers
- Published and unpublished research addressing these issues.

Defining and quantifying violence against sex workers

Defining violence against sex workers presents problems: should all violence against sex workers be included or only violence committed *because* the victim is a sex worker? Sex workers may be attacked because they are in vulnerable places or situations, typically, on the street, at night, perhaps affected by alcohol or drugs – but these circumstances also apply to victims who are not sex workers. Even the court process may not be able to determine why attacks happened. Offenders may misrepresent their motivations, juries may not convict, and some convictions are later overturned. It is therefore often difficult to decide if a crime against a sex worker relates directly to her occupation. This paper concerns violence committed *against* sex workers, rather than violence committed *because* the victim was a sex worker.

Quantifying violence also poses problems. Sex workers are a hidden population so obtaining representative data is difficult. However, surveys of sex workers' experiences provide some information, whereas no data is available through the criminal justice system. Sex workers frequently do not report attacks to the police, and even when they do, police do not routinely record the occupation of the victim, even when the crime is murder (Brookman and Maguire 2003).

Finally, categorising types of violence is problematic. For example: clients frequently take back the money they have paid after sex. Since consent was given on the basis of payment, some women view this as rape, others regard it as robbery. Some incidents defy categorisation: the man who clambers over the sex worker, fully clothed, then defecates in his trousers, may be an unwelcome customer, but has he committed assault? If yes, is it sexual assault? What about the client who tries to kiss the maid?[4] Is he committing an assault? If so, it is not comparable to the assault where a client "kicked and punched (a sex worker) for an hour, until her friend came and shouted for an ambulance" (London Ugly Mugs List April 2001).

Different analysts will adopt different approaches to defining categories of violence, so some variations between results in different groups of sex workers can be expected.

Context of violence

In the UK there are no locations where sex work can take place legally, although a woman working alone, in premises she owns herself, who does not advertise, is probably only liable to prosecution for "keeping a disorderly house", under a law passed in 1751, or under civil planning regulations, for running a business without planning consent. The Sexual Offences Act 1956, and subsequent legislation, criminalise the management of indoor work, making the premises in which sex work occurs, and those deemed responsible for the premises, the focus of criminalisation.

The Street Offences Act 1959 and subsequent legislation on kerb-crawling[5] criminalise street work, through criminalising sex workers and clients for their use of public space. Both strands of law lead to covert behaviour by sex workers, their clients, and anyone involved in organisation of the business, or provision of indoor premises for the purposes of sex work, but policing strategies in relation to sex work vary from place to place.

Many towns and cities have areas of street soliciting, and some have brothels which advertise themselves as saunas or massage parlours. There are also numerous private addresses where sex workers operate, attracting custom by word-of-mouth, advertising in coded (but widely understood) language in the personal columns of newspapers or in contact magazines, or on the internet.

This type of work happens in rural and suburban areas, as well as in towns and cities. There are escort agencies through which sex workers may meet clients in hotels, restaurants, or in the clients' own homes. Sex workers may also work from pubs and clubs, in lorry parks, and at motorway service stations. Whichever work style is adopted, the criminalisation and stigmatisation of sex work leads to covert behaviour by both sex workers and their clients and the avoidance of contact with the police, or others who might report them to the police. In this criminalised, stigmatised, and covert world, it is not surprising that violence takes place, but it is clear that some sex work environments are more dangerous than others.

Experience of violence amongst sex worker populations appears variable, but although different methods may account for some variations, most results indicate that street workers are much more vulnerable than indoor workers. Research in Glasgow, Edinburgh and Leeds (Church, Henderson, Barnard 2001) found that 81 per cent of street workers had ever experienced violence from clients, compared to 48 per cent of indoor workers.

Similar results were found in Birmingham in 1993 (Kinnell 1993), where 83 per cent of street workers had experienced violence at work, compared to 53 per cent of indoor workers, most of whom were reporting on violence experienced at a time when they did street work.[6] Benson (1998) also found high prevalence amongst mainly street workers in Nottingham, as did May (2001) amongst street workers in London, where 54 per cent had been attacked within the previous 18 months. A multi-centre survey of street workers for Channel 4 TV in 2001 (*Guardian* 16.9.02), found that 73 per cent had been attacked in the previous year.

The relative safety of indoor work highlighted in Birmingham and Edinburgh has been questioned by London-based researchers and project workers, as escalating levels of violence have been reported at indoor premises in London during the 1990s (da Silva 2000). However, only 17 per cent of sex workers attending a central London service (Azevedo, Ward, Day 2002) had ever experienced violence at work.

Analysis of 243 reports to the London Ugly Mugs[7] List from May 2000 to January 2002 (Kinnell 2002) shows that, while indoor workers made many more reports (84 per cent), only half of these involved violence, and under 7 per cent involved sexual assault (see table). In contrast, despite the small number of reports from street workers, they were much more likely to report sexual or other assault not involving robbery than were indoor workers: 82 per cent of street incidents involved violence and 37 per cent of these were sexual assaults.

London Ugly Mugs reports, May 2000 to January 2002

Incidents reported	Indoor (%)**	Street (%) **	All
Sexual assault/rape*	13 (6)	14 (37)	27
Robbery with violence	64 (31)	7 (18)	71
Assault	15 (7)	10 (26)	25
Theft	16 (8)	2 (5)	18
Other (non-violent)	97 (47)	5 (13)	102
Total	205 (99)	38 (99)	243

* including reports where robbery and/or other violence were combined with a
    sexual attack.
** Figure in brackets is percent of all assaults by work sector

Indoor workers were more likely than street workers to report robberies, 81 per cent of which involved violence much of it extreme. Robbers may view sex work premises as 'soft targets', perhaps because they do not expect crimes to be reported to the police. This may be related to rising numbers of foreign women at premises in central London, since the presence of 'illegal status' women may deter the reporting of crimes to the police. Nevertheless, although under 40 per cent of crimes at indoor premises were reported to police, this was double the rate of reporting by street workers in London, and by indoor workers in Leeds and Edinburgh (Church et al. 2001).

Many reports from indoor workers described the effectiveness of CCTV and the presence of others in averting or reducing the severity of incidents, such as one of attempted rape where the women present managed to lock the assailant out of the room, and: "The maid and others in the building kicked the door open when they heard the woman call out. . . He didn't see the camera and the maid saw him come back in. . ."

Escort sex workers, unlike many other indoor workers, are usually alone with clients, in premises they do not control. Only nine reports to the London Ugly Mug List were made by escorts. However, six of these nine incidents involved violence: a much higher proportion relative to the number of reports than amongst other indoor workers, but lower than amongst street workers.

Neither are the presence of others, doors, locks and CCTV available to street workers. Street workers, although they may solicit in sight of other sex workers, are usually alone when they encounter problems. Once they have a client, street workers usually leave the soliciting area, so that sexual encounters take place elsewhere. They may be safest in their own homes, if other people are about to help should clients turn violent. However, most avoid this because they can be evicted from social housing for taking clients to their homes, so other locations are used: alleyways, industrial estates, lorry parks, derelict buildings, country areas, and sometimes hotels or other indoor premises. Once in clients' cars, they have little control over where they are taken, and may be trapped by clients parking their cars against walls, or using central locking devices.

Hostility or indifference to sex workers from the general public may inhibit helpful interventions. One account noted, "the woman screamed to people in the vicinity but nobody came to help her" (London Ugly Mugs List October 2001).

But "people in the vicinity" can save lives. Noel Dooley, who stabbed a sex worker in Bradford 43 times (October 2000), was confronted by passers-by, leading to his swift arrest and to prompt attention for his victim, who survived; Gary Allen, who attacked sex workers in Plymouth in 2000, was interrupted on two occasions because "people in the vicinity" intervened.

What kind of people attack sex workers?

Benson (1998) and Pearce and Roach (1997) have described a range of people who attack sex workers: other working women; "predatory men", "people on the streets", including vigilantes, those intent on property crime, as well as clients. The Birmingham survey (Kinnell 1993), found that at least 70 per cent of incidents of violence were ascribed to clients in all categories except kidnapping, while other investigators appear to have only measured violence from clients.

The high proportion of attacks ascribed to clients has led to assumptions that a high proportion of clients are violent. However, attempts to explore this question have found the reverse to be true. Brooks-Gordon (1999) checked over 1,000 kerb-crawlers in central London (1998/1999) against the Criminal Records database. Sixty-three were found to have criminal records (less than 6 per cent). Low rates (8 per cent) of previous convictions for violent and sexual offences were also found amongst men apprehended for kerb-crawling in Southampton (Shell, Campbell, Caren 2001).

This suggests that a small proportion of clients may be responsible for a large number of attacks. Data from the London Ugly Mugs List supports this hypothesis. Thirty per cent of attackers were known as clients, as having attacked other sex workers, or as being known to the police.

Examples of repeat offenders include:

- MO who raped two sex workers in Coventry in 2000 (*Coventry Evening Telegraph* 19.6.01), eight months after his release from prison for attacking another sex worker in 1996.
- ND who stabbed a Bradford sex worker 43 times in 2000, had murdered a woman in Coventry in 1979 (*Bradford Telegraph & Argus* 6.11.01.).
- JW, convicted in 2001 of two rapes, four indecent assaults, four false imprisonments and other offences against sex

workers in Plymouth (*Plymouth Evening Herald* 1.12.01), had appeared in court on 56 previous occasions since 1962.

- DB, given a life sentence for sexual assaults on three Liverpool sex workers (*Liverpool Echo* 25.1.02), had been convicted of rape in 1990, and serious assaults on his partner in 1996.

- KS, who raped two sex workers in Aberdeen in 2000, had been convicted of four previous assaults on sex workers in 1997 (BBC News website 6.2.01.).

- VF was given twelve years in 1988 for rape, false imprisonment, grievous bodily harm and unlawful wounding. Released in November 1995, the following month he attacked a sex worker in Hampshire, and six weeks later murdered another woman who was not a sex worker (BBC News website 29.1.98.).

- KV, convicted of murdering a Bradford sex worker in Bradford in 1996, was previously convicted of the manslaughter of another woman in Leeds in 1991, and for indecent assault, robbery and burglary (*Yorkshire Post* 27.3.98).

- PB, who murdered a Wolverhampton sex worker in February 1999, and raped a 17-year-old shortly after, had served 15 years for beating a shopkeeper to death in Essex, and strangling a bus driver in Denmark (BBC News website 21.7.00).

- DS, who murdered a London sex worker in April 1999, had previously raped a woman at knifepoint, in front of her children (1976), and had been acquitted of murdering another sex worker in 1993 (BBC News website 8.12.99.).

- AK, convicted in March 2000 of the murders of two women from the Midlands (December 1993 and March 1994), was serving seven years for rape when DNA linked him to the Midlands murders (*Observer* 19.3.00.).

Murder of sex workers

Information collated from sex work projects and press reports about 73 murders or unlawfully killings of sex workers between January 1990 and December 2002 shows that 52 (71 per cent) were street workers and eleven (15 per cent) were indoor workers. The work style of ten is not known. In 46 of these 73 cases (63 per cent), it is known that charges have been brought or suspects named, and it appears that the majority approached their victims as clients (52 per cent), a similar proportion as found by Lowman (2000) in Canada (56 per cent). Nine (21 per cent) were partners, and in nine other cases (21 per cent), persons with other relationships to the victims were charged.[8]

Of 45 people known to have been charged or named as suspects,[9] 42 per cent (19/45) have known previous or subsequent convictions for violence, including rape, manslaughter and murder. It is important to note that these previous offences were committed against non-sex workers as well as sex workers, and against both women and men. There is a common assumption that people who murder sex workers do not usually murder other people, that sex workers live lives which expose them to the criminally insane, and therefore that the rest of us are safe. It is perhaps far less comfortable to recognise that those who attack and murder sex workers frequently attack others, and are rarely classed as 'insane' by the courts, so are regularly released back into the community, where they re-offend.

Despite limited information about many of these deaths, available data appear to confirm the vulnerability of street workers, and patterns of repeat offending amongst aggressors. However, clients were not the only offenders. Both in the UK and elsewhere, killings have been attributed to partners, pimps, traffickers, drug dealers, other sex workers, acquaintances, robbers, vigilantes and homophobes.

While sexual violence and partner homicide have been much studied, other causes of extreme violence towards sex workers are less understood. It may be that some aggressors are undeterred since they believe that police will not accord such crimes much priority, and perhaps, that acts which are normally considered crimes are not crimes if committed against a sex worker (O'Neill and Barbaret 2000 and Sanders 2001).

Violence and control policies surrounding street work

A few areas in the UK operate unofficial tolerance zones, but in most places police and courts harass, arrest, fine and imprison street workers and their clients.[10] These strategies increase the dangers of street work in several ways.

Hostile policing reduces the vital assessment period when sex workers try to judge if a client may become violent, as one of Benson's interviewees explains:

> if the guy's driven around a couple of times, and he hasn't stopped and then he's come back round again, that sends a little signal to you, 'cause you think 'What's he keep driving round

for? Why hasn't he stopped before?' Then when you open the car door. . .if they're tense, or too relaxed, you know, like 'Come on then get in I haven't got time to mess about' or even just the way he flicks his eyes at you, or you know like, if he's shuffling his legs, or he looks real sort of nervous and you think 'Well what's he nervous for?' that sort of sets your alarms off as well . . . (Benson 1998: 30).

To be told to get in the car quickly sounds reasonable if kerbcrawling measures are being enforced, instead of alerting the sex worker to potential trouble. A customer who is nervous, or looking over his shoulder, may also seem to be behaving reasonably under the circumstances.

Police crackdowns mean fewer clients, so women spend longer in dangerous locations to make their money. Amongst women interviewed for Channel 4, 65 per cent worked longer hours, 71 per cent later at night, and 66 per cent earned less money anyway (*Guardian* 16.9.02.). Reduced earnings leads to more violence: pimps may beat women for not earning enough; women made desperate may rob clients, who then turn violent: "he thought the woman was someone who robbed him before . . . he raped and assaulted (her)" (London Ugly Mugs List November 2001).

Anti-kerbcrawler policies disrupt sex workers' contact with regular clients, whom sex workers regard as less risky (Sanders 2001; Benson 1998): in the Channel 4 sample 90 per cent said they had never done business before with men who attacked them. However, regular clients are more vulnerable to anti-kerbcrawler initiatives than occasional visitors, leaving sex workers fewer 'regulars' to do business with.

Sex workers and clients are also likely to disperse from familiar areas during crackdowns, simply displacing problems to other neighbourhoods:

Kerbcrawlers have been forced out of Hull, police chiefs claimed today. . . . A spokesman for South Yorkshire Police said officers had never before stopped such a significant number of motorists from East Yorkshire in Sheffield's red light district. (This Is Hull and East Yorkshire website 20.1.99.)

The displacement effect of the 1998/9 Leeds Kerb-Crawler Rehabilitation Programme was acknowledged in the West Yorkshire Police evaluation:

> Intense high visibility policing of any problem that occurs in a public place will obviously have a displacement effect. This is clearly illustrated with the displacement that has been noticed in Chapeltown. . .prostitutes have moved their business into surrounding divisions. . . (West Yorkshire Police 2000).

Displacement can have far more serious consequences. During the anti-kerbcrawling activity in Leeds (April 1999), one local sex worker went to work in London, where she was murdered by DS, a convicted rapist (BBC News website 8.12.99.). DS was known to be dangerous by local women, but an outsider would not have known his reputation. A similar case occurred in Stoke-on-Trent in 1994, when a Wolverhampton woman was murdered by KW, known to local women as a dangerous client, but not to an outsider.

Several more recent murders have occurred in places where hostile policing strategies have been adopted. Not only do such strategies increase sex workers' vulnerability and social stigmatisation, they also appear to interfere with police investigations of violence, by reducing the willingness of potential witnesses to come forward.

A Bradford sex worker was found murdered in April 2001. Within two weeks the senior vice officer was quoted as saying: "I issue this warning to anybody who does undertake kerb crawling or pimping – the police will always press for prosecution at court."

A week later the officer leading the murder investigation complained: "We've had a disappointing response to our appeal so far . . . Our detectives do not care under what circumstances you knew Becky, but if you did, please come forward" (*Bradford Telegraph & Argus* 8.5.01. & 14.5.01).

The Bradford crackdown on street prostitution has continued, but the murder is still unsolved, as are similar cases in Middlesborough, Stoke-on-Trent, and Sheffield.

There is then a contradiction in police work between their enforcement of anti-prostitution strategies which exacerbate violence against sex workers, and their duty to protect all citizens, including sex workers.

Police and judicial responses to violence

Sex workers are often unwilling to report violence to the police. They may not expect sympathetic treatment. Police may say they "shouldn't be out there anyway", and refuse to take a statement.

Women with outstanding warrants, those subject to Antisocial Behaviour Orders (ASBOs), or illegal immigrants may fear incarceration if they contact police. Those without prostitution-related convictions may hesitate to identify themselves as sex workers; indoor workers may not wish to draw attention to their working address. If they do approach the police, they may be detained for long periods, and questioned about unrelated matters.

Government-set performance indicators for the police exclude violent crimes and sexual offences. Also, police efficiency is measured by the relationship between crimes reported and crimes solved, but no weighting is given to different types of crime. Consequently, solving a murder has no more importance than solving a theft in measurements of police efficiency.

Encouraging the reporting of crimes that would otherwise go unreported, especially when the prospect of solving them is uncertain, would make police efficiency appear worse. From the police perspective, vigorous arresting policies towards sex workers and kerbcrawlers may be far more attractive options, since they produce good 'clear-up' rates, are cheap to run and also politically popular, both at local and central government levels.

Even when attacks are reported to the police, and arrests made, the judicial system can continue to expose potential victims to danger.

The case of JW, eventually convicted of eleven offences against sex workers in Plymouth, illustrates the effect of failure to remand suspects in custody. JW was charged with indecent assault and false imprisonment in December 2000, but was not remanded in custody until arrested a fourth time. Had he been remanded in custody after the initial arrest, the subsequent offences, including two rapes, three indecent assaults and three false imprisonments, would not have occurred (*Plymouth Evening Herald* 1.12.01.).

The decision to remand in custody someone who has been charged, though influenced by police advice, lies ultimately with the court. Decisions about what charges are brought depend on the Crown Prosecution Service (CPS). The record of the CPS for refusing to prosecute, or downgrading charges against those accused of rape was documented by the English Collective of Prostitutes in 1995 (Women Against Rape and Legal Action for Women 1995) and there are still occasions when CPS decisions raise questions. For example, Gary Allen's attacks on sex workers in Plymouth in 2000 made both women fear for their lives, but he was only charged with indecent assault and actual bodily harm, rather than grievous bodily harm, or attempted murder. He was found guilty, but the charges brought limited the sentencing options available to the court (*Plymouth Evening Herald* 9.12.00.).

Sentencing policy for sexual and violent crimes is currently under review. British courts hand down swingeing sentences for property crime – one of those recently convicted for a failed robbery at the Millennium Dome, where no one was hurt, was sentenced to 18 years in prison, but sentences for violence against sex workers often seem inadequate. One of Benson's interviewees expressed the effect that lenient sentencing can have:

> I would never go to court again. I would never even make a statement to the police, I wouldn't go through with it again, just for that, 'cause at the end of the day, they've only got four years and they're only gonna do two. What's that? I mean that's affected me for the rest of my life and all they get is two years. I don't think that's right (Benson 1998: 45).

Several cases of rape and murder given above involve offenders released early from sentences for previous violent offences, including ND (*Bradford Telegraph & Argus* 6.11.01.), JW (*Plymouth Evening Herald* 1.12.01.), VF (BBC News website 29.1.98.), KV (*Yorkshire Post* 27.3.98.) and PB. The Chief Constable for the West Midlands attacked the decision to parole PB, saying:

> it seems inconceivable that a man who has previously been convicted for a litany of offences since 1968, including two counts of manslaughter and wounding for which he received three life sentences, can still be allowed to wander around the streets (Guardian 22.7.00).

Failure to monitor violent offenders appropriately after release is also evident. KV, convicted of manslaughter in 1991 but released in 1995, had been rehoused in the Bradford street soliciting area, where he encouraged sex workers to use his flat for business. Here he murdered one sex worker and, when arrested, police found another woman imprisoned in his flat.

ND, a paranoid schizophrenic, having served 19 years for murder, was released on licence in 1998. In 2000 he stabbed a Bradford sex worker 43 times. At the time of the attack he was in breach of his licence conditions, having missed probation and psychiatric appointments (*Bradford Telegraph & Argus* November

2001). The judge at his trial said, "the authorities' failure to trace him had enabled him to try to kill again".

Vigilantes or respectable residents?

Many people are obsessed with hatred of sex workers. But in the UK, more people opposed to prostitution join residents' groups to deter street prostitution than commit murder. However, the potential for such activities to turn into violent vigilantism is illustrated by a report from Bradford (1996). A woman told the local paper:

> . . . the mob piled out of five cars and set upon the vice girl who fell into the pub. . . . the vigilantes demanded that we throw the prostitute back outside to them. Because we didn't, they got really nasty and were threatening to do things to the pub. They seemed to think that because she was a prostitute, she had no rights. . . I've seen car loads of people who spit and throw things at prostitutes, and I've seen them trying to grab the women . . . One day the vigilantes are going to pick on someone who isn't a prostitute. . . . Someone is going to get badly hurt (*Bradford Telegraph & Argus* November 1996).

Despite her opposition to violence, this woman's comment that, "One day the vigilantes are going to pick on someone who isn't a prostitute" illustrates the automatic distinction made, even by well-intentioned people, between violence against sex workers and violence against others. The assumption that the former violence is legitimate is so widespread, it has even been incorporated into a popular computer game (*The Independent* 9.1.03.).

Lowman (2000) describes the 'rhetoric of disposal' used by Canadian media and action groups opposed to street prostitution. He draws associations between the intensity of such rhetoric and the incidence of murder of sex workers, arguing that the social acceptability of using language which equates sex workers with rubbish legitimises the actions of those who attack and kill them. Similar rhetoric has characterised innumerable press stories on street sex work in the UK, for example, in Hull where five sex workers have been killed since 1996: "Hull has *declared war on vice girls* operating on a city estate . . . . Humberside Police is launching a major new initiative to *wipe out street prostitution*." (*Yorkshire Evening Post* 10.8.01).

Police also make public statements that reinforce prejudice against sex workers. In November 1999, Aberdeen police warned clients that they risked being robbed by sex workers (BBC News website 25.11.99.). Not long after this, Kenneth Smith, convicted of four assaults against sex workers in Aberdeen in 1997, raped again, in February and in June 2000 (BBC News website 6.02.01.). Police in Wolverhampton used the arrest of a multiple rapist to raise fears about HIV:

> A police force today warned men about the possibility of contracting HIV from prostitutes after a man with the condition was charged with rape . . . A police spokesman said men who have had sex with prostitutes in the city within the past six months needed to be made aware of the situation (Press Association News 27.04.01).

Politicians may also use fears of HIV to bolster support for punitive control measures. When the possibility of tolerance zones was discussed in Walsall in 2001, the MP told a local newspaper, "Who is going to clean up the mess, the condoms and needles that are left behind? This could create a health epidemic (sic)." (*Walsall Advertiser* 26.04.01.)

The deliberate fomentation of public fears about the supposed dangers sex workers pose to the rest of society suggests there is a fine line between the self-justification of someone who attacks sex workers, and the attitudes of some police, politicians, media, and residents' groups. Current state policies also show a similar disregard for sex workers' safety and could even be interpreted as legitimising violence.

Conclusions

Levels of reporting of violence against sex workers are poor, despite the efforts of many sex work projects to improve matters. Failure to apprehend offenders, or to remand them in custody, has led to further violent crimes, including murder. Charges brought by the CPS may not reflect the seriousness of the offences, limiting the sentencing power of the court, if a guilty verdict is returned. At least 73 sex workers have been killed in the UK between 1990 and 2002, several by offenders with previous convictions for assault, rape, manslaughter and murder, against both sex workers and others. This suggests that current practice in sentencing violent offenders, the availability of therapy when incarcerated, and their monitoring after release, are dangerously inadequate.

Sex workers experience violence from many sources, whether engaged in street soliciting or indoor work, but this violence is neither documented in official statistics, nor addressed by public policy towards prostitution. The deleterious effect of current law is acknowledged, if obliquely, in recent Home Office research on homicide: "The feasibility of many preventive strategies depends largely on the legal position of prostitutes and police enforcement practices" (Brookman and Maguire 2003: 11).

Indoor workers are endangered by legislation which criminalises their working environments. The threat of brothel-keeping charges discourages those who work in groups from reporting crimes against them, and leads others to operate alone, which exposes them to greater violence.

Street workers are even more vulnerable. While some police and local authorities express interest in adopting 'tolerance' zones, these are officially opposed by central government and the Association of Chief Police Officers. Street prostitution is usually policed solely to remove sex workers and their clients from public areas. These control policies increase sex workers' vulnerability by increasing levels of client anger and public hatred towards them, and by decreasing their ability to limit their own risks. In several cases hostile policing has coincided with murder, or interfered with murder investigations, through decreased co-operation between sex workers, clients and police.

Politicians, police and the media routinely use 'the rhetoric of disposal' to promote anti-prostitution policies, and deliberately foment public fears about the supposed dangers posed by sex workers to the rest of the population, without regard for the effect their words may have on public attitudes towards sex workers. Such rhetoric has coincided with serious violence against sex workers, including murder. This suggests that there is a fine line between the self-justifications expressed by those who attack and murder sex workers, and the attitudes of many in society towards sex workers.

Since most public policy towards sex work in the UK reflects fear and hatred of sex workers, exacerbates their vulnerability, and hinders the investigation of crimes of violence against them, it is possible to conceptualise violence against sex workers as one aspect of public policy in the control of prostitution.

The argument that policies and legal changes to promote safer working conditions are unacceptable, since they might 'encourage'

194

sex work, demonstrates that violence is seen by many as a deterrent, as well as a punishment to those involved. Only a vigorous reshaping of public policy towards sex work, promoting safe working environments, and treating violent offences with the seriousness they deserve, could alter this situation.

Notes

[1] Women are described as sex workers if they are known to have engaged in sex work, not on the basis of whether they exercised any meaningful choice in their involvement in sex work.

[2] Male sex workers also experience violence, as illustrated by the massacre of eight male masseurs in Cape Town in January 2003 (*Guardian* 21.01.03.).

[3] The Sexual Offences Act 2003 has redefined several prostitution-related offences. None of the changes promote safer working conditions for sex workers.

[4] Maids (who act as receptionists for sex workers), by definition, do not perform sexual services.

[5] Clients who approach street sex workers in cars are known as kerb-crawlers.

[6] Birmingham data includes all violence at work, not only from clients.

[7] The term "Ugly Mug" was coined by the Prostitutes' Collective of Victoria, Australia, in the 1980s, for a report of an attack on a sex worker. The system of turning these reports into a flyer for distribution to other sex workers was taken up by UK projects from 1989 onwards, and is now common, though not universal practice.

[8] No information about person/s charged in four cases.

[9] "Known to have" means known to the author, from the sources stated. In three cases police have named suspects but charges or prosecutions are not thought possible at the time of writing.

[10] Imprisonment for street prostitution, discontinued in 1983, has been re-introduced through Anti-Social Behaviour Orders, which ban the subject of the order from an area. If the order is breached, this can result in a prison sentence of up to five years.

References

Books, Articles, Reports

Azevedo J, Ward H, Day S (2002). Health risks for sex workers: results of a European study. Paper presented to *Sex work and health in a changing Europe* Conference, January 2002.

Benson, C (1998). *Violence against Female Prostitutes: Experiences of Violence, Safety Strategies and the Role of Agencies.* Published by the Dept of Social Sciences, Loughborough University, Leicestershire, UK. ISBN 0 907274 23 4.

Brookman F, Maguire M (2003). *Reducing homicide: Summary of a review of the possibilities.* January 2003, RDS Occasional Paper No 84, Home Office.

Brooks-Gordon, B (1999). *The Criminal Careers of Kerb-Crawlers.* Paper presented to the National Police Vice Conference, June 1999.

Church S, Henderson M, Barnard M (2001). Violence by clients towards female prostitutes in different work settings: questionnaire survey, *BMJ*, Vol. 322, 3 March 2001.

da Silva, C (2000). *Prostitution in the Nineties: Changing Working Practices, Changing Violence* MA Criminology dissertation, Middlesex University.

Jeffreys, S (1997). *The idea of prostitution.* North Melbourne: Spinifex Press.

Kinnell, H (1993). *Prostitutes' exposure to rape: Implications for HIV prevention and for legal reform.* Paper presented to the VII Social Aspects of AIDS Conference, South Bank University, London, June 1993.

Kinnell, H (2002). Violence against sex workers in London: the London Ugly Mugs List. Europap-UK, February 2002. Unpublished paper.

London Ugly Mugs List, April 2001. Sex worker's report of attack, February 2001.

London Ugly Mugs List, October 2001. Sex worker's report of attack, September 2001

London Ugly Mugs List, November 2001. Sex worker's report of attack, September 2001.

Lowman, J (2000). Violence and the Outlaw Status of (Street) prostitution in Canada, *Violence Against Women*, Vol. 6, No 9.

May T, Harocopos A, Turnbull PJ (2001). *Selling Sex in the City: an evaluation of a targeted arrest referral scheme for sex workers in Kings Cross*, June 2001. London: South Bank University, Social Science Research Papers, No. 14.

O'Neill M, Barbaret, R (2000). Victimisation and the social organisation of prostitution in England and Spain, in R. Weittzer (ed) *Sex for Sale*. London: Routledge.

Pearce JJ, Roach P, et al (1997). *Report into the links between Prostitution, Drugs and Violence*. A SOVA publication in collaboration with Middlesex University.

Sanders, T (2001). Female street sex workers, sexual violence and protection strategies, *Journal of Sexual Aggression*, Vol.7 (1): 5-18.

Shell Y, Campbell P, Caren, I (2001). *It's Not a Game: a report on Hampshire Constabulary's Anti-Kerb Crawling Initiative*. Hampshire Constabulary.

West Yorkshire Police (2000). *The Kerb-Crawlers Rehabilitation Programme: An Evaluation from the Police Perspective.*

Women Against Rape and Legal Action for Women (1995). *Dossier: The Crown Prosecution Service and the Crime of Rape.*

Newspaper articles

Bradford Telegraph & Argus, November 1996. "Party horror after vice girls is attacked."

Bradford Telegraph & Argus, 8.5.01. & 14.5.01

Bradford Telegraph & Argus, November 2001. "Double life term for knife maniac."

Bradford Telegraph & Argus, 6.11.01

Coventry Evening Telegraph, 19.6.01

Guardian, 22.7.00. "Chief Constable attacks jail system."

Guardian, 16.9.02. "Law increases danger, prostitutes say."

Liverpool Echo, 25.1.02. "Sex beast preyed on vice girls."

Observer, 19.3.00. "Midlands Ripper unmasked."

Plymouth Evening Herald, 1.12.01

Plymouth Evening Herald, 9.12.00

Press Association, 27.4.01. "HIV warning to men using prostitutes."

The Independent, 9.1.03. Natasha Walker, "All victims of murder should be treated equally."

Walsall Advertiser, 26.4.01.

Yorkshire Evening Post, 10.8.01. "New drive to keep vice girls off streets."

Yorkshire Post, 27.3.98. "Minimum of 22 years for prostitute's killer."

Websites

BBC News website, 29.1.98. Rapist gets life for murder. http://news.bbc.co.uk /1/hi/uk/51747.stm. (accessed 17.7.03).

BBC News website, 25.11.99. Sex clients' robbery risk. http://news.bbc.co.uk /hi/english/uk/scotland/newsid_536000/536141.stm. (accessed 17.7.03).

BBC News website, 8.12.99. Prostitute murderer gets life David Smith. http://news.bbc.co.uk/1/hi/uk/552350.stm. (accessed 17.7.03).

BBC News website, 21.7.00 Freed killer murders again. http://news.bbc.co.uk /1/hi/uk/845211.stm. (accessed 17.7.03).

BBC News website, 6.2.01 Rapist jailed for prostitute attacks, http://news.bbc.co.uk/1/hi/scotland/1156724.stm. Accessed 17.7.03).

This Is Hull and East Yorkshire website, 20.1.99. Link no longer available. (accessed by author 20.10.00).

Policy

Chapter 13
Prostitution seen as violence against women
Liv Jessen

Oscar Wilde said the way to truth is through paradoxes. I have never come across any subject as full of paradoxes and contradictions as prostitution. It is very real but at the same time it is a grand illusion. It is closeness, but nonetheless distance, sex and total sexlessness. It is truth, but still full of lies. Joy and sorrow can be present in the same moment. Nothing that happens in prostitution has only one obvious meaning. Prostitution is a subject that I for one am not soon done with. It is a subject with very many variations and many possible interpretations.

In the first place, it has to do with gender relations, with our sexuality and what boundaries we have for it – it has to do with our longings and dreams, our wish for love and intimacy. It has to do with excitement and with the forbidden. It has to do with joy, sorrow, need, pain, flight, oppression and violence. First and foremost it has to do with poverty – and politics, in particular. It is no wonder that people are interested in this subject.

Prostitution can be approached at many different levels. We can discuss it from a socio-political point of view, from a historical point of view, from an anthropological angle and from the point of view of legislation. There are many ways of looking at it. I am going to discuss prostitution from a feminist point of view but based on my own experience as a social worker, all in a Scandinavian setting.

I am the head of the Pro Centre, a national centre for prostitutes in Norway. I am a social worker by profession and for twenty years I worked daily among Norwegian and foreign women and men who sell sex. I have also worked among some of their customers. In writing about prostitution and society's view of this phenomenon, it is natural for me to base myself on my experiences in Norway and, more broadly, Scandinavia.

I am fully aware that we are a small corner of the world and that other and perhaps more important discussions about prostitution go on elsewhere. The reason why I would still like to say something about the view that prostitution is sexual violence against women is that in the past I believed so myself. But as a result of meeting thousands of women and men in prostitution I have come to take a critical view of this theory.

From moral to social deviation

Since the 1970s, parallels have been drawn between prostitution, pornography, rape and domestic violence. Radical feminists suggest that prostitution should be regarded as violence against women. I will argue that this is an imperfect or, at worst, an oppressive theory that can continue to stigmatise prostitutes. Furthermore, this theory can go hand in hand with the view that prostitution is a moral problem – a stance that the feminists have disagreed with. For the sake of simplicity, I will write only about women who sell sex and men who buy it.

In the 1970s and 1980s, the position of women in Scandinavian societies was the subject of vigorous debate. Most importantly women wanted financial independence and they invaded the labour market. As time passed, many areas of society became subject to feminist critique and influence. Many battles were won and a number of measures were implemented. Legal abortion was an important victory.

There were heated discussions about rape, domestic violence, sexual abuse and prostitution. This concern gave rise to women's shelters, rape centres, centres for victims of incest and, not least, support centres for prostitutes. The Pro Centre was established to rehabilitate prostitutes.

Feminist thinking infused much of the progressive politics of that time. The Swedish Government published its first major Report on Prostitution in 1981. In Norway, the book *Back streets: Prostitution, Money and Love* (Høigaard and Finstad 1992) first appeared in 1986. Both of these works were underpinned by feminism and laid the foundation for the establishment – in both Norway and Sweden – of special rehabilitation centres for street prostitutes.

Two kinds of women

After some years at the Pro Centre I met Anna. She was my age and had begun selling sex when she was thirteen. She worked for years in Norway and abroad. When she got pregnant she decided to stop. She got herself a job in the health service and had this job for ten years before she contacted me. One conversation I remember well went something like this: "You know, it's written on my forehead. I am a whore." "But Anna, it's not something you are; it's something you do or have done."

I realised that many women like Anna regard being a prostitute as a quality some women have. Is it only Anna who imagines that there are two kinds of women: Them and Us, the respectable women and the whores? I would maintain that 'every woman' knows what I am talking about. There are few of us who have not understood the negative implication that lies in having the word 'whore' slung at us.

When I visit secondary schools and talk about prostitution, all the young girls nod their heads when I ask them if they know what I mean when I talk about the tightrope we girls have to tread. We cannot be seen to be too prudish, on the one hand, and certainly not too easy, on the other. We have got to be sure to stay on the right side. Anna did not, and she has suffered for it all her life. That is why she never tells anyone. The cost is too high.

For as long as there have been records, women have been ashamed of working as prostitutes. The belief that some women have qualities that make them prostitutes is very much alive, and not just among women in prostitution. This view maintains that female prostitutes are different from most women and they are whores due to bad morals or to a biological defect.

A radical feminist view

Feminists in the 1980s objected to this. Prostitution was sexual violence against women and there was no reason to divide women into the respectable ones and the temptresses, unless it was to keep women disciplined and divided. We believed that women were forced into prostitution for various reasons – material and spiritual. Prostitution was also a class question. It is working class women who were, and remain, more available. Therefore, prostitution has to be abolished.

This radical feminist understanding is pervasive in Scandinavian societies. Prostitution became the ultimate symbol of the oppression of women. Feminism insists that the balance of power between men and women determines their different positions in society. Women were, and still are, inferior to men in financial, social, political and cultural fields. Although much has changed since the 1980s, research shows that there is still a long way to go. This structural imbalance affects both our thinking and society's many institutions.

Areas of people's lives that had previously been regarded as private were now politicised: domestic violence, rape and sexual abuse among them. Men's violence against women in the home was an expression of men's power over women and thus a social issue. Previously, it was the woman's fault for putting herself in a position where she was raped and abused.

Now this violence was interpreted within the context of the power imbalance between the sexes, the need of men to discipline the female. Viewed this way, women were the victims and men the abusers. So far, so good. But we also looked at prostitution the same way. A female prostitute was a victim of the (male) client.

This outlook presumes that men have power, are subjects, can act and make choices. Women by contrast are mere victims, objects who are more or less 'forced' into prostitution for a variety of reasons, such as sexual abuse, poverty, drug dependence and an unhappy childhood. Moreover, prostitution – selling sexual services – was seen as synonymous with selling part of you and therefore done at great emotional cost. Our sexuality was very closely associated with our identity or our very being.

It was accepted that the people who organise this business, the 'ringleaders' and 'pimps', should be punished; the further tightening up of anti-prostitution regulations was not designed to harm the weak party, i.e. the sellers. Disagreement arose as to whether the client alone should be prosecuted – and that disagreement remains to this day.

Mary taught me a lesson.

"By objectifying the other person, you attack the other person's freedom" - Hans
Skjervheim, Norwegian Philosopher (Skjervheim 1976: 56)

I must tell you about a meeting I had with a woman called Mary, a young, attractive woman in her late twenties. She had eventually completed higher education and made a position for herself in society. However, she continued as a prostitute in addition to holding down a well-paid job. Mary had never worked on the street or had drug problems. She was seven when a close member of her family sexually abused her. She tells me about it. In my eagerness to assuage her guilt, I say that naturally she was in no way responsible for the sexual abuse when she was only seven years old. I notice that she becomes stubborn and tends to argue with me. Finally, she says, rather annoyed: "But the prostitution, Liv, at least I am responsible for that."

The years pass by and thanks to my day-to-day work at the Pro Centre I learn more, understand more, read more and, not least, meet women who are not wretched and miserable as we supposed they all were. I feel the need to broaden the picture.

Prostitutes are not all drug-addicted streetwalkers with a difficult past and few options, who think prostitution is hell on earth. The prostitute is a person with many different faces. She no longer talks with only one tongue.

I meet women who tell me they have both 'chosen' prostitution and that they do not lack anything because of it. I do not believe them. I think they are saying this because they do not know what is good for them: "It is only human to want to defend what you are doing. Just wait, one day they will discover we were right." WE KNOW what traumas are involved.

How often can we say or think this without wondering what view of humankind is hidden here? Hans Skjervheim has wisely said that if we objectify another person, it is not easy to take her and what she is saying seriously. He says:

> By objectifying the other person, you attack that other person's freedom. You turn the other person into a fact, an object in your world. In that way you can gain control of the other person. The person who objectifies the other in the most sophisticated way is the master. (Skjervheim 1976: 56)

This leaves a nasty taste in my mouth. I do not want to objectify anyone or take control of anyone. Who am I to say to these women that I know better than they do what their lives are like, what they feel and think? Mary was a good teacher. She clearly needed to have power and control over her own life. I was in the process of taking that away from her. I made her an object – a passive, apathetic, resigned person who could not make her own choices. Mary objected. I learned an important lesson. Never 'steal' the other person's story. Have respect for her version.

How can I know whether or not she chose prostitution deliberately? Why should my traditional, narrow interpretation that "with such a background it was quite natural for her to drift into prostitution" be the correct one? She taught me a great deal about how important it is for everyone to be in control of his or her own life.

As time goes on, we meet more and more people who describe their life in prostitution in a rather different way from the picture drawn by radical feminist research, a picture I myself had obstinately stuck to throughout my initial years at the Pro Centre. The picture becomes more varied and therefore more complicated. It is no longer so black and white. The horizons become wider.

Can different realities be true at one and the same time? I think, at any rate, that the feminist perspective of the 1980s alone does not provide a satisfactory answer to all the complex questions we come up against, or explain the paradoxes we encounter, nor is it a sufficient basis on which to formulate policy for the future. The starting point was too narrow.

The mistake we had made was to believe that our view embraced the whole world of prostitution. Until then, the prostitutes we had seen were among the downtrodden women on the streets whose need was greatest. It was easy, as a social worker, to regard her as a victim of men's oppression.

This was particularly true when it fitted in with our theoretical conceptions. Feminist research in Scandinavia had chosen to research the 'obvious victims' of street prostitution. But to widen one's horizons, not to just stick to one opinion, to doubt, to ask questions, to provoke discussion – all this can be threatening.

That is what happened when the Pro Centre dared to raise some questions. Criticism from feminists was quick in coming. It allowed no room for disagreement, doubts or other opinions. Resistance to anti-prostitution feminism was labelled pro-prostitution lobbyism. Before I knew what was happening some of us were labelled that way. Twenty years of helping women and men to get out of prostitution counted for nothing.

That is what sometimes happens in debates - far more is attributed to an opponent than the opponent actually believes. We objectify the other person, as Skjervheim says. We interpret and twist views, until sometimes they become quite unrecognisable, often to promote our own political views. At any rate, I am more afraid today of the people who possess the whole truth about prostitution than I am of those who have the courage to doubt.

A social constructionist perspective of prostitution

One person who has challenged the prominent Scandinavian view on prostitution is Finnish researcher, Margaretha Järvinen (1991). She asks us to look at prostitution as part of society, from the inside not the outside. She claims that there are several possible feminist views of prostitution. Some complement each other, while others are in direct conflict.

The sex trade reflects the gender and power structure that exists and is thus not abnormal. It is important not to attach importance to what distinguishes prostitutes from other women. Instead we should focus on the fact that women in general have a great deal in common, such as our role as mothers, the fact that we are financially worse off than men, the female role in the sex game, commercialisation of the female body, the disciplining of women's sexuality, and so on.

She calls her view a social constructionist perspective and she says it is not very helpful to explain a prostitute's participation in prostitution by her background, upbringing or by the detrimental effects prostitution is claimed to have. She asks some controversial questions: Can prostitution be seen as one option for work, or is it always undertaken where there is no other choice? Are sex workers deviants or normal people? Is the buying of sex itself an expression of power or of powerlessness? Can criminalising the buying of sex prevent prostitution and protect women?

I would like to consider some of these questions.

Does prostitution always have to be linked with a no-choice situation? As Hans Skjervheim has said, "The first thing you have to choose is to make the choice yourself" (1976: 64). Women are in some ways subordinate to men. But it is easy to confuse the structural view of women as victims and objects of men's abusive power with the picture of individual wretchedness in some street prostitutes. We naturally have no difficulty in understanding that her wretched situation 'forces' her to prostitute herself. To her, however, prostitution may seem like a strategy for solving a problem that is even worse.

In their book *Back streets* Høigard and Finstad (1992) are unable to accept voluntary prostitution because they believe that no-one could ever choose to take part in such activity: "no one wants to rent out her vagina as a rubbish bin for hordes of anonymous men's ejaculations". Nevertheless, to apply the social victim-object view to individuals in prostitution can at best arouse our sympathy, but at worst can result in the prostitute no longer seeing herself as a person, a subject with a choice. To be able to choose she must be ascribed humanity, subjectivity and identity. But in doing so we run the risk that she may choose prostitution.

The sex trade today involves many different degrees of volition and exploitation. That is why it is fruitless to take a general victim view of prostitution. Free will and force vary in different cultures in the past and in the present, within any one country and perhaps also in any one individual.

We know today that women choose prostitution for a variety of reasons. Some are more coerced and dominated than others.

Some hate what they do, think it is hell on earth, but see no other course. Others think it is easy enough to do for the money concerned. Prostitutes come from different backgrounds; most of them belong to the working class or lower. Some feel they have a genuine choice, for others it is an unconscious choice; some see it as a choice between cholera and the plague, and some are forced into it.

Some are extremely unhappy with what they are doing, become deeply troubled and need years of support to repair the damage done to their mental health. Some seem to sail through it without a problem. But they all have one thing in common. They all know that society around them condemns them for what they do. They are a pariah race, branded as outcasts and feared.

Combating this should be a major preoccupation for all feminists. Instead, radical feminists continue to talk about prostitutes as victims. If a woman defends her participation in prostitution, they say that she is not credible. Eva Lundgren, a feminist professor, refers to a "false consciousness syndrome".[1] The only women who are to be trusted, are the 'repentant sinners', who are called Survivors.

Women in prostitution naturally have different views on the subject of prostitution, but to say that only the ones who agree with us are right, while the prostitutes who think differently are not ascribed human qualities like the right to make their own choices or to be believed, is oppressive.

Are prostitutes deviants or normal people? Prostitutes have traditionally been regarded as morally deviant. This was something feminists objected to. They disagreed that the prostitute's participation in prostitution could be explained by individual characteristics and pathology. But what happens if we explain her participation solely by background factors such as a difficult childhood, drug abuse in the home, psychological problems, sexual abuse, etc?

Or if we analyse the social and psychological deviance and harmful effects caused by prostitution, such as split personality, loss of self-respect, sexual problems, social isolation etc.? What then? We are getting dangerously close to defining her as a social deviant. She is certainly not like us. She is still the Other Woman, with whom we do not have to identify. We are careful not to show our contempt. Instead she becomes the object of our pity.

If she is in a situation where she has no choice, is he always in a position of power? In 1989, Arnhild Taksdal and Annick Prieur published their book, *Å sette pris på kvinner – menn som kjøper sex*

(Putting a Price on Women – Men Who Buy Sex). This book has unfortunately not been translated. At last, the focus shifted for a brief moment. Since then both the Swedes and the Danes have written books and reports on those who buy sex.

Research shows the client is no different from other men as regards age, marital status or occupation, although there is an overrepresentation among men who travel a great deal. The client's reasons for buying sex vary. However, the feminist interpretation of men as the subject, active and power-wielding, does not fit in very well with the motives given by interviewees. Their actions can be interpreted as those of powerless men as easily as anything else. In some ways, the women themselves believe that prostitutes are the ones with power, not clients.

Client research has shown that the client cannot solely be seen and interpreted as someone who abuses their power. But there are areas of prostitution that attract criminals and abusers. But placing them outside public supervision will aggravate this.

Since power and the exercise of power vary so much between different forms of prostitution and in different cultures, it is not easy to paint an unambiguous picture. I think that many of us who trouble ourselves with these questions agree that far more social effort must be directed at the clients in the years ahead, both in the form of more research into the market and into the buyers' motives, and we should perhaps implement some social measures for certain groups of customers (Smette 2003).

Aspects of criminalisation.

Every society tries to control prostitution through various laws and regulations. The Scandinavian legal system has chosen to outlaw pimping, procuring and, recently, advertising and renting out premises for prostitution. Their approach to prostitution is more or less an abolitionist one.

For many years it has been generally accepted that we do not want to criminalise women involved in prostitution. The situation for street prostitutes is already wretched enough; no one wants to make it any worse. Some political lobbies advocate total criminalisation, but it does not seem as though this has much support among people in Scandinavia.

However, there are many people who, out of feminist solidarity and sympathy for street prostitutes, advocate criminalising the clients. Sweden passed a law in 1999 prohibiting the buying of sexual services. The main reasons for passing the law were to signal that women are not for sale and to reduce prostitution. After four years not one report has been published in Sweden that documents a decline in prostitution. But more than 80 per cent of the population seem to be in favour of the law.

Since Sweden has granted no extra money for the rehabilitation of sex workers, we can only guess at their situation. The police have focused on street prostitution and reports by Malmø police suggest there is increasing violence against the women there. Furthermore, any kind of criminalisation will hurt the weakest party, the women. In 1985 changes were made to the penal code in Canada, prohibiting the sale of sexual services in public places. They tried to apply the law equally against prostitutes and their clients but more sellers than buyers were caught.

In Sweden some women report that the police keep them under surveillance in order to catch clients. They feel that this is harassment. In principle, the law should support them. Street prostitutes I have spoken to in Oslo do not see criminalisation of the clients as supportive of them. They say that they do not make any distinction between criminalising prostitution as such and criminalising the purchase of sex alone. They already feel their activity is a criminal one, so if the purchase alone is criminalised in Norway, they know that their situation will get worse.

We have to wonder whether tightening up the legislation will have the desired effect, or whether other measures might prove to be better. No country I know of has managed to abolish prostitution with the help of a few legal provisions. I have never seen such widespread sale of sex as there is in Thailand where prostitution is prohibited.

In any event, there is a scarlet thread running from the view that prostitutes are victims and social losers to the idea that buying sex is 'violence against women' to the suggestion that the activity of clients should be criminalised. Seen from this point of view, criminalisation recognises that prostitutes have no choice and the blame is heaped where it belongs – the client.

Järvinen says: "Prostitution is not a marginal phenomenon on the edge of society, carried out by deviant individuals. It does not represent a break with the male society's central values and norms. It is a social construction which corresponds with the male and female roles in society. Therefore, there is no obvious and universally applicable line dividing prostitute-client relationships from other heterosexual relationships." (Järvinen 1991: 86)

Some future challenges!

We must talk about all types of prostitution. Street prostitution is not representative of the whole trade in sex throughout the world, as we tend to think in Scandinavia. It is perhaps only a small part of it. Nor are street prostitutes a homogenous group. Male prostitution, which I have not touched on at all, presents more new angles, even more so when we talk about women buying sex. The time for simplifying things is over. If we are to implement effective and adequate measures, we must see the variations and the different parts of the whole.

We must not look for one universal cure for the whole of this difficult problem. We must accept the fact that the steps we take can be effective in limited areas. But whatever we do, we must base all our efforts on solidarity. We must make sure that our measures do not add to the stigma.

What do we need today in our work on prostitution? Our society's humanistic traditions should be the basis for all our work. We need to demonstrate our solidarity with women and men who sell sex. Every prostitute suffers from the way society brands her. Furthermore, we must initiate measures, which can help to strengthen prostitutes' civil rights. We must abolish any laws that prevent this.

Whatever we do, we must ask ourselves whether the measures we take intensify the stigma or make the situation worse for those who sell sex. We must keep their health and well-being in mind. We need to fight those aspects of prostitution that are oppressive and degrading.

We must formulate a social welfare policy that gives a helping hand to prostitutes who want to get out of it; that applies to both buyers and sellers. While prostitution itself should not be a crime, coercion, violence and deception should be.

Women's subordinate position to men in society applies way beyond prostitution. We also know that being oppressed is not the same as being weak and passive. We have to distinguish between understanding prostitution at a structural level and at an individual level. But whatever we do it is of utmost importance not to reinforce the Whore/Madonna dichotomy, which in itself is oppressive.

Prostitutes, like all people, must be given the freedom to choose. That is what makes you human. It also means that you are allowed to take the responsibility for your actions. Prostitutes will no longer be looked upon as victims to pity or rescue – but as heroines in their own lives.

Notes

[1] Lundgren, Eva, Professor, at a open feminist meeting in Oslo, 8 March 1999

References

Remark: the titles of books, magazines and chapters in these references have been translated by the author from the original Norwegian.

Bernstein, Elizabeth (1999). What's Wrong with Prostitution? What's Right with Sex Work?: Comparing Markets in Female Sexual Labor. *Hastings Women's Law Journal* 10 (1):91-119.

Chapkis, Wendy (1997). *Live Sex Acts: Women performing erotic labor*. New York: Routledge.

Ericsson, Kjersti (1993). Kvinner om handlende offer (*Women as active victims*). *Nordisk Tidsskrift for Kriminalvitenskap* (Nordic Journal of Criminology).

Høigaard, Cecilie and Finstad, Liv (1992). *Backstreets; Prostitution, Money and Love*. Pennsylvania University Press.

Høigaard, Cecilie (1993). *The victim as expert: active and captive*. Scandinavian University Press, ISSN 0803-8740.

Järvinen, Margaretha (1991). Könsperspektiv på prostitution. (A Gender Perspective on Prostitution). *Nordisk Tidsskrift for Kriminalvitenskap* (Nordic Journal of Criminology).

Jessen, Liv (1995). *Prostitution is no longer a simple question*. International HIV / Aids conference, Copenhagen.

Jessen, Liv (1998). *Om prostitusjon. Hvordan forstår vi den? Hva gjør vi med den?* (Prostitution – how do we understand it? What do we do with it?) Innledninger fra Pro Sentrets jubileumskonferanse (Papers presented at Pro Senter conference in 1998).

Jessen, Liv (2000). Vi og horene (We and the whores) *Kronikk i Dagbladet*.

Kampadoo, Kamala and Doezema, Jo (1998). *Global Sex Workers. Rights, Resistance and Redefinition*. New York: Routledge.

Pheterson, Gail (1996). *The whore stigma. – Female dishonour and male unworthiness*. Dutch Ministry of Social Affairs and Employment, ISBN 90 363 9592 5.

Skjervheim, Hans (1976). *Deltakar og tilskodar og andre essays* (Participant and spectator and other essays). Oslo: Tanum-Norli. Author's translation

SOU 1995: Official Swedish Report: *Könshandelen. Betänkande av 1993 års prostitutionsutredning*. Ministry of Social Affairs, Stockholm, Sweden.

Smette, Ingrid (2003). *Den seksuelle slavestand? En rapport om kundene i prostitusjonen* (Report on customers in prostitution, Pro Sentret, Oslo 2003 – Available in Norwegian only).

Stenvoll, Dag (2002). *From Russia with Love?* Newspaper Coverage of Cross-Border Prostitution in Northern Norway, 1990-2001. *European Journal of Women's Studies.* Vol. 9 (2) p. 143-162.

Taksdal, Arnhild, Prieur, Annick (1989). Å *sette pris på kvinner – menn som kjøper sex* (Putting a price on women – men who buy sex). Oslo: Pax Forlag A.s.

Chapter 14
Sex in the new Europe: the criminalisation of clients and Swedish fear of penetration
By Don Kulick

This article was first published as "Sex in the New Europe: the criminalisation of clients and Swedish Fear of Penetration" in Anthropological Theory, *Vol. 3, Issue 2, June 2003, pp 199-218.*

> "Sweden is going through an identity crisis these days which has become acute with our entry into the EU" - Dag Sebastian Ahlander (1997) in the journal *Moderna Tider*
>
> "Prostitution doesn't belong in our country"(*Prostitution hör inte hemma i vårt land*) - Minister for Gender Equality, Ulrika Messing (Kvinnofrid website, 1997)

On May 29, 1998, the Swedish Parliament passed a law that made it a crime to purchase or the attempt to purchase "a temporary sexual relationship" (*tillfällig sexuell förbindelse*). This law was the culmination of nearly a decade of work by feminist groups and center/left politicians to convince lawmakers that they should 'send a message' that 'society' does not accept prostitution. But it was also a law that flies in the face of increasingly non-punitive approaches to prostitution that have been gaining ground in other European countries. At the same time that Sweden was criminalising the clients of prostitutes, Italy was debating whether or not to repeal a 1958 law which prohibited bordellos[1], Denmark decriminalised prostitution, Norway was abandoning its decades-old policy of trying to 'rehabilitate' prostitutes, and was encouraging them to organise (Bodström & Zweigbergk 1994: 142-62), and the Netherlands and Germany were taking the truly radical step of placing the regulation of prostitution under labour law, instead of criminal law.

In passing a law that criminalised clients, Sweden made a decisive move from an abolitionist legislative model (i.e. a legal system that holds that prostitution in itself is not an offence, but the exploitation of the prostitution of others is; thus any third party recruiting, profiting from, or organizing prostitutes is penalized) towards a prohibitionist model that criminalises the actual transaction of selling sex.

In a contemporary European context, this is exceptional. It is also remarkable given the small numbers of prostitutes in Sweden.

By all accounts, the total number of street prostitutes in all of Sweden has never numbered more than about 1,000. In other words, there are substantially fewer street prostitutes in the whole of Sweden than there are in any large or even medium sized European city such as Milan, Copenhagen, or Madrid. Given that, why the flurry of political and legislative activity around prostitution?

The argument that I will make here is that the law criminalising the clients of prostitutes is in large measure a response to Sweden's entry in to the EU. During the two years leading up to the country's referendum in 1994, the press was filled with reports warning that eastern European women were poised to invade the country. "A new form of prostitution is spreading in Europe" announced an article in *Dagens Nyheter*, the country's largest daily newspaper (circulation ca. 380,000 daily), in early 1993 (*Dagens Nyheter* 2.2.93).[2] "It is a mobile prostitution where about 100,000 young women from the Eastern bloc (*öststatskvinnor*) travel out into Europe to make money by prostituting themselves". This prostitution was linked to organised crime, drugs, and a "new wave of HIV" which threatened Sweden (see also *Dagens Nyheter* 7.1.92, which also cites the figure 100,000).

This threat of 'Eastern bloc' women was compounded by the political gains throughout Europe of what in the Swedish press was referred to as "the pro-prostitution lobby". To the distress of Swedish feminists, journalists, social workers and politicians, this lobby, which was portrayed as powerful and financed by a conglomerate called by the vague but sinister name: "the international sex industry", was managing to convince policy makers and legislators on the Continent that prostitution was a profession, and that prostitutes should organise to demand rights and recognition.

This was consistently portrayed as a fundamentally incomprehensible position: "It isn't up to individuals to decide whether or not they want to sell their bodies", snapped the Minister for Gender Equality in a discussion of European policies on prostitution. The combination of 'Eastern bloc' women eager for intercourse in Sweden, and 'pro-prostitution' policies in other European countries raised the truly frightful spectre of Sweden being penetrated on all fronts. Even children were at risk. Invoking what appears to be the epitome of the scary Other, one report on prostitution in the EU informed readers in an incredulous tone that:

> Today it actually happens in Holland that two lesbian prostitutes who live together and work in a sadomasochistic sex service can adopt children or legally become inseminated, something that under Swedish law would be completely unthinkable.

"What will happen", this report continued, darkly, "if Sweden becomes part of the EC?" (Månsson & Backman 1992:24, 25)

What happened, I argue, is that Sweden took concrete steps to make sure its borders were not penetrated by lesbian sadomasochistic prostitute mothers, once it became clear that the country would become part of the EU.

Let me return now to the law that forms the basis of my discussion, the law that criminalises the purchase of a temporary sexual relationship.

Before I detail that law, I need to situate it in the wider context of what Gayle Rubin (1993) would call Swedish sex law. It is necessary to make it very clear at the outset that the widespread images that many people have of Sweden as a kind of sexually liberated wonderland are utterly misguided and wrong. Sweden has some of the harshest sex laws in the world. It is the only European country, for example, where during the early years of the AIDS epidemic, a national law was passed abolishing existing gay bathhouses and prohibiting the establishment of new ones.

It is also one of the few countries in the world where persons with HIV can still be forcibly incarcerated without a criminal trial, simply because doctors believe that they will not follow instructions to inform their sexual partners that they are HIV+. Sweden is also one of the few countries in Europe – perhaps the only one – where it is impossible to remain anonymous as a person with HIV: if you test positive at any state funded or private clinic, your physician is legally obliged to report your identity to the health authorities, and you are then legally obliged to report to a doctor regularly with information about your sexual encounters and relationships.

Numerous laws regulate activities such as erotic dancing and posing, which are more or less illegal under the Swedish legal code. According to the latest police reports, there are a total of *five* sex clubs in the entire country. The strongest beverage served in these clubs is Coca Cola, and the most scandalous sexual act that undercover policemen have been able to document consisted of a woman flashing her vagina at a man from behind a barrier made of chicken wire (SoS 2000:5, p. 56-57).

Even prior to the new law criminalising the purchase of a temporary sexual relationship it was illegal to purchase or attempt to purchase sex from anyone under 18 years of age. Anyone under 19 years of age caught selling sex can be incarcerated in special youth facilities.

The law dealing with what in Swedish is referred to as "procuring" (*koppleri*) is very harsh, and can result in a maximum prison term of four years. It is illegal to profit in any way from sexual services performed by anyone else. This is positive in the sense that it makes the exploitation of sex workers and others by unscrupulous profiteers illegal. But it also makes it illegal for sex workers to rent apartments or commercial spaces for work. It makes it illegal for them to hire anyone to book their appointments, and it makes it illegal to openly advertise their services in newspapers and magazines. It even makes it difficult for them to live with anybody, since their lover, roommate or friend could be seen as profiting from the sex worker's income, in cases where they share expenses or have joint bank accounts.

This is the framework of sex law in which the law criminalising the purchase or attempt to purchase "a temporary sexual relationship" must be understood. The law was passed as part of a broad package of laws entitled *Kvinnofrid*, which is officially translated as "Violence Against Women", but which actually means something like "Peace or Serenity for Women", or "Women Left Alone" (*Kvinnofrid* 1997).

The first sentence in the government bill that presented the package states that the Serenity for Women laws were all designed to "counteract violence against women, prostitution, and sexual harassment in the workplace". The laws prescribed harsher penalties for wife battering, they expanded the definition of rape, they replaced the legal term "female circumcision" with "genital mutilation" and made the penalties much more severe, they defined the term "sexual harassment" and prescribed penalties, and they prohibited the purchase or the attempt to purchase a temporary sexual relationship.

This is the actual text of the law (italics in original):

Den som mot ersättning skaffar sig en tillfällig sexuell förbindelse döms – om inte gärningen är belagd med straff enligt brottsbalken — *för köp av sexuella tjänster* till böter eller fängelse i högst sex månader.

> Anyone who for remuneration procures a temporary sexual relationship will be guilty – if their action is not punishable by some other offense according to the penal code – *of purchasing sexual services*, and will be sentenced to fines or prison for not more than six months.

There is also a short paragraph that states that an attempt to purchase sex will be treated just as severely as the actual purchase of sex.

It should be immediately apparent that there are a number of quite serious problems with the way this law is formulated; problems that make it extremely difficult to interpret and enforce. The four key words "remuneration", "procures", "temporary", and "sexual relationship" are far from clear-cut. What constitutes remuneration? A nice dinner in a fancy restaurant – is that remuneration? (Actually, in this case, the courts have been instructed that remuneration includes non-monetary remuneration, "such as narcotics, alcohol or furs"; BRÅ 2000:4, p.39). What about "procure"? If I give a sex worker money for sex with me, that's clear. But what about if a company pays for escorts for visiting businessmen, or I pay for my best friend to have a big night out on the town just before he gets married? Who is prosecutable? The one who paid and didn't have sex, or the one who didn't pay but had sex? What does "temporary" mean exactly? Should it cover regular clients, who maintain long-term relationships with individual sex workers, or are they exempt from prosecution? And, finally, what exactly constitutes "a sexual relationship"? One might recall, in another context, how a certain US president managed to complicate that question, admitting that a certain White House intern had performed fellatio on him on a number of occasions, but steadfastly denying that oral sex constituted "sexual relations" (Time.Com) The issue is not much clearer here: what exactly has to be done to whom for a given interaction to be considered "sexual"?[3].

The law prohibiting the purchase of temporary sexual relationships became effective on 1 January 1999. It is noteworthy that the law was passed despite the fact that a number of weighty organisations, including the National Board of Police, the National Social Welfare Board, the Attorney General, and the National Courts Administration, advised against it.

The vote was 181 votes for the law, 92 against, and 13 abstentions (63 Members of Parliament were absent and cast no vote). The parties that voted for the law were those on the Left – Social Democrats (*Socialdemokraterna*), the Swedish Left

(*Vänsterpartiet*, formerly the Communist party), the Greens (*Miljöpartiet*) and a centrist party with a largely rural constituency (*Centern*). The three liberal/rightist parties (*Moderaterna, Folkpartiet*, and *Kristdemokraterna*) either opposed it or abstained from voting.

A basic difference between the Left and the Right on this issue was that the Left portrayed the issue as one of 'taking a stand' against what they asserted was a reprehensible social practice. The Left consistently drew parallels with a much-discussed 1979 law that prohibited the spanking of children, even in the home. The effects of that law are contested among researchers and policy makers (Larselere and Johnson 1999), but there is a widely disseminated and popularly felt consensus in Sweden that the law had a positive impact: it made spanking socially unacceptable, and rates of child abuse have dropped.

The same will happen with prostitution, so the argument went: if 'society' speaks, citizens will listen. Note how this parallel between laws prohibiting the spanking of children and laws prohibiting clients to purchase sex depends on and sustains an analogy between children and prostitutes. Just as society has a duty to protect children – victims without a voice of their own who need others to speak for them and the state to protect them – so does society have a duty to protect prostitutes who, in Swedish debates, are unvaryingly portrayed as exploited victims who need others to speak for them and the state to protect them.

This parallel between prostitutes and children is highlighted even more starkly by the fact that under Swedish law, "[c]hildren under 15 years of age can...never consent to sexual acts with the effect of exonerating the offender from criminal liability" (SOU 2001:14, p. 584). In other words, children under 15 have no "right of sexual self-determination" (SOU 2001:14, p. 584). As a result of the law prohibiting the purchase of sexual services, neither do sex workers.

Political parties on the right framed their opposition to the law as an opposition to the state infringing on individuals' right to privacy. Parties on the right also highlighted the difficulties that legal representatives like the Attorney General predicted that police and the courts would face in actual enforcement. They pointed out that under the law contact with a prostitute is not illegal, and neither is sex with a prostitute. What is illegal is purchasing or attempting to purchase "a temporary sexual relation" – a specific action that is extremely difficult to document or prove, particularly when both parties deny it occurred, which of course they both have a strong incentive to do.

In fact, this kind of practical difficulty has dogged the law since its passage. A recent study by the National Council for Crime Prevention reported that during the first year of the law's existence, 91 police offence reports were filed throughout the country. Of those 91 cases, most of the investigations were discontinued on the grounds that there was insufficient evidence to press charges. By the beginning of 2000, only seven cases had gone to court. Of those seven cases, six defendants were found guilty and one was acquitted (four of those found guilty had confessed, two denied it but were convicted anyway).

The guilty men were fined sums of between 1,600 and 13,600 kronor, that is to say, between about $150-$1,200 USD. In practice, this means that the penalty for purchasing sex is more or less equivalent to the penalty for petty shoplifting (Nord and Rosenberg 2001:13).[4]

What has been the effect of the law on sex workers in Sweden? First, it is important to note that the issue of how the law would affect sex workers was of relatively little interest to the Social Democratic League of Women and other groups who were instrumental in getting it passed. Although many of these groups supported the move to criminalise only the clients of prostitutes – on the grounds that prostitutes themselves are oppressed victims – when they were confronted with the possibility that the law might drive sex work underground and make sex workers more vulnerable to exploitation by profiteers, representatives consistently responded in one of two related ways: either they said that the purpose of the law was first and foremost to 'take a stance' or 'send a message' that 'society' did not accept prostitution; hence, the impact of the law on prostitutes was of secondary concern, or they interpreted the phrase 'driven underground' not to mean 'made vulnerable to exploitation and abuse', but, instead, to mean 'not visible', 'not be known to the police'. Hence, they argued that most prostitution was already 'invisible' anyway – it took place away from police awareness in massage parlours and through escort services. For this reason, the new law would make no real difference to prostitutes. If one then asked why the law was necessary if it would make no real difference, representatives would return to their first argument that 'society' needed to 'send a message' that prostitution was unacceptable.

Immediately after the law began to be enforced, police noted a drop in the numbers of street prostitutes (again, we are not talking about massive numbers to begin with – in 1999, reports indicate that there were less than 800 sex workers in the entire country).

This may have something to do with the fact that policemen, who had been allotted 7m Swedish kronor ($650,000 USD) to enforce the new law, immediately began making their presence felt on the streets where sex workers worked. Armed with video cameras, which they ostentatiously pointed at any car that slowed down near a sex worker, they effectively frightened away clients, thus driving the sex workers off the streets.

By the middle of 1999, however, it seems that many of the sex workers who initially left the streets were back again. In August 2002, social workers in Malmö, Sweden's third largest city, estimated that there were about 200 street prostitutes there, which is the same number that was estimated before the passage of the law in 1999 (*Kvällsposten* 9.8.02) Since the law came into effect, three government reports have been commissioned to evaluate it and to recommend how it might be enforced (BRÅ 2000:4; Nord and Rosenberg 2001; SoS 2000:5) None of these reports has concluded that the law has resulted in a significant drop in prostitution in Sweden.

While street prostitution was initially (and, it seems, temporarily) affected (see note 6), researchers report that the passage of the law corresponded with an increase of the number of sex ads on the internet. The number of brothels – which in practice means apartments on the periphery of large cities, in which Baltic women work, often under oppressive conditions – appears to have increased since the law was passed.

Prostitutes interviewed in the mass media report that women with drug problems have been driven to desperation and even suicide by the new law, since they have been unable to put ads on the internet and make up for the clients they lost as a result of the law. Social workers agree that the law has made it more difficult for them to reach prostitutes.

Police report that their efforts to prosecute pimps and traffickers has been made more difficult because clients, who before the passage of the law were sometimes willing to serve as witnesses, are now disinclined to cooperate, since they themselves are guilty of a crime (Nord and Rosenberg 2001:4). Social workers and street prostitutes say that the quality of clients has declined, and a recent report commissioned by the National Board of Police has concluded that that women are now forced to accept not only more clients (since prices have dropped), but also more unstable and dangerous clients than they would have accepted before the law, when there were more clients and, hence, more choice (e.g.

GT/Expressen 22.4.00; *Dagens Nyheter* 2.8.98, *Dagens Nyheter* 18.1.99; Nord and Rosenberg 2001:27).

Police harassment of prostitutes has increased. They can be forced to appear in court to provide testimony against the client (they can refuse to give evidence, but they are still summoned and sometimes escorted to courtrooms), and whenever they are caught with a client, their belongings are searched and they may be frisked. Anything that police think they can use as evidence against clients (such as condoms) is confiscated. This practice clearly has consequences for condom use among sex workers. It provides them with strong incentives to avoid using them.

The law has been a catastrophe for non-Swedish sex workers – if the prostitute found with a client is not a citizen or legal resident of Sweden, she is immediately deported; in fact government prosecutors complain that in a number of cases they were unable to gain convictions against clients because the prostitutes they were found with had been deported before they could even give a statement (BRÅ 2000:4, p. 44; also *Expressen* 30.9.01).[5] This fact affects the willingness of non-residents to report on violence. A police chief in the north of Sweden observes that, "I don't think for example that a Russian woman would dare to report a man for violence against her, because then she would risk not being given a visa if she ever wanted to come back to Sweden, because it would have become known that she is a prostitute" (*Tidningen Svensk Polis* 18.4.02).

The only positive thing for sex workers that perhaps can to be said to have emerged from this law is that it seems that some of them have used it to rob clients or blackmail them, telling them that if they didn't cough up more money, they would turn them into the police (*GT-Expressen* 21.1.99). Of course, if these robberies or blackmail attempts are reported to the police, the sex worker risks much harsher penalties than the client she attempts to blackmail (*Dagens Nyheter* 30.12.99).

Despite these obvious negative impacts on the lives and working conditions of street sex workers, and despite the ludicrously small numbers of convictions for breaking the law against purchasing a temporary sexual relationship, the feminist organisations and the politicians who advocated the law still support it, claiming that any negative impact on sex workers is outweighed by 'the message' conveyed by the law.[6]

As I have argued, that 'message' is an unambiguous one, and it is most succinctly summarised by Ulrika Messing, then Minister for Gender Equality, who declared in 1997 that "Prostitution doesn't belong in our country".

But are there perhaps also other messages being conveyed by the Swedish law that criminalises the purchase of sexual services?

One of the most striking dimensions of the debate that occurred in Sweden in the early 1990s about whether or not to join the EU was the way that prostitution emerged as an argument for staying out. In the two years leading up to the referendum in November 1994, numerous articles were published in Swedish newspapers asserting that Sweden would be overrun with foreign prostitutes if the country entered the EU. I have already mentioned reports like the one that claimed that 100,000 'Eastern bloc' women were gathering like storm clouds on the horizon, waiting to get into Sweden and spread HIV.

The same year that article appeared, the threat was explicitly enunciated by Karin Starrin, then-President of the Center party's League of Women. In a public speech, Starrin announced that "The biggest threat is the outpouring of prostitution from the former communist countries. A Russian woman can earn half a yearly salary from a couple of acts of intercourse in Sweden. There are those who think that it's OK to come here and sell themselves" (*Dagens Nyheter* 18.6.93). The National Chief of Police concurred. "13-year old prostitutes are something we have to get used to in Sweden", he remarked, explaining that Sweden would have to brace itself in the wake of the collapse of the Soviet Union (*Expressen* 18.6.93).

A report from Helsinki, neighboring Finland's capital city, seemed to foreshadow what Sweden had in store: "These days", the article explained, "sex clubs, private bordellos and street prostitution are the most flourishing businesses in Helsinki". The success of these new businesses was due to the influx of Russian and Estonian women, and the increasing presence of eastern bloc "Mafias" in Finland (*Dagens Nyheter* 23.11.93, *Dagens Nyheter* 2.11.93).

There were also a number of reports that claimed that Eastern women and organised crime had already infiltrated Sweden, e.g. 'Eastern Bloc Women Sell Themselves in Sweden: Secret Investigation on Mafia's Prostitution in Swedish Hotels' (*Expressen* 4.5.94, also *Expressen* 21.6.94, 7.4.93; *Dagens Nyheter* 6.9.93).

At the same time that 'Eastern bloc' prostitutes and organised crime were colonising Finland and threatening Sweden, a new view of prostitution was reported to be 'spreading' in Europe. A newspaper article with the rubric "Liberal view of prostitution spreads" (*Dagens Nyheter* 28.5.94) is a representative example. This article appeared in *Dagens Nyheter* five months before the referendum on whether or not Sweden should join the European Union. It begins like this:

"The female prostitute is seen nowadays as a free woman in most parts of Europe. A 'sex worker' who is smart enough to get paid for what other women give away for free. In Norway and Denmark, prostitutes have started unions that want to make 'sex work' a job like any other."

Any reader who would see this development as something positive is immediately disabused by two feminist journalists, who explain: "There's a big risk that these new ideas could take hold even in Sweden". The rest of the article details these journalists' opinions, which were developed in detail in a book they published on the topic, entitled The Price One Pays To Avoid Love (*Priset Man Betalar För Att Slippa Kärlek*, Bodström and von Zweigbergk 1994). In this and other newspaper articles that appeared with the publication of their book, the two journalists expressed dismay and anger that several EU countries were considering legalising prostitution, adding ominously that "it can be difficult for Sweden to stand against this wave of European liberalisation" (*Expressen* 12.5.94).

Anxiety that Sweden would drown in a "wave of European liberalisation" regarding prostitution reached its most distilled form in a pamphlet with the says-it-all title "Bordello Europe". *Bordell Europa* was printed and distributed by a lobby group called 'Nej Till EG' ('No to the EC [European Community]).[7] In August 1992, *Nej Till EG* began publishing a series of 20-60 page pamphlets in which journalists, academics and leftist politicians discussed what would happen if Sweden were to become a part of the European Community. Thirteen pamphlets were published, with titles ranging from "Europe's Dark Heart" (*Europas Mörka Hjärta* [Larsson and Rasch 1992]), which featured a photo of Helmut Kohl and François Mitterand on the cover, to "Sweden for Sale" (*Sverige Till Salu*; Eriksson and Torstensson 1992).

Each one of these pamphlets invite detailed analysis for what they reveal about the ways in which Sweden's relation to Europe could be expressed at the time – the "Sweden for Sale" pamphlet, for example, begins with a section entitled "The wolf's freedom is the lamb's prison" (*Vargens frihet är lammets ofrihet*; Eriksson and Torstensson 1992:8). It doesn't take an enormous amount of imagination to guess which of these animals represents Europe, and which is supposed to characterise gentle and meek Sweden.

Nej Till EG had about 12,000 members, all of whom would have been politically on the left (in Sweden, unlike for example the UK, opposition to the EU has always been from the political left, not the right).

The pamphlets present articulate opposition to the EU and, as such, they entered public and media discussion (*Bordell Europa*, for example, is discussed in *Expressen* 22.5.93; *Dagens Nyheter* 5.4.93, *Dagens Nyheter* 14.12.93).

In a language of contagion similar to that used by the two feminist journalists mentioned above, *Bordell Europa* argues that a "pro-prostitutions [sic] lobby" is now "spreading throughout Europe" with disturbing consequences: "[t]he truth is", the pamphlet argues, "organised trafficking in sex is not only tolerated, but is also actively encouraged [*aktivt främjas*] by most of the countries in the European 'community'" (Månsson and Backman 1992:15)."With the active support of authorities and working closely with prostitutes' 'own' organisations,[8] [the pro-prostitution lobby] is working for the decriminalisation of procuring and a professionalisation of prostitution" (Månsson and Backman 1992:16).

This theme is repeated later on in the pamphlet, when one of the authors discusses a "Whore Congress" that took place in Frankfurt Am Main in 1991. As reported in *Bordell Europa* (Månsson & Backman 1992:22):

> An important section of the conference program was concerned with EC work, how the [different prostitutes'] unions would cooperate when the borders become open, how they, together with other support groups, will influence people who make decisions in directions they want. The German union HWG presented a proposal about how "the whore" should be able to work in a future society, as a taxpayer and receiver of a pension.

Rather than see anything positive in the fact that prostitutes are organizing and demanding recognition and rights, this development is regarded as perverse and threatening. "From a Swedish perspective", the authors conclude:

> the issues raised at the conference in Frankfurt Am Main raise despair (*tvivel*), to say the least. Can trade unions for prostitutes really become a reality even in our country? What will happen

if Sweden becomes part of the EC? (Månsson and Backman
1992:26)

Is there not something profoundly ironic about leftist Swedes
expressing "despair" over the fact that groups of people are
organizing into trade unions?

I hope it is apparent by now that in the early 1990s, as Sweden
was debating whether or not to join the EU, talk about prostitution
had a subtext – in addition to being about the prostitution, it was
also about the EU, and Sweden's relationship to it. What is
noteworthy about that talk is first of all that it was resoundingly
and exclusively negative – in over 4,000 articles from the country's
largest newspapers and from a number of publications and
magazines from 1993-2000, there are only a handful of examples
where anyone claims that other EU countries' policies on
prostitution might be positive.

Where this positive spin does appear, the person making that
claim is dismissed by a Swedish journalist, politician or social
worker, who is always given the last word to assert that anyone
who would claim that German or Dutch law is reasonable is either
self-deluded (e.g. *Dagens Nyheter* 11.3.96, Ulmanen 1998),
"disagreeable and cynical" (*Dagens Arbete* 18.4.02; also *Dagens
Nyheter* 26.9.97, 2.7.02), hypocritical (*Veckans Affärer* 21.5.01),
socially irresponsible and evil (e.g. Eek 2000), or, the ultimate
dismissal: a spokesperson for "the international sex industry" (e.g.
Dagens Nyheter 5.5.95).

It is impossible to stress enough the monologic nature of
Swedish discourse on this topic. Indeed, the fact that there is no
debate – or even information about – alternative legal and social
approaches to prostitution[9] is the reason I feel justified in
presenting a complex polity like Sweden as a kind of monolithic
(or, rather, hegemonic) whole.

The question I would now like to consider briefly is: why
prostitution? In one sense, this question is not difficult to answer.
Throughout modern history, prostitution has been a reliable grist
for the mill of moral panics. The white slavery panic of the early
1900s, the First World War panics about venereal disease, and the
panic about AIDS in the 1980s were all expressed, in different
ways, through discourse about and repressive measures directed
towards, prostitutes (Gilman 1988; Guy 1990; Hobson 1990;
Phoenix 1999).

With the help of anthropological theory, it is easy to see why this should be the case – sex workers are very much "matter out of place" (Douglas 1966). They confound and challenge boundaries of public and private, scandal and decorum, gift and commodity, agent and object. As such they are electrifyingly taboo – in both senses of that word: forbidden and powerful. So in a sense, it is no surprise that during a period of public anxiety about social change, prostitution should come into focus as a channel through which that anxiety might be expressed.

Be that as it may, moral panics will always have their own local social dynamics and cultural forms. And to my knowledge, prostitution has not figured in any significant or even noticeable way in the debates about the EU that have been occurring in other European countries during the last decade. Why then has it been so important in Sweden? Why did prostitution emerge as a way of talking about the relationship between Sweden and the EU? What does a focus on prostitution give those Swedes who use it as a way of addressing that relationship?

At this point in my research, all I can offer are some hypotheses. One concerns the role that Swedes desire to have in the EU. If the EU can be conceptualised as a political body, then Sweden, I would argue, would like to install itself as that body's conscience. As happened in 1979 with the law against spanking children, and as happened again in 1998 with the law criminalising the purchase of sexual services, Swedish politicians made it clear that they see one of their roles as a fostering one, one of legislating particular moral stances that the populace, guided by them in this way, will come to adopt. This is a form of governmentality that dominated 20th century Swedish politics (e.g. Hirdman 1989), and that continues today.

Since the 1930s, but particularly during the 1960s and 1970s, Sweden developed a number of related self-images that have proven important and durable. One of the most important has been *neutrality*, which until recently was a cornerstone in Swedish foreign affairs and in Swedish understandings of self. Fear that Sweden would abandon its policy of neutrality was one oft-raised reason why Swedes should remain outside the EU (e.g. Fred 1996:46, Karlslund och Torstensson 1992: 5-12, Larsson och Rasch 1992).

Directly related to neutrality has been a strong sense of *internationalism*. This was embodied and symbolised by internationally known and respected political figures like Dag Hammarsjöld, Raoul Wallenberg, and Olof Palme. It was also to be seen in a downplaying of nationalism: in a telling observation, an ethnographic study in Swedish schools from the 1970s reports that if classrooms contained flags at all, they were the UN flag, or else the flags of many countries, never just the Swedish flag (Narrowe 1998).[10]

Related to both neutrality and internationalism is the sense that was actively cultivated in Sweden of *moral righteousness*. Sweden's vocal opposition to the Vietnam war, the government's support of and foreign aid to Cuba, the Allende government in Chile, and the ANC in South Africa, coupled with what Swedes in the 1970s and 1980s believed were unusually generous policies towards immigrants, provided an entire generation of Swedes (the generation that for well over two decades has controlled the country's political establishment and the overwhelming bulk of cultural production) with a strong sense that the Swedish polity was politically more aware, humane, and moral than many other nations, especially the US.

And in addition to these three dimensions of Swedishness, Swedes carried with them the idea of the *folkhem* (literally, 'people's home'), a core Social Democratic concept that depicted the nation as a home, and the state as both the providers for and the caretakers of that home.

Referring to the tight link between 'Swedishness' and the characteristics just listed, a recent writer observed that "no other European nation has invested so much of its identity in such a specific social system tied to such a specific historical period", as Sweden has (Rosenberg 1997). A predictable crisis resulted when all of this began to be challenged in the 1980s, as the Swedish economy declined, the policy of neutrality began to be questioned, popular suspicion of the United States gave way to a younger generation's largely uncritical admiration of it, and the welfare state that epitomised the *folkhem* began to be dismantled (Stråth 1992, 2000, 2001). As one commentator trenchantly observed:

> With the decline of the Swedish economy and the end of the Cold War, Sweden has been hit by the equivalent of what happened to France and England after they lost their colonies. We are no longer the center of a world that we have made ourselves. We suddenly see ourselves as the victim of forces – the EU, the USA, South Asia's [economic] tigers, Islam's fundamentalists. Our role as [political and social] mediators is gone. The foreign delegations [who came to study and admire the *folkhem*] are gone. The moral grounding of neutrality is

chipped away with each revelation of the neutral countries'
gold-transactions with Nazi Germany...Today...we belong to
the poorer half of Europe and we find ourselves far from the
center of European politics. Yes, one can say that the existence
of the EU makes Sweden provincial. (Ahlander 1997: 34)

In this context, what does Sweden have to offer the EU? One
answer is that, with little else to offer, Swedish politicians might
fall back on a familiar and time-tested role of fostering particular
moral stances in those who have not yet acquired them. By
identifying particular issues as morally clear-cut ones, and by
'taking a stand' on those issues, Sweden can portray itself as a kind
of moral beacon that others will want to follow.

It is interesting that many of the issues on which Sweden has
maintained a high profile in the EU – children's rights, prostitution
(trafficking) and the environment – all focus on people or entities
that Swedish politicians insist cannot speak for themselves. That
Sweden could use its position in the EU to influence the policies of
less enlightened member countries was a frequently marshalled
argument during the referendum campaign for why Sweden
should join the EU.

Indeed, while the political right maintained that Swedes
should vote to join the EU because membership would
'Europeanise Sweden' after too many years of Social Democratic
rule, the Social Democratic counter-appeal was the messianic
vision to 'Swedenise Europe' (Fred 1996:45; Stråth 2000:28-29, 2001:
200). Although sober voices warned that "[w]e should not fool
ourselves into thinking that we will be so strong in the EU as to
change 300 million other people" (Wallin 1992, cited in Fred 1996),
the hope that other member states will follow Sweden's lead on
issues it holds important continues to circulate in the country:
"Sweden has to be a role model" (*föregångsland*) as one article put it
(*GT/Expressen* 3.2.01).

Tellingly, Swedish politicians are reported to be 'perplexed' by
the less-than-enthusiastic reception that the law criminalising the
purchase of sexual services has received from other EU countries
(*Expressen* 18.2.97; *Dagens Nyheter* 2.7.02). But hope springs eternal:
under the headline "Law Against Buying Sex Can Become an
Export Product", a short article in early 2002 reported that:

the Minister for Gender Equality, Margareta Winberg, hopes
that France will be the first country after Sweden to criminalise
the purchase of sexual services. The reason is a recent statement

from her French colleague that prostitution has to be stopped. 'This is gratifying (*glädjande*)' says Margareta Winberg, who yesterday participated in a debate for Ministers on violence against women. (*Metro* 8.3.02)[11]

The second reason why I believe that prostitution emerged as a way for Swedes to talk about and negotiate their relationship to the EU is because of the way in which prostitutes are portrayed in the Swedish mass media. The relentless portrayal of innocent exploited victims forced to commit acts against their will bears, I think, a not arbitrary resemblance to the role that lobby groups like *Nej Till EG* argued that Sweden would have if it joined the EU. The "No" side argued exhaustively that Sweden would be a mere "fiefdom" (*lydrike*) in the EU, a "garbage dump" (*sopstation*; Eriksson och Torstensson 1992: 18, 28), and that the EU would force Sweden to do everything from abandon its gender-progressive legislation to accept nuclear waste from environmentally unenlightened countries like France.

In all of these discussions, it is striking that the EU was uniformly gendered as masculine. The titles of some of the pamphlets published by *Nej Till EG* are typical: *The Executives' Europe* (Nyberg 1992), *The Generals' Europe* (Karlsund och Torstensson 1992), *Europe's Dark Heart* (this is a reference to Joseph Conrad's *Heart of Darkness*, and it is the pamphlet with Mitterrand and Kohl on the cover), *Is the EU a Trap for Women?* (the answer is 'yes'; Eriksson 1993), and, of course, *Bordell Europa*, which asserts, as I have noted, that "organised trafficking in sex is not only tolerated, but is also actively encouraged by most of the countries in the European "community"" (Månsson and Backman 1992:15).

In all of this, there is a clear, if unspoken, sense that if Mother Sweden were to join the EU, she would be, to put it indelicately, fucked. Even after the "yes" side won the referendum (by a small margin)[12] and Sweden joined the EU, concerns about being exploited by the EU did not vanish, as is indicated by Sweden's resistance to joining the EMU, and continued uncertainty about what the outcome of the forthcoming referendum on that issue will be.[13]

The thought with which I wish to conclude this paper is that prostitution may provide Swedish politicians, policy makers and journalists with a metaphor for Sweden's relationship to the EU. As Dag Ahlander (1997) noted in the passage I cited above, "[Swedes] suddenly see ourselves as the victim". As a small, weak, innocent victim threatened with exploitation by a dirty masculinised foreigner like the EU, Sweden suddenly begins to look very much like a prostitute – at least the kind of prostitute that uniformly circulates in the Swedish press.

The law criminalising the purchase of sexual services was passed in 1998. But it was first proposed in late 1992 (*Expressen* 8.12.92, *Dagens Nyheter* 21.6.93, *Dagens Nyheter* 13.3.93, *Dagens Nyheter* 21.1.93), just as the campaign for the EU referendum was getting underway. Perhaps the identification of prostitution as a major social problem (despite the small numbers of prostitutes actually known to work in the country) and legislation against it that runs counter to trends in other EU member states is a channel for Swedish anxieties about its role in the EU; a way of symbolically distancing itself from an EU that offers it rewards but threatens to exploit it. Although social processes are not reducible to psychodynamic processes, to the extent that we subscribe to Benedict Anderson's dictum that "communities are to be distinguished not by their falsity/genuineness, but by the style in which they are imagined"(1983: 15), we can acknowledge that imaginings also involve psychosocial processes like repression and projection.

There certainly seems to be an element of projection involved here, in the Freudian sense of "the attribution to another (person or thing) of qualities, feelings or wishes that the subject repudiates or refuses to recognise in himself" (Laplanche and Pontalis 1988: 352). In other words, prostitutes and prostitution may be the focus of so much attention in Sweden partly because they are portrayed as embodying the very qualities that Swedish politicians and policymakers fear might characterise Sweden in relation to the EU. If this is plausible, then the Swedish case is an important one showing how sexuality is one site where boundaries and roles in the New Europe are being imagined and negotiated.

What is unacceptable and tragic is that while Swedes are busy working out their role in the EU in this way, the laws they pass and the attitudes they promote are profoundly harmful to those individuals who actually sell sex on their city streets at night.

Notes

[1]This debate, which was initiated by the center-left government of Guiliano Amato, continues today in the right-wing government of Silvio Berlusconi. In early January 2002, Berlusconi proposed reviewing the law, arguing that regulated brothels might well be preferable to having so many prostitutes soliciting on city streets. The city of Venice, partly in response to Berlusconi's suggestion, was preparing to set up officially sanctioned zones for prostitutes (*BBC News* 6.1.02 and 14.1.02; see also *la Repubblica* 15.7.02). Prostitution is not illegal in Italy, but profiting from the prostitution of another person (e.g. as a bordello proprietor) currently is.

[2] The dates of the articles cited are written in the Swedish convention of day-month-year.

[3] All these issues have been addressed by a government committee that in 1998 was given the directive to review all law on sex crime in Sweden. The 700 page report that the committee delivered in March 2001 discusses everything from incest and rape law to the new law prohibiting the purchase of sexual services. For the law prohibiting the purchase of sexual services (SOU 2001:14, pp. 303-17; 562) the committee recommends plugging up the loopholes and making it stricter: it recommends that the law be understood to include even regular clients, that it be expanded to include anyone who allows a sexual service to be purchased for him (and that the purchaser be liable to prosecution for being an accessory to and facilitator of a crime), and that sexual relations be precisely defined as "intercourse, [and] activities that involve the fairly sustained touching (*någorlunda varaktig beröring*) of the other's genitals or the other's body with one's own genitals. The purpose of the activity is to entice or satisfy the sexual urges of the perpetrator or some other person. Generally, direct physical contact is necessary" SOU 2001:14, p 296 – see also pp. 150-52, where exceptions to this rule of "direct physical contact" are enumerated, in the context of the sexual abuse of children. The committee proposes a new wording of the law as follows:

För köp av sexuella tjänster döms den som i annat fall än som sägs förut i detta kapitel skaffar eller låter skaffa sig en sexuell tjänst under förhållanden som utgör prostitution. Straffet är böter eller fängelse i högst sex månader.

Aside from any other crime committed under this chapter [of the Swedish penal code pertaining to sex crime], a person shall be punishable for the purchase of sexual services if that person obtains or allows to be obtained a sexual service under circumstances of prostitution [defined as "temporary sexual relations for remuneration", SOU 2001:14, p. 317]. The sentence is fines or prison for not more than six months.

To my knowledge (as of October 2002), this new wording has not yet been approved by Parliament

[4] Nord and Rosenberg 2001 was published a year after the report by the National Council for Crime Prevention (BRÅ 2000) referred to in the text, and it has more up-to-date statistics. According to Nord and Rosenberg 2001:13, by 2001, there had been a total of 160 police offence reports, of which 43 went to court (this includes the statistics I have cited from the BRÅ report). No information is given in Nord and Rosenberg 2000 about the outcome of those court cases.

[5] This fact highlights a certain disingenuousness in one recurring Swedish criticism of the recent prostitution laws in Denmark, the Netherlands and Germany. Swedish commentators argue that the laws are cynical because they only apply to EU nationals, therefore leaving illegal immigrants without legal

status and hence "under the pimps' control" (*Kvällsposten/Expressen* 9.7.02). What these commentators never mention is what happens to illegal sex workers when police find them in Sweden.

[6] Another reason they support it is because they assiduously ignore all information that might fly in the face of their assertions that the law is good. A speech given by the Minister for Gender Equality, Margareta Winberg, on 15 May 2002, is typical. In that speech, Winberg (who since the September 2002 elections is also Sweden's Deputy Prime Minister) asserts that the law "has significantly reduced street prostitution and made it possible for the police to take measures against brothels and other markets". Police, of course, had power to take measures against brothels before the passage of the law prohibiting the purchase of sexual services. None of the three reports on the law commissioned by the government in which Winberg is a minister claim that the law has had any effect on the police's role in this area. On the contrary, there are indications that the law has made it more difficult to locate and prosecute traffickers and exploiters (Nord and Rosenberg 2001; *Tidningen Svensk Polis* 18.4.02). And while those reports note a drop in street prostitution (a drop that seems to have been temporary; e.g. *Kvällsposten/Expressen* 9.8.02), they all say that there is no evidence that the law has reduced the total numbers of prostitutes or acts of sex for remuneration in Sweden. Winberg's speech can be accessed on http://www.regeringen.se/galactica/service=irnews/action=obj_show?c_obj_id =45159.

[7] *Nej Till EG* retained their name even after the European Community (EG in Swedish, for *Europeiska Gemenskapen*) changed its name to the European Union (EU in Swedish, for *Europeiska Unionen*) on January 1, 1993.

[8] Note the dismissive quotes around 'own', implying that those organisations are simply ventriloquist dummies controlled by someone else. Any culturally competent reader would know that that ventriloquist invoked by the quotes around 'own' is "the international sex industry".

[9] In the over 4,000 newspaper and magazine articles I have examined, I have not found a single instance of a dispassionate summary of the political process that persuaded Dutch or German politicians to remove prostitution from their criminal codes and regulate it, instead, under labour laws. Whenever German or Dutch policies appear in the Swedish press, they are mentioned only to facilitate their immediate dismissal by a Swedish commentator. The inference that must be drawn, given the context in which this lack of information occurs, is that German and Dutch parliamentarians must either be stupid, evil, or in cahoots with "the international sex industry". This latter association is made explicit in publications like *Bordell Europa*, and newspaper articles which assert that regulating prostitution under labour laws turns the state into a Big Pimp (see footnote 16). A similar situation pertains to Swedish discussion about drugs and drug laws. Dispassionate information about drug laws that are not totally prohibitionist in nature is virtually non-existent in the Swedish mass media. In a way exactly parallel to prostitution, non-prohibitionist ideas and laws are only ever mentioned so as to facilitate their immediate dismissal by a Swedish authority figure. The epithet "*drogliberal*" (lit. 'drug-liberal') is similar to 'spokesperson for the international sex industry' in that its invocation immediately disqualifies anyone so labelled from being taken seriously in any debate. And needless to say, 'drogliberal' and 'spokesperson for the international sex industry' are linked in Swedish discourse, the one implicitly suggesting the other.

[10] The opening scene of the popular Swedish movie *Tillsammans* (English 'Together'; Moodyson 2000) is another shrewdly observed example of this. The

movie takes place in 1975, and it opens with a scene of preschool children rejoicing at the news that Franciso Franco has died. What I refer to here as Swedish internationalism is also referenced by the name of one of the children in the film: Tet, after the Tet offensive in Vietnam. Although *Tillsammans* takes place in a leftist commune, that commune was widely interpreted to represent a microcosm of Sweden in the 1970s. It was regarded as a generous film in Sweden, and it raised a bittersweet mix of nostalgia and embarrassment in many viewers belonging to the generation it portrayed.

[11] The frosty reception given the Swedish law by EU countries is certainly one reason why Swedish efforts to export the law prohibiting the purchase of sexual services have now begun to focus on the Baltic countries, which are portrayed in Sweden as impoverished neighbors who look up to Sweden as an advanced and benevolent agent of inspiration and social change. During the summer of 2002, the government sponsored a "Nordic-Baltic information campaign" that was designed to raise awareness about issues related to prostitution, and to disseminate what were asserted to be the positive effects of the Swedish law. See *Expressen-GT-Kvällsposten* 15.5.02 and the webpage cited in note 6.

[12] 52.2% voted 'yes', 46.9% voted 'no'.

[13] I think it is not a coincidence that as the inevitability of the EMU referendum becomes clearer, attention is once again becoming focussed on prostitution, and the exact same language that structured the discourse in the early 1990s is being recycled. Articles about eastern European women flooding the country (particularly the north) are back (e.g. *Dagens Nyheter* 16.2.01; *Expressen* 8.1.01, 21.11.00;*Tidningen Svensk Polis* 18.4.02; *Kvinnotryck* 4/2000; *NIKK magasin* 1-2002). And during 2002, the 'EU as pimp' trope also acquired a new lease on life: "Europe's countries become pimps", trumpeted the headline of one article published in July 2002 (*Kvällsposten/Expressen* 9.7.02). Another op-ed article published by a respected daily around the same time could have been lifted verbatim from texts written in 1993. "EU herds Sweden into legalized prostitution" was the headline. "Strong forces in the EU are at work", the article noted ominously, "so that prostitution might become part of the labour law, like in Germany. According to this way of seeing things", it continued, "prostituted women's work earns the right to a pension. The prostitute also pays taxes, which means that the state earns money from her work. By extension, we all become her pimp. Now when the EU's internal market is being harmonized, will all women be prostitutionable? Will one be forced to "work" in a bordello if one has collected too much unemployment benefits?" (*Svenska Dagbladet* 8.6.02; see also *Expressen* 7.5.99;*Veckans Affärer* 21.5.01).

Articles about high rates of HIV in eastern European countries have also begun to reappear in the Swedish press. One from 3 July 2002 opens in bold print with: "The worst nightmare scenario about HIV has become reality. 40 million people today live with the infection. Every day, 14,000 more – the majority of them young – are infected. The most rapid increase is happening in our neighboring country, Estonia. A ticking bomb, 350 kilometers from Stockholm" (*Svenska Dagbladet* 3.7.02). Predictably, this article focuses on how prostitutes supposedly spread the virus to others: "Sex tourists in Estonian cities, among them many Swedes, are living dangerously. The women are young, readily available, and often desperate in their hunt for money for their daily fix [of heroin]".

235

References

Books, Law Texts and Government-sponsored Reports

Ahlander, Dag Sebastian (1997). En svenskhet i upplösning. *Moderna Tider*, September 33-35.

Anderson, Benedict (1983). *Imagined communities: reflections on the origin and spread of nationalism*. London: Verso.

Bodström, Cecilia & Helena von Zweigbergk (1994). *Priset man betalar för att slippa kärlek: en bok om prostitution på 90-talet*. Stockholm: Nordstedts.

BRÅ (Brottsförebyggande Rådet) (2000:4). Förbud mot köp av sexuella tjänster: tillämpning av lagen under första året. Stockholm: Brottsförebyggande Rådet (contains summary in English).

Chapkis, Wendy (1997). *Live sex acts: women performing erotic labour*. London: Cassell.

Douglas, Mary (1966). *Purity and danger: an analysis of the concepts of pollution and taboo*. London: Routledge and Kegan Paul.

Eek, Louise (2000). Världens äldsta lögn. *Arena* 1:33-38.

Eriksson, Billy & Gösta Torstensson (1992). Sverige till salu. *Nej Till EG:s skriftserie* 6-7. Göteborg: Nej Till EG.

Eriksson, Marianne (1993). Är EG en kvinnofälla? *Nej Till EG:s skriftserie* 10. Göteborg: Nej Till EG.

Fred, Morris (1996). Becoming Europeans: Sweden enters the EU. *Europea* II-2: 33-59.

Gilman, Sander L. (1988). AIDS and syphilis: the iconography of disease. In Douglas Crimp (ed.) *AIDS: cultural analysis, cultural activism*. Cambridge, Mass.: MIT Press, 87-107.

Guy, Donna (1990). *Sex and danger in Buenos Aires: prostitution, family and nation in Argentina*. Lincoln and London: University of Nebraska Press.

Hirdman, Yvonne (1989). *Att lägga livet till rätta: studier i svensk folkhemspolitik*. Stockholm: Carlsssons.

Hobson, Barbara Meil (1990). *Uneasy virtue: the politics of prostitution and the American reform tradition*. Chicago: University of Chicago Press.

Karlslund, Willy & Gösta Torstensson (1992). Generalernas Europa. *Nej Till EG:s skriftserie* 4. Göteborg: Nej Till EG.

Kvinnofrid (1997). Regeringens proposition 1997/98:55.

Laplanche, Jean & J.-B. Pontalis (1988). *The language of psychoanalysis*. London: Karnac Books.

Larsson, Maria Bergom & Ingrid Rasch (1992). Europas mörka hjärta. *Nej Till EG:s skriftserie* 1. Göteborg: Nej Till EG.

Larselere, Robert E. & Johnson B. (1999). Evaluation of the effects of Sweden's spanking ban on physical child abuse rates: a literature review. *Psychological Reports* 85: 381-92.

Moodyson, Lukas (2000). *Tillsammans*. Film produced by Lars Jonsson, Memfis Film.

Månsson, Sven-Axel och Susanne Backman (1992). Bordell Europa. *Nej Till EG:s skriftserie* 3. Göteborg: Nej Till EG.

Narrowe, Judith (1998). *Under one roof: on becoming a Turk in Sweden*. Stockholm: Stockholm *Studies in Social Anthropology* 43.

NIKK-magasin 1-2002. Bodies across borders: prostitution and trafficking in women. Oslo: Nordic Institute for Women's Studies and Gender Research.

Nord, Anders & Tomas Rosenberg (2001). Rapport: Lag (1998:408) om förbud mot köp av sexuella tjänster. Metodutveckling avseende åtgärder mot prostitution. Malmö: Polismyndigheten i Skåne.

Nyberg, Mikael (1992). Direktörernas Europa. *Nej Till EG:s skriftserie 5*. Göteborg: Nej Till EG.

Phoenix, Joanna (1999). *Making sense of prostitution*. Basingstoke: Palgrave.

Rosenberg, Göran (1997). Vad är svenskhet? *Moderna Tider*, September: 22.

Rubin, Gayle (1993). Thinking sex: notes towards a radical theory of the politics of sexuality, in Henry Abelove (ed.) *The gay and lesbian studies reader*, Michèle Aina Barale & David M. Halperin. NY & London: Routledge. 3-44.

SoS (Socialstyrelsen) 2000:5. *Kännedom om prostitution 1998-1999*. Stockholm: Socialstyrelsen.

SoS (Socialstyrelsen) 2001:14. *Sexualbrotten: ett ökat skydd för den sexuella integriteten och angränsande frågor*. Stockholm: Socialstyrelsen (Summary in English, pp. 583-96).

SOU (Statens Offentliga Utredningar) 2001, nr. 14. *Sexualbrotten. Betänkande av 1998 års Sexualbrottskommitté*. Stockholm: Fritzes Offentliga Publikationer.

Stråth 1992. *Folkhemmet mot Europa: ett historiskt perspektiv på 90-talet*. Falun: Tidens förlag.

Stråth 2000. Neutralitet som självförståelse. In Kurt Almqvist och Kay Glans, red. *Den svenska framgångssagan?* Stockholm: Fischer & Co, pp 186-204.

Stråth, Bo 2001. The Swedish Image of Europe as the Other, in Bo Stråth, (ed.) *Europe and the other and Europe as the other*. Brussels: PIE-Peter Lang.

Ulmanen, Petra (1998). Vem ska man lyssna på? *Arena* 5, p. 49.

Wallin, Ulf (1992). *EG- hot eller löfte?* Stockholm: Almqvist & Wiksell International.

Newspaper articles

Dagens Arbete 18.4.02 Reportage: den lagliga bordellen.

Dagens Nyheter 7.1.92 "Könshandeln är modern kolonialism". Krafter i Europa på kollisionskurs med grundläggande svenska värderingar, varnar professor.

Dagens Nyheter 21.1.93 Jämställdheten. Nye ministern skällde på m.

Dagens Nyheter 2.2.93 "Ny hiv-våg hotar". Professor Per-Anders Mårdh presenterar nya skrämmande siffror om den europeiska prostitutionen.

Dagens Nyheter 13.3.93 Prostitution utreds igen. Kriminalisering svår fråga för före detta JämO

Dagens Nyheter 5.4.93 Varning för EG-prostitution

Dagens Nyheter 21.6.93 Koppleri

Dagens Nyheter 6.9.93 Rysk maffia i Stockholm. Polisen måste ges befogenheter att möta brottsligheten från det tidigare Sovjetunionen.

Dagens Nyheter 2.11.93 Toppolitiker i bordellhärva.

Dagens Nyheter 23.11.93 Sexhandeln frodas i Finland. Polisen varnar för rysk och estnisk maffia i Helsingfors.

Dagens Nyheter 14.12.93 Svenska flickor på svenska bordeller

Dagens Nyheter 28.5.94 Liberal syn på prostitution breder ut sig.

Dagens Nyheter 5.5.95 "Prostituerade är inte bara offer". "Glädjeflicka" kräver erkännande.

Dagens Nyheter 16.2.96 "Hjälp kvinnorna till vanligt Svenssonliv". Anmäl fastighetsägare och kriminalisera torskarna. Men framför allt – hjälp tjejerna.

Dagens Nyheter 5.3.96 "Massösen" Margareta försvarar sig: "Vårt arbete är lagligt".

Dagens Nyheter 11.3.96 Ingen kvinna väljer frivilligt prostitution.

Dagens Nyheter 26.9.97 De gröna oense om bordeller. Debatt i EU. Holländsk legalisering ställs mot svensk kriminalisering.
Dagens Nyheter 18.12.97 Kriminalisering av könsköpare. Tvist om lagens effekt. Brott kan bli svårt att bevisa, anser åklagare.
Dagens Nyheter 2.8.98. Prostitution: sexhandeln blir brutalare.
Dagens Nyheter 3.8.98. Politiker försvarar krimialisering. Nya lagen slår inte mot de prostituerade utan mot de männen som köper sex, hävdar Inger Segelström (s).
Dagens Nyheter 18.1.99 "Nya lagen dödar missbrukartjejer". Prostitution. Kommunerna får inga extra pengar för att hjälpa utsatta kvinnor.
Dagens Nyheter 30.12.99 Få sexköp leder till åtal. Ett år med den nya lagen. Trots att fyra av tio polisanmälningar skrivs av ser spanarna resultat.
Dagens Nyheter 16.2.01 Prostitution: gränserna vidöppna för kvinnohandel.
Dagens Nyheter 2.7.02 Svårt exportera svensk kampanj mot sexhandel.
Expressen 8.12.92 Westerberg till attack mot könshandeln
Expressen 7.4.93 Ryska maffians lyxhoror i stan
Expressen 22.5.93 Brev till ledarsidan: Att utså rädsla för EG.
Expressen 18.6.93 "Detta är något vi får vänja oss vid"
Expressen 4.5.94 Östkvinnor säljer sig i Sverige. Hemlig utredning om maffians protituion på svenska hotell.
Expressen 12.5.94 De skrev boken om prostitution.
Expressen 21.6.94 Mentalsjuka, hivsmittade slavinnor från öst.
Expressen 28.2.97 Svensk – nya skällsordet i EU.
Expressen 7.5.99 Staten är torsk.
Expressen 21.11.00 Hit kördes de prostituerade. Ryska sexmaffian har redan startat verksamhet inne i Sverige.
Expressen 8.1.01 EU-mötet. Ökad sexhandel när EU kommer. Prostituerade från österuropa väntar redan på pamparna i Stockholm.
Expressen 30.9.01 De utvisas direkt – därför är det svårt att stoppa kvinnohandel
Expressen-GT-Kvällsposten 15.5.02 Margareta Winberg, jämställdhetsminister: Så ska du ha sex.
GT/Expressen 21.1.99 Prostituerad pressade kund på pengar
GT/Expressen 22.4.00 "Kvinnorna sviks av den nya sexköpslagen". Forskaren: De har lämnats utan hjälp.
GT/Expressen 13.2.01 Debatt. Kvinnor är ingen handlesvara.
Kvällsposten/Expressen 9.7.02 Frislag. Europas stater blir hallickar.
Kvällsposten/Expressen 9.8.02 Allt fler prostituerade i Malmö
La Reppublica 15.7.02 Il governo prepara la legge per riaprire le case chiuse.
Metro 8.3.02 Sexköpslag kan bli exportvara.
Svenska Dagbladet 8.6.02 EU driver Sverige in a legal prostitution.
Svenska Dagbladet 3.7.02 Hivsmitta sprids fort i Estland.
Tidningen Svensk Polis 18.4.02 Norrland ny marknad för sexhandel.
Veckans Affärer 21.5.01 Prostitution och dubbelmoral.

Websites

BBC News 6.1.02 Berlusconi suggests legal brothels. (http://news.bbc.co.uk) Accessed 6.1.02
BBC News 14.1.02 Red light district for Venice. (http://news.bbc.co.uk) Accessed 14.1.02
Kvinnofrid 1997. http://www.kvinnofrid.gov.se/regeringen/UMInforos.html

Kvinnotryck Ryska kvinnor transporteras till män i Norbotten 4/2002
(http://wvvw.roks.se/kvinnotryck/kt4_02_prokamp_norrbotten.html).
Accessed 4/2002
Time.Com, http://www.time.com/time/daily/scandal/testimony.html.
Accessed 1.8.03

Chapter 15
Policies towards the sex industry in Europe: new models of control

Jan Visser, with Arne Randers-Pehrson, Sophie Day, Helen Ward

Introduction

It is not easy to acquire reliable information on the nature and scope of the sex industries in the European Union, nor how they change over time. It is equally difficult to agree a common vocabulary and set of concepts to describe this picture. Should we be asking, "how many women, men and children are selling sexual services" or should we formulate this question in other terms: "how many are sold into prostitution?" Some ask, "what kinds of clients buy these services?", whereas others inquire instead, "how many men abuse these victims of sexual exploitation, and what kind of men are they?"

We might ask about "the businessmen who organise or facilitate encounters in brothels, escort agencies and the streets" or we might refer instead to "the pimps who turn human beings into slaves in order to exploit them as commodities".

Where do "migrant women" come from, "who try to earn a better living in the entertainment industries of European cities"? Or is it better to describe these women as "poor trafficked victims sold into slavery by organised criminal organisations"?

Important questions about the contemporary sex industry can be asked in fundamentally different ways according to one's perspective. There seems to be no neutral vocabulary with which we can discuss prostitution as simply another sector of the economy, since many commentators consider the exchange of sex for money incompatible with the dignity and value of human life.

The main purpose of this chapter is to clarify these questions rather than answer them. We shall note recent developments in prostitution that have created major problems for policy makers and other officials who have to deal with these developments on behalf of the state and the public. We show that different states have proposed different solutions to similar problems. We reflect on the consequences of government action for workers in the sex industry.

In this chapter we will restrict ourselves to female prostitution. Male prostitution is much more hidden as both sex workers and their clients have to deal with the additional stigma attached to homosexuality. This results in a different kind of organisation, generally integrated with the social organisation of homosexuality. There, it is largely hidden to the general public and ignored by policy makers.[1]

Changes in prostitution

In the second half of the twentieth century, prostitution had a low profile, largely confined to specific areas in the bigger cities of Europe. The milieu described a largely self-contained world in both social and geographical terms; a special world with its own rules and codes of conduct, relatively isolated from mainstream society.

Although public morality was opposed to prostitution and the law did not accept procuring and pimping, it was tolerated. Prostitution sometimes seemed to serve a positive function, providing a 'safety valve'. Men (often thought to be unmarried) 'let off steam' on their visits to monitored areas of prostitution. Prostitution could even posses a touch of innocence and romance, as in the motion picture *Irma la Douce*.[2]

In subsequent decades, at the time of the civil rights movements and the second wave of feminism, prostitutes' rights groups were formed in many European countries. These women defined prostitution as work and argued for human and civil rights (Pheterson ed 1989). The term sex worker stresses that prostitution is a form of labour (Alexander and Delacoste 1987) and advocates have challenged the double standard that is prevalent in most European countries whereby prostitution is accepted *de facto* as an inevitable social phenomenon but morally condemned at the same time. This mechanism means that prostitutes are blamed for the existence of prostitution, and are stigmatised and criminalised in consequence.

By the 1980s, the prostitution milieu was changing in many countries, including The Netherlands.[3] Heroin and other illicit drugs appeared on the streets and in other parts of the sex industry and there was a public outcry about soliciting on the part of young addicts. In The Netherlands, as in other European countries, men had more money to spend and there was a demand for luxurious brothels. At the same time, the pornography, sex shops and sex theatres that were associated with the sexual revolution of this period had become more publicly acceptable.

Prostitution became more visible in city centres and grew internationally. During the Vietnam War, a large sex industry had developed in South East Asia. After the war, men continued to visit the region as sex tourists (Odzer 1994, Truong 1988). Not long after, 'exotic' women from South East Asia arrived at European brothels, joined in the following decades by women from other parts of the world.

The milieu became closely connected with the underworld trafficking of drugs and women: from South East Asia, Latin America and Africa, as well as Central and Eastern Europe after the fall of the Berlin Wall (Doezema and Kempadoo eds 1998). Some sex workers fell victim to traffickers, lured under false pretences with promises of well-paid jobs in European hotels and restaurants. Others come as migrant workers to improve their standard of living, aware that they would have to work temporarily in the sex industry but equally aware of the need to support their families at home.

Both types of women face gross economic exploitation as they cannot control their working conditions (The European Network for HIV/STD Prevention in Prostitution (Europap/Tampep) 1998: 41). The vast majority are additionally vulnerable because they have no legal right of residence, which might grant them some security as workers (ibid: 41-45).

By the end of the twentieth century, technological developments also had an impact on the structure of the sex market and relations between participants. New forms of negotiation between sex workers and clients and new forms of communication among clients, such as the internet and mobile telephones, have intensified a tendency toward individualisation and may have promoted a weakening of norms and codes within the milieu.

These developments have made the sex industry more diverse, more hidden in some ways and yet more public in others, more extensive and above all, as far as state representatives are concerned, more difficult to monitor. As a result of all these developments politicians felt obliged to control prostitution more actively. Policy makers urgently promote regulation because the growth and diversification of the industry has made it more difficult to draw the line between what might be acceptable in private and what might be admissible in public. The blurred boundaries between prostitution, tourism, business and entertainment have led authorities to establish rules and regulations.

The discussion about what prostitution is and what societies should do about it is largely a debate about morality. The fact that most people work in the sex industry to earn money is of course obvious but it is not really reflected in the political discussions of monitoring and control.

We are not aware of any studies that attempt to explain developments in prostitution using concepts from economics. The sex industry is not analysed in the same way as other industries. We are convinced that we would understand much more of the background and the forces that shape prostitution today if we knew the size of the market, the number of workers, the mechanisms that balance supply and demand, how the market is segmented, how innovation is implemented, and the profits in prostitution.

Laws, policy and their application

How do governments try to control the sex industries currently? It has been customary to contrast four broad approaches to prostitution control in Europe: regulation; abolition; decriminalisation (West 2000); and prohibition.

The first type of policy is named after the state regulations governing licit prostitution, which generally include rules governing where sex can be sold, registers of prostitutes working legally in those places, and mandatory medical examinations for prostitutes.

Abolitionism describes opposition to this system of state regulation, coined in the nineteenth century and applying to most penal codes in Europe today.[4] Prostitution is considered to be immoral and oppressive to prostitutes; therefore, the state should not benefit financially, nor should it condone prostitution. Anyone who organises or benefits from prostitution is criminalised while prostitutes are seen as victims to be re-integrated into mainstream society.

Decriminalisation describes a possible system of control in which all laws against prostitutes are repealed and governed instead by laws relating to business, public order, violence, abuse and exploitation. This option has been backed by prostitutes' rights organisations and partially implemented in various Australian states, New Zealand and, in Europe, The Netherlands. But the effects of these legal changes are not yet clear (see below).

A fourth approach is the suppression or prohibition that characterises many US policies where all aspects of the sex trade are illegal.

In principle, these approaches to prostitution control appear distinct but, in practice, they can be very hard to tell apart. There are discrepancies between the laws and policies on the one side, and everyday practice on the other. It is in the interplay between the one and the other that prostitution in Europe is controlled today.

Most European states practice forms of regulation, but these vary in their details and have different effects on the lives of sex workers. For example, it is against the law to organise the prostitution of anyone else in the majority of the EU, but the sex industry thrives openly in most of them.[5] The law is not applied in the strict sense; instead, an overt or covert policy of condoning prostitution is practised since national and local governments have found it impossible to uphold the law in the absence of universal public support or a policeman in every bedroom.

Local governments, with limited law enforcement capabilities, have had to work out a compromise. In practice, the sex industry has been tolerated and allowed to market its products in a discreet manner, as long as public order is preserved and provided no other criminal activities take place (for example, the prostitution of children, trafficking of women, trading in or using illicit drugs).

A fragile equilibrium has developed that requires constant rebalancing by local authorities as they respond to continual fluctuations in the market. By and large, rights organisations consider these *de facto* policies as at best unsympathetic to prostitutes and at worst often explicitly hostile. This is in sharp contrast to the close relationships that have developed between state officials and the businessmen who organise prostitution. Because of this contrast, most sex workers have argued that the state should refrain from any interference in the sex industry.

The need for state control

European states have increased surveillance of the sex industry and introduced more sanctions and more regulations in recent years. Many officials have found that pragmatic toleration of the sex industry is inadequate to deal with the apparent threat to public order presented by organised crime and its role in trafficking women. In addition, they seem troubled by the growth of the industry and its increasing visibility. Moreover, many are concerned to address the occupational health and safety of sex workers, particularly in response to AIDS.

Sweden, for example, has intensified an abolitionist approach and The Netherlands a regulationist approach. Other countries in

Europe are monitoring evaluations of these developments closely, with a view to developing their own (Kilvington et al 2001).

The Swedish approach

In 1999, the Swedish parliament passed a law criminalising the purchase of sexual services.[6] Reform was justified by the argument that prostitution is not merely immoral, and unworthy of a 'modern' society, but also a form of (sexual) violence against women in and of itself (Gould 2001, Jessen and Kulick, this volume). Prostitutes are held to be victims of psychological, physical, sexual, emotional, and social violence. Therefore, it is not simply a crime to enable or force women to work in the sex industry but also to pay them for sex. The client is a criminal, an offender, who violates the individual prostitute and transgresses public morality.

Police in major cities have been given additional resources to patrol street and indoor prostitution but, in practice, most are targeting the more visible sectors, namely street prostitution. Police liase with social workers working with women who want to leave prostitution. There have been mixed reports on the results of intensified police activity. Clients of prostitutes have been arrested, but the few convictions that have resulted relied largely on guilty pleas from clients, owing to problems of evidence. Some reports suggest that prostitution has become less visible rather than less common (Europap 2000: 16).

Such reports are consistent with past attempts to repress prostitution; it does not disappear but rather changes, like a chameleon. If prostitutes continue to work but in more hidden ways, they are likely to have less access to health and social services. In addition, more hidden and surreptitious forms of work are likely to have a negative effect on the ability of sex workers to negotiate their health and safety, for instance, in safer sex practices.

The Dutch approach

In The Netherlands, the government has developed a modern form of the regulationism that characterised nineteenth century efforts to control prostitutes, mainly for public order reasons. In addition, there was strong pressure to legalise the sex industry so as to give sex workers the protection of labour legislation.

The current Dutch position, laid down in a law that came into effect in 2000, argues that prostitution itself is not the problem but that social issues associated with the sex industry do need to be tackled.[7]

The first debate on legalisation took place in 1983 and three main arguments emerged in the long debate that followed. The first pragmatically accepted that the sale of sex could not be eradicated from Dutch society; rather than fighting a battle that it could not win, the state should try to minimise associated problems. The new law states that the role of the state is not to outlaw and prosecute behaviour that some and perhaps most citizens dislike, but to enforce sanctions against persons who violate human rights through violence and fraud. It prohibits these activities but not the organisation of prostitution per se, as the state has no moral interest in criminalising the exchange of sex for money by consenting adults.

The second argument, put forward by sex workers and feminist supporters, is based upon the legitimacy of sex work and claims that the concept of *work* should be central to reform. If a woman decides to make her living through sex work, then she should not be exposed to criminal sanctions but should enjoy full rights as a worker in the same way as other citizens and legal residents who do different kinds of work.

The new law meets demands from both pragmatists and sex workers by recognising the legitimacy of sex work. It acknowledges that prostitution is a profession, and sex workers can now claim workers' rights as employees and self-employed workers. However, the full implementation of this law is far from being realised in terms of taxation, social security provision and labour inspection or in relation to the chamber of commerce and the labour exchange.

The technical problems of integrating a new profession into the complicated arrangements of social and economic provision are compounded by the reluctance of many officials in The Netherlands to co-operate fully and to prioritise this area of work. While legal recognition of sex work is a decisive step towards emancipation, public opinion remains generally unsympathetic towards the new profession. The majority of prostitutes have not yet noticed benefits from their new legal status and report tension and stigma in meetings with state officials and employers.[7]

The third argument contributing to the reforms maintained that it was in the state's interest to settle upon a definition of permitted and prohibited behaviours so that more effective surveillance and control could be undertaken. By defining what is right or permitted and what is wrong or prohibited in prostitution, it was thought that it would be easier to combat illegal activities.

The new law has legalised the organisation of sex work on the grounds that this change will distinguish acceptable and unacceptable forms of prostitution more effectively. Brothels must obtain a license from city councils, which gives local authorities the right and duty to use their by-laws to monitor and control the industry.

Child prostitution, forced prostitution and the trafficking of persons are not deemed acceptable and have been made clearly illegal. The government aims to fight crimes in the sex industry and the penalties against these phenomena have been increased. Each regional police force now has a special department that is responsible for monitoring the sex industry and prosecuting criminals. Victims, especially women from other countries, are given protection and temporary permits to reside in The Netherlands while traffickers are prosecuted. This is primarily to help the public prosecution strengthen its case; victims do not automatically receive resident permits and face deportation as soon as traffickers are sentenced. Only in Italy do victims have a real chance of obtaining residence and work permits.

The argument about how best to control illegal activities revolves around a distinction between so-called voluntary and forced prostitution. Voluntary prostitution is treated as just another sector of the economy under the new policy. Local councils design a licensing system, which prescribes where a brothel or sex club is allowed, what safety and sanitary conditions are required and how the management will have to treat sex workers.

Nationals of the European Union have the same rights as Dutch sex workers under this legislation. They are free to work in the Dutch sex industry in the same way as other jobs. However, brothel owners cannot recruit from abroad. This restriction relates to treaties against international trafficking for the purpose of prostitution, dating back to the 1930s, which make no distinction between voluntary and forced prostitution. As The Netherlands is a partner to various treaties of this kind, any involvement in bringing prostitutes across national borders continues to be prohibited.

Sex workers from outside the European Union constitute a large section of the total prostitute population in The Netherlands; up to 50 per cent in some regions (see chapter 8, and Brussa 1999). Before the reforms, they were tolerated largely because law enforcement had been directed towards public order offences rather than the amorphous world of prostitution, in which it was very unclear what was legal and what illegal. It was not a priority for state officials to hunt down illegal workers.

But it is now a general police practice to check the identities of sex workers regularly and to deport those who do not have the appropriate documents. The Netherlands is less tolerant towards asylum seekers and illegal immigrants in general than before, and this stance has been institutionalised since the new law came into effect. It is justified largely in terms of the appalling conditions that victims of trafficking face but should be recognised more broadly as part of a concerted effort to control immigration. It is impossible for migrants to obtain work papers for prostitution as this line of work is not considered to make a useful contribution to the Dutch economy. The implementation of the new licensing system has made it much easier for the police to control immigration since it is now in the interests of brothel owners to do the policing themselves. Before the reform, it was of little consequence to a businessman whether or not sex workers had papers. Today, getting and keeping a licence from the local municipality depends, among other things, on providing the documentation to prove your employees have the right to work in The Netherlands. As we have seen, this is only possible for Dutch and EU citizens. Breach of these conditions allows the local mayor to revoke the license. This new measure has led most brothel owners to check the identity of sex workers carefully before they offer them work.

The Dutch reforms have been criticised from various quarters. Some, including small religious parties, have lobbied the Dutch government to follow in the footsteps of Sweden since they do not agree with any legalisation of prostitution. Others are sceptical that laws and policies alone will bring about full occupational rights for sex workers. They feel that 'the public' is still unwilling to accept and integrate prostitution into mainstream society and, therefore, sex workers will continue to work illegally.

The more difficult it is for brothel owners and sex workers to join mainstream society, the more likely it is that they will continue to operate underground. The strongest criticism has come from those who speak on behalf of non-European Union migrant sex workers. They claim that the majority of these women are not naïve victims of trafficking but migrant workers who have made a rational decision to come to the EU in order to earn a better living in better conditions than they could at home.

It is widely agreed that there is a demand for such migrant labour. It might be possible to grant work permits to migrants, as they have decided to work in prostitution and prostitution is legally regarded as work. But there are no signs that the government is about to adopt such a policy, because it fears an uncontrollable inflow of sex workers once the strict ban is lifted. Meanwhile, migrants are 'forced' to work in illegal, hidden circuits where they have to rely on the services of facilitators, who are often highly exploitative.

The impact of these reforms on sex workers' health is difficult to assess. Preliminary evaluations suggest both positive and negative results in different local areas. Mandatory testing for STI and HIV has not been considered viable or desirable since it was abolished in 1911. It is widely accepted that one person cannot be held accountable for transmitting a venereal disease to another; both parties share the responsibility for safer sex. This precept applies to sex between a sex worker and her client in the same way as any other sexual transaction. In addition, medical authorities believe that mandatory health checks would prove counterproductive as they would most likely drive those who are already hard to reach, including the very young, drug users, migrants without papers, and victims of abuse even further away from health care agencies. The reforms have not introduced any legal compulsion for regular health checks, and are intended to enable health care providers to establish health promotion at the workplace in addition to the centres already established by the Municipal Health Service and private doctors.

STI prevention is embedded in the new prostitution policy as part of the effort to improve the position of sex workers. The Netherlands Foundation for STD control (*Stichting soa-bestrijding*) has added a safer sex policy to the licensing system. Each brothel must develop a safer sex policy including the following elements: sex workers should be able to refuse customers; all sex must be 'safe' and this rule should be made clear to customers. In addition, health workers should have free access to brothels and a brothel or club owner should give sex workers the opportunity to be screened for STI.

Each municipal health service covers an average of eleven municipalities and the safer sex policies introduced to date vary widely. Van den Berg (2002) reported this variation with reference to three different municipalities. Rotterdam had a clear policy on safer sex which it resourced adequately, for example, by appointing four health educators in the field. Leiden had not formulated a policy but faced a demand for mandatory screening in its five sex clubs. The municipal health service for Zwolle had a safer sex policy that was followed by some municipalities and not others; it was limited above all by the refusal of municipalities to provide any resources for the new policy.

These examples show wide variation in local interpretations of the law such that reform is read in terms of the old regulationism in Leiden while, in Rotterdam, better working conditions for sex workers have become a clear priority. Licensing enables local councils to approach the new regulations in terms of the old abolitionism as well and some refuse licenses for brothels or clubs and refuse to designate safe working areas for sex workers outdoors.

Councils are interested primarily in restricting the number of businesses and controlling them in such a way as to minimise nuisance to residents. Street prostitution is only allowed in designated areas, where there is no disturbance to the neighbourhood. It is as yet unclear whether the licensing system will become a means of enforcing the health and safety regulations that will improve work conditions in general.

Comparison

At first sight, the Dutch and Swedish approaches seem to be diametrically opposed. The latter has extended abolition and may even end in US-style prohibition where all parties, including prostitutes, are criminalised. The Netherlands, in contrast, has introduced an apparently liberal form of regulationism. The new law is informed by concerns about the health and well-being of sex workers, about state intrusion into private life, including issues of sexuality and sexual transactions between consenting adults, and it is based on the pragmatic conclusion that the sex industry cannot be abolished.

It is not possible as yet to provide empirically grounded evidence on the success or failure of either the Swedish or the Dutch approach or to predict future outcomes, as noted by other contributors to the volume. But it is questionable whether the fundamental aims behind these approaches are very different.

The approaches themselves certainly differ. In The Netherlands, prostitution has been brought under the administrative control of local municipalities while, in Sweden, prostitution is largely governed by criminal law. But, both types of reform are intended to improve state control of the sex industry, and both are guided by concerns about public order, migration and the control of drugs and trafficking, and money laundering.

What differences there are between the Swedish and Dutch reforms might be attributed to traditions of governance rather than a fundamental difference in goals. Compared to The Netherlands, Sweden has a history of greater state intervention in the private sphere. This tradition may have promoted a consensus among the majority of the population that some kinds of behaviour are 'wrong' and should be corrected by the state. In the more pluralistic Netherlands, there is little support for intervention on the part of the authorities in the way citizens choose to live; the Dutch boast a wide range of sexual, gender and other identities, amongst which prostitution can be seen as a lifestyle choice as well as a form of work.

The governments of many other European nations face the same problem as the Swedes and the Dutch. Agencies responsible for law enforcement no longer find that they can turn a blind eye to the sex industry; they can no longer tolerate, regulate and criminalise different aspects in roughly equal measure according to the varying strength of different interest groups. For example, there are growing concerns in most of Europe about trafficking and international organised crime; hence the interest that is shown in the results of the Swedish and Dutch reforms. Several other states have experimented with new legislation and policies. Scandinavian countries are tending to follow the Swedish example and seem likely to synchronise their laws (International Abolitionist Federation 2001). Denmark has decriminalised prostitutes without giving sex work the status of a profession, so that sex workers do not enjoy full occupational rights comparable to other workers. (www.europap.net, Country Report for Denmark).

The German parliament has overruled a verdict by the Supreme Court that the contract between a prostitute and her client was invalid because it was immoral and so prostitution is now legally accepted as a profession. But the German government, in contrast to The Netherlands, has not made a co-ordinated effort to ensure that the change of legal status is reflected in local and national systems of taxation and welfare (chapter 4).

In Belgium, both the Swedish and Dutch approaches have been proposed but it remains unclear what legislation parliament will adopt (www.europap.net, Country Report for Belgium). The French Minister of the Interior has recently ushered in new legislation successfully to sanction and, in the case of aliens, deport those who solicit on the streets. The Italian government has recently introduced laws that likewise criminalise street prostitution and 'push' prostitution indoors, mostly to apartments (La Marca 2003).

Some cities in the United Kingdom experimented briefly with courses for men caught in the process of soliciting prostitutes. Arrested for what is known locally as 'kerb crawling', potential or actual clients of sex workers can be required to attend a 'John school', modelled on US practice, where they are told why they should not buy sex (Campbell and Storr 2001). Other UK cities have expressed interest in the Dutch regulations that allow street prostitution only within designated zones.

Austria and Greece are the only European countries where traditional forms of regulationism still operate: prostitution is legal provided that women have work permits through registration and attend clinics for mandatory health checks as required. In both countries, unregistered women, often from non-EU countries, exceed the number of registered sex workers by a factor of ten or more.

Effects on prostitutes

It is unclear how far government interventions are governed by concern for sex workers but benefit to the worker must serve as a key principle for evaluating these developments. Observers have concluded that little has changed as far as sex workers are concerned. Europap has found that repression nearly always has a negative effect on the safety, well-being and working conditions of prostitutes. Some people who are opposed to prostitution as such argue that the best and only way to help sex workers is to get them out of prostitution and into a decent life. They are suspicious about many campaigns, such as interventions for safer sex, which are not directed at stopping prostitution.

Europap, by contrast, is committed to supporting sex workers whether they choose to change their 'careers' or to continue working in poor conditions within the sex industry. We do not consider ourselves mandated to make decisions for sex workers, only to inform, support and encourage them in the lives they decide to lead. The effect of various policies and laws on individual sex workers are summarised in an earlier book on Europap's experiences, focusing primarily on health in Europe, defined broadly to encompass concepts of well-being (Mak ed 1996, Conclusions and Recommendations pp. v-xviii). These findings may be relevant to current debates about reform as well as the evaluation of those reforms that have already been introduced.

Conclusion

Many governments in Europe are determined to control the sex industry more closely than before. This will have negative effects on sex workers unless sex work is recognised legally as a profession. Even where sex workers have been legally recognised as workers and freelance, self-employed operators, they have been unable to gain the rights enjoyed by others at work to date and they are unlikely to achieve them in the near future. Greater attention is required to the position of sex workers in national and local reforms whether these concern laws, policies or practices of law enforcement.

A personal note, Jan Visser

After I obtained my degree in sociology in 1979 from the University of Amsterdam, I responded to a small job advertisement from de Mr A. de Graaf Stichting in Amsterdam. I joined the institute, which was heir to the abolitionist movement in The Netherlands, but had recently transformed. The new director introduced the concept of work to the prostitution debate; and proposed to tackle problems associated with sex work rather than prostitution itself.

This shift was to prove fruitful, and was welcomed by a new generation of professionals (politicians, policemen, health and social workers). In the early 1980s prostitution developed rapidly in many directions and people dealing with 'the problem' were determined to be pragmatic. But they felt uneasy with the prevalent moral condemnation of prostitution.

The proposed definition of prostitution as work provided an alternative ideological formulation. If a grown person decides to do sex work then it is not the business of the state to interfere; rather the state should guarantee that this work is done under the protection of labour legislation.

This view of sex work coincided with strong beliefs about the proper role of the state in the Netherlands more generally: many thought that the state should not prescribe on moral beliefs and intimate behaviour. In Dutch politics of the early 1980s a consensus was soon formed around this view of sex work, and translated into a draft law. The Graaf Foundation studied the sex industry and developed theoretical and practical proposals. The foundation played a leading role in bringing together players with different perspectives on and different relationships to prostitution.

As a representative of the foundation I was one of the spokespersons and organisers of this movement. I also became, like other professionals, personally involved in the struggle for sex workers' rights. My contact and collaboration with sex workers, independent and self-confident sex workers, supported my belief that sex work could be a profession without victimisation, if only it were organised rationally. We helped establish a Dutch sex workers rights' organisation, *De Rode Draad*, and promoted the concept of sex work in international forums. (Since 2001, I have worked for *De Rode Draad*, The Red Thread in English).

In the 1980s, prostitutes could be heard and legalisation of sex work seemed to be imminent. But, the prostitution debate became much more complicated at the end of the 1980s. We were arguing for the rights of adults to earn a living without being criminalised, an argument that was met with growing sympathy by the general public. Other issues then emerged: HIV/AIDS, drugs, migration and trafficking of children. It was no longer possible to have a discussion or analysis of what I call 'pure' prostitution, sex for money among consenting adults. Many opponents of prostitution claim that exploitation, violence, physical and psychological trauma are intrinsic to prostitution. For them, the logical and necessary solution is to fight prostitution altogether.

Despite this setback, it is remarkable that we have preserved any consensus at all on prostitution as work in The Netherlands. Few Dutch people want to 'abolish' prostitution. The policy norm continues to focus on dealing with the problematic aspects of prostitution and not prostitution itself.

Nonetheless, it has become more difficult to argue for the legalisation of prostitution, just as it has become more difficult to analyse and differentiate the developments in the sex industry that I have described. The debate has become more complex. The cultural climate has become less tolerant and less open to social experimentation. We can see that prostitution has become connected to criminality, abuse and exploitation. But still I believe, as an academic and as a member of this society, that the only way to improve the situation is to give sex workers human and workers' rights, and to legalise and integrate the sex industry into mainstream society. It will take time and it will require more energy to inform and influence a somewhat reluctant public opinion.

In Europe, we are in the midst of an ideological battle, initiated by the 'Swedish' side, between those who want to criminalise prostitution in order to abolish it and those who want to legalise prostitution in order to sanitise it. It will soon be clear which approach has the upper hand. At the national level I expect that governments will retain a great deal of autonomy in dealing with the sex industry. But, in view of the increasing problems associated with prostitution, it is unlikely that governments will ignore this industry in the way they have in the past. Let us hope that promoting and safeguarding prostitutes' rights is one of the central concerns of all governments in the years ahead.

Acknowledgements

The data for this chapter were collected for a Europap project during 2002 in which we reviewed laws, policies and their application in participating countries. These data are available at www.europap.net. We wish to thank Dieuwke James for her assistance in carrying out the inquiry and Maura Graff for her help in preparing this chapter.

Notes

[1] For detailed information on the current situation in Europe, see the website for European Network Male Prostitution, www.enmp.org.
[2] In the film, starring Shirley Maclaine and Jack Lemmon (1963, directed by Billy Wilder), a policeman becomes obsessed with cleaning up a Parisian red-light district, loses his job, and ends up falling in love with one of the prostitutes.
[3] See the website www.mrgraaf.nl for all references to Dutch history in this chapter.
[4] See the United Nations: Convention for the Suppression of the Traffic in Persons and of the Exploitation of the Prostitution of others (1949).
[5] See the website www.europap.net for reference material about current and recent policies in different European countries.
[6] See www.qweb.kvinnoforum.se/misc/iaf.rtf, Petterson, E. & Sjogren, T. (2001) "Sweden: Early Effects of Changing Legislation on Prostitution" *International Abolitionist Federation Newsletter: Special Issue: Prostitution in the Nordic Countries*, p. 10; Gould, A. (2001) "The Criminalisation of Buying Sex: The Politics of Prostitution in Sweden" *Jnl Soc. Pol.*, Vol. 30, No. 3: 437-456; plus chapters 13 and 14 of this volume.
[7] Evidence from a series of evaluation studies that were published by the Scientific Centre of the Ministry of Justice (Wetenschappelijk Onderzoeks en Documentatie Centrum) in Dutch in October 2002. See also Tampep websites at: http://www.mrgraaf.nl/tampepframe.htm and www.femmigration.net

References

Alexander, Priscilla and Delacoste, Frederique eds (1987). *Sex Work: Writings By Women in the Sex Industry*. Pennsylvania: Cleis Press.

Brussa, Licia (1999). *Health Migration Sex Work: The Experience of Tampep*. Amsterdam: Tampep International Foundation.

Campbell, R and Storr, M (2001). Challenging the Kerb Crawler Rehabilitation Programme. *Feminist Review*; 67, 94-108.

Doezema, Jo and Kempadoo, Kamala (1998). *Global Sex Workers: Rights, Resistance, and Redefinition*. New York: Routledge.

Europap (2000). Northern Region Report in *Europap Final Report 2000*. available on http://www.europap.net/dl/archive/reports/regional/Report_from_the_N orthern_Region.pdf (accessed Dec 2003).

International Abolitionist Federation (2001). Prostitution in the Nordic Countries. IAF Newsletter; special issue, August, 2001. on http://www.qweb.kvinnoforum.se/misc/iaf.rtf, accessed December 2003

Kilvington J, Day S, Ward H (2001). Prostitution Policy in Europe: A Time of Change? *Feminist Review*; 67:79 - 85.

La Marca, P (2003). "02 March 03: New law on prostitution in Italy?" Europap News; 4. on http://www.europap.net/dl/news/news_apr_2003.pdf (accessed Dec 2003).

Mak, R ed (1996). *Europap: European Intervention Projects, Aids Prevention for Prostitutes*. Gent: Academia Press.

Odzer, Cleo (1994). *Patpong Sisters: An American Woman's View of the Bangkok Sex World*. New York: Arcade Publ: Distributed by Little Brown and Co.

Pheterson, Gail ed (1989). *A Vindication of the Rights of Whores*. Seattle, Washington: The Seal Press.

Thanh-Dam Truong (1990). *Sex, Money and Morality: Prostitution and Tourism in South East Asia*. London: Zed books.

The European Network for HIV/STD Prevention in Prostitution (Europap/Tampep) (1999). *Hustling for Health: Developing Services for sex workers in Europe*. Department of Public Health and Epidemiology, Imperial College School of Medicine, London, UK.

van den Berg, R (2002). The impact of legislation on STI-prevention activities. Paper presented at conference on *Sex work and health in a changing Europe, Milton Keynes, UK, 14 – 16 January 2002*.

West, J (2000). Prostitution: Collectives and the Politics of Regulation. *Gender, Work and Organization*; 7(2):106.

Conclusion

Chapter 16
Reflections
Priscilla Alexander

Recent changes in Europe have influenced prostitution both in terms of the workforce and the contexts of sex work. These changes include increases in migration. Women and men move between countries of the European Union; they move from one part of Europe to another, especially from the newly independent states to the European Union and they also migrate from Asia, Africa, and Latin America in increasing numbers. Partly in response to these population shifts, but also in response to concerns about public health and activism on the part of sex workers and observers, some countries have begun to discuss alternatives to existing policies. For example, two countries in Europe, the Netherlands and Germany, have broadened the legal context of sex work, even as one country, Sweden, has narrowed it. In Europe, a range of experiments in regulating prostitution, from repression to toleration, do not seem to have improved conditions for sex workers, at least not in any unambiguous way. The reasons may lie in the formulation of prostitution as a 'problem'.

Competing Discourses

For most of recorded history, prostitution has been considered inherently problematic, and prostitutes have been thought deviant. For most of that history, dominant discourses have defined prostitutes as female, although there are hints from various times and places that some were male and, in many cultures, there have been persons who cross gender lines, some of whom have performed variations of prostitution.

One statist discourse has defined prostitution as a threat to public order, and there is a long history of laws designed to place prostitutes in specific, controllable places such as specific streets, or near, in, or outside city walls. There have been laws requiring prostitutes to wear specific clothes or other markers of their profession or identity, laws banishing or excluding them from communities, and laws confining them to brothels.

A second discourse has identified prostitutes as a threat to public health and, associating prostitutes with disease, inspired laws closing brothels in the 16th century (bathhouses or, in England, stews) and, in the 17th century, requiring prostitutes to register with police or health agents, forcing them to be examined for evidence of venereal diseases, and quarantining them if they appeared to be infected. The descendants of these reglementary laws continue to operate in some countries, mostly in Latin American and Asia, but also in Greece and Austria. At various times and places, prostitution and slavery have overlapped although, in all the historical records, there have been independent prostitutes. In the 19th century, inspired by the effectiveness of discourses about the enslavement of Africans in the United States, the Caribbean and Europe, as well as widespread discomfort with voluntary international migration, an 'abolitionist' discourse about prostitutes as 'white slaves' began to compete with discourses about morality, public disorder, and public disease. These discourses dominated the international approaches to prostitution in the mid 1970s, when Margo St. James, a former prostitute, started the organization in San Francisco, COYOTE, that began to talk in terms of prostitutes' rights: the right of sex workers to speak on their own behalf, the right to control their own bodies, the right to work legally, the right to relationships, the right to travel and the right to safe working conditions. By the end of the 20th century, there were sex workers' rights organizations, organized and led by sex workers, on every continent.

When epidemiologists first speculated that what came to be called AIDS might be sexually transmitted, many concluded, without much evidence, that prostitutes and prostitution would play a role in the spread of the disease, with female prostitutes spreading AIDS to what they called the 'general population'. Many countries allocated funds to study the epidemiology of AIDS in prostitutes, almost exclusively among women. Indeed, a hegemonic discourse in the first decade of the epidemic considered female prostitutes to represent a "core group of high frequency transmitters". However, some countries sought out sex workers, and funded sex workers' organisations, to enlist their help in fighting the epidemic. As a result, sex workers in a number of countries, including Germany, Italy, the Netherlands, the United Kingdom, Australia, New Zealand, Mexico, Brazil, and the United States have played an important role in discussions of the best way to reduce the risk of HIV transmission—to prostitutes as well as to clients—emphasising the role of working conditions and the detrimental impact of the laws and other repressive policies. No longer confined to being the subjects of studies by others, sex workers have designed projects, conducted research, written papers, and spoken out at numerous conferences, forcing the public health community to listen to their points of view.

Nonetheless, at the beginning of the 21st century, as at the beginning of the 20th, discussions of prostitution reflect several competing discourses: prostitutes as a threat to public order, prostitutes as a threat to public health, prostitutes as victims of violence and exploitation, and prostitutes as agents entitled to civil and human rights. Each discourse has an impact on the ability to organize effective health promotion efforts.

Migration

Although migration has always been a factor in sex work, the proportion of sex workers who have migrated from another country has increased significantly over the last ten years in many European countries, as reported in the chapters of this book. While abolitionist discourse constructs this migration as 'trafficking,' and defines migrant sex workers as helpless, passive bodies who have been duped or coerced into prostitution, in fact, organizations that work with migrant sex workers in a variety of countries have found that most of them have either consciously made the decision to engage in sex work or have understood prior to migrating that it was likely that the work available to them in the receiving countries would be some form of sex work. However, it is clear that working conditions for migrant sex workers are often problematic, and that many brokers and managers are exploitative and abusive, particularly where the work is illegal and, therefore, underground, out of the purview of such regulatory agencies as occupational health and safety bodies.

The response to this migration is varied, on the parts of states, feminists, public health analysts, and others. To states, uncontrolled in-migration represents a threat to public order. To public health authorities, it represents a potential for the migration of disease. To some feminists, as well as to most fundamentalist Christians, it seems inconceivable that women could choose to work as prostitutes, so they define the phenomenon as 'traffic' and coercion, and they personify the prostitute as victim. Although people migrate to work in many sectors of the economy, including construction, information technology, domestic labour, industrial labour, and formal sectors providing services related to tourism, much of the anxiety expressed in the receiving countries, and to a lesser extent in the sending countries, has focused on sex work in the form of a panic about 'traffic' in women. However, people who want to move - sometimes driven by the need to make money, sometimes by the desire to see other places and cultures - often see sex work as a way to facilitate their migration. Thus, many consciously choose or see migration and sex work as a risk worth taking. Some are terribly surprised when they arrive, and what then happens is profoundly affected by the legal context.

Both the migration and the response take place in the context of inherited laws and policies related to prostitution, and the efforts of sex workers to change those policies. But such efforts have had unanticipated consequences. For example, governments concerned about migration have taken advantage of both feminist discourses about trafficking and sex workers' discourses about the right to safe working conditions to enact legislation that they think will give them more control.

The Legal Context

Projects designed to reduce the spread of HIV do not happen in a vacuum. They are directly affected by public policies and discourses. The laws, regulations, and ordinances reviewed above, designed to prohibit or control various aspects of prostitution, have also affected HIV prevention.

In the 18th and 19th centuries, many European countries enacted health-related regulations, both in their home countries and in their colonies or war zones, requiring female prostitutes to register or be licensed by police or health officers, and to be regularly examined for evidence of venereal infections, primarily syphilis, in some cases confining prostitutes to closed brothels. France ended the closed house (brothel) system in 1946, and the health reglementation system in 1960. Italy ended its reglementation system in 1958. Greece and Austria still maintain traditional systems of regulation, although the majority of sex workers do not and never have registered. In most European countries, however, in conformance with the 1949 United Nations "Convention for the Suppression of the Traffic in Persons and of the Exploitation of the Prostitution of Others",[1] engaging in prostitution, by itself, is not a crime. Nonetheless, most countries have laws either prohibiting the promotion of prostitution by, for example, running a prostitution business, renting premises for the purposes of prostitution, receiving income from prostitutes, soliciting and/or advertising related to prostitution, or laws regulating prostitution such as zoning laws, licensing or registering prostitutes, and/or mandatory examinations for sexually transmitted diseases. Some countries, including the Unites States, bar anyone who has worked as a prostitute from entering the country, either temporarily or permanently, while others provide temporary visas or work permits to sex workers, often disguised as 'artists' visas.' After the Second World War, Germany took the approach of barring prostitutes from specific city neighbourhoods, which made it possible for prostitutes to work in other areas. As a result, most cities have a well-recognized red-light district with dense concentrations of super brothels or 'Eros centres' in cities such as Frankfurt and Hamburg while, in the cities without prohibited zones such as Berlin, prostitution is more diffused. In the Soviet Union and much of Eastern Europe, prostitution was often not specifically prohibited by law, but prostitutes could be arrested as 'parasites on the state' for not having a recognized source of income. Nonetheless, until recently, no states recognized prostitution as work.

Partly in response to health concerns in the age of AIDS, as well as the increases in migration, and partly as a result of sex workers' activism, various countries in Europe have begun to reconsider the legal context, and three countries have now reformed at least some of the laws. Two other countries in Australasia have also introduced reforms. However, the approach is far from uniform.

In The Netherlands, which has long taken the position that toleration is a more effective way to approach nonconformist activities than interdiction and repression, a new law legalizing brothels took effect in October 2000. Although the government claimed it wanted to "improve the conditions of prostitutes", with the enactment of some occupational health and safety regulations, the primary focus of the law was to give the government more control. Thus, despite the fact that before the new law, most prostitutes in The Netherlands were from somewhere else, the law bars the newly legal brothels from employing (or allowing to work on their premises) prostitutes from countries that are not members of the European Union. As a result, such migrants do not use public clinics as they did in the past (see chapter 8). Although there are strict regulations regarding migrant workers in all occupations in The Netherlands, it is only in prostitution that it is completely prohibited to employ migrants from countries outside the EU. Since the law came into effect, police have been entering brothels, checking workers' papers, and sending non-EU residents (defined as 'victims of traffickers') back to the sending country. Nonetheless, the new law has made it possible to begin to address other issues, including how to pay taxes, obtain social security, register as a business with the Chamber of Commerce, open commercial bank accounts, and implement rational occupational health and safety regulations (chapter 15). De Rode Draad, the sex workers' rights organization, is in the process of forming a union, to represent both sex workers employed by third parties and independent sex workers.

The Federal Republic of Germany also enacted a new law. Although they stopped short of legalising brothels or drafting occupational health and safety regulations, the new law recognized prostitution as a legitimate economic activity, and extended health insurance and social security to prostitutes (chapter 4). The new law has another important effect: under the old law, although as in most of Europe, engaging in prostitution was not a crime, the courts held that prostitution represented an 'immoral' contract. As a result, prostitutes were barred from filing a claim in court in the case of a dispute with a client or a manager, at the same time that the courts permitted clients to sue for a refund 'if the performance agreed upon was not accomplished'. The new law gives prostitutes the right to use the courts to resolve contractual disputes for the first time. However, as Maya Czajka has pointed out (chapter 4), this change in the law is not without problems, foremost being a continued unwillingness to recognize sexual labour as work, subject to the same kinds of rights and responsibilities as other forms of work.

Sweden has taken a completely different approach. Exploiting some feminists' definition of prostitution as violence against women, a law was passed to criminalise the purchase of sexual services, with a penalty of a fine or up to six months in prison (chapter 14). Although the government has argued that the purpose of the law is to reduce violence against women, sex workers in Sweden say that the new law actually harms them. Prostitution has gone further underground, and both sex workers and clients have been crossing borders to avoid its effects. Although some other countries in the region are considering following Sweden's example, sex workers have protested the law and called for its repeal.

These reforms suggest comparisons with other reforms, such as the Disorderly Houses Amendment Act of 1995, which legalised brothels in New South Wales, Australia and the similar reforms enacted in 2003 in New Zealand. In New South Wales, occupational health and safety regulations were adopted that covered the prevention of sexually transmitted diseases and other factors that affect physical safety, including drug and alcohol use, physical safety and security, injury management, and workers' compensation, as well as relationships with clients, and the rights of employees vs. sub-contractors. As a result of the law reform, sex workers are eligible for workers' compensation, if injured on the job. In collaboration with WorkCover,[2] the Sex Workers Outreach Project (SWOP) produced a book advising sex workers of their rights, and informing them how to get help if their rights are violated, as well as a videotape advising brothel owners and managers on how to create a safe workplace. New South Wales also permits and regulates street prostitution in some neighbourhoods, under some conditions. Although it is possible to apply for permission to open a brothel from local planning councils, independent sex workers who work alone in their own homes, or in pairs (for safety), have been arrested and charged with running an illegal brothel, with police using possession of condoms as evidence of intent. A bill that would have exempted up to two prostitutes working outside licensed brothels from prosecution was defeated.

Advocacy on the part of the New Zealand Prostitutes Collective led to the New Zealand reform permitting up to four sex workers to work together in an apartment without having to apply for a formal brothel permit. Currently, sex workers' rights activists are campaigning elsewhere, for example in the state of California, USA, to convince state legislatures to enact similar laws.[3]

A number of countries, including The Netherlands, the United States, and Italy, have enacted laws giving migrants who have been 'trafficked' into the country permission to remain if and while they testify against their 'traffickers.' However, during 2001, police in Milan, Italy, conducted intensified raids against foreigners 'without papers,' and forcibly repatriated them immediately. Many of the migrants targeted by the police had been prostitutes, many from North Africa and Latin America, including both women and transsexuals. The level of violence during the raids was high, with the police pressuring NGOs that provide services to prostitutes to stay out of the area when raids are planned (with obvious implications for sex workers' health). Despite laws allowing victims of trafficking to remain in the country during the prosecution of their traffickers, many continue to be summarily deported. Prime Minister Silvio Berlusconi has been calling for changes in the Italian law—by either eradicating prostitution, as if that were possible, or reopening the brothels. Although some speculated that he had raised the issue to deflect press attention from accusations of malfeasance in office, his remarks provoked extensive discussion in Italy, including a discussion of proposals put forth by the Comitato per i Diritti Civili delle Prostitute (chapter 5).

In Edinburgh, Scotland, for two decades, there was a policy of toleration allowing prostitutes to work in specified neighbourhoods. Under this policy, health promotion activities were quite effective in the zone, so that the incidence of sexually transmitted infections had become lower among female sex workers attending medical outreach clinics than among non-prostitute women attending a Genitourinary Medicine Department. In addition, while the number of young girls working increased in other cities in Scotland, the average age of sex workers in the toleration zone rose, and none under the age of 16 had been seen since January 2000. The toleration policy also made it easier to address violence against sex workers, the incidence of which declined. In August 2001, in response to pressure from people moving into the neighbourhood, the police changed the designated area of toleration, demanding that sex workers move to the new area. Almost all of them did. However, despite overwhelming cooperation, the police declared the transfer a failure, and ended the policy of toleration in December 2001. Since then, Scot-PEP, a local sex worker led education project, has been closely monitoring the effect of the closure, and in 2003, the legislature began considering reforms to authorise cities in Scotland to set aside zones of toleration to reduce the level of violence.

A new era?

Any sense of optimism about a new era has become tarnished by these preliminary assessments of the impact of reforms. In Amsterdam, for example, the government closed down street work in the famous red light district in downtown Amsterdam and set aside an industrial area as the zone of toleration, and in November 2003, voted to close this street zone as well, marking a major change in Dutch policy. In addition, police have been rigorously enforcing the bar against immigrants by intensively checking workers' papers, both on the street and in the newly legal brothels. This repression has encouraged most Dutch sex workers to continue working outside the law, out of sight of the police, and has increased the power of the brokers of migrant sex work, who simply move workers from one city or country to the next in an effort to stay ahead of the police. This has made it extremely difficult for the Huiskammer (Living Room) Project and the Dutch STD Foundation to effectively provide health and social services to sex workers, with obvious consequences for sex workers' physical and mental health.

These reports show how difficult it is to change the context of sex work. As the example from Edinburgh shows, informal progressive modifications in law enforcement practices are easily reversed. Even when the law is changed, governments remain anxious about prostitution, and the idea of prostitutes being out of control, and so it is difficult to consolidate or expand on the improvements. Sometimes, police implement old, long-since repealed policies as in Leiden, in the Netherlands, where the local government requires quarterly STI screening, although the national law does not. Similarly, in Lyon, France, the Police des Moeurs pressured brothel owners to require their employees to register with the police, despite the repeal of reglementation more than 50 years ago.

Implication for Sex Workers' Health

Policies on prostitution have a tremendous impact on sex workers' health. In virtually every country, researchers have reported that sex workers are wary of health projects and health care providers. Illegality increases sex workers' dependency on third parties whether club owners, street managers, husbands or boyfriends, and makes it difficult or impossible for sex workers to organize against exploitation. They experience long working hours, unsafe and unprotected working conditions, denial of the right to turn down abusive clients, and pressure to drink alcohol or use drugs. Illegality increases sex workers' isolation and stigma. Immigration restrictions compound the difficulties since they increase the likelihood of frequent migration when visas run out, or when laws distinguish between 'legal' and 'illegal' prostitutes and make it very difficult to provide any social support or health services.

Among street-based sex workers in New York City, it is not uncommon to be arrested 100 or 150 times over six or seven years of sex work. With some regularity, sex workers tell outreach workers about police confiscating condoms and/or destroying them, or using possession of condoms as evidence of intent to commit prostitution, particularly when arresting them for 'loitering with intent'. As a result, in some neighbourhoods, sex workers refuse to take more than three condoms. Sometimes, police park their cars behind AIDS prevention project mobile units and observe people who come for services. From time to time, police stop women as they leave these mobile units, and search the bags containing condoms, information, and food. Some sex workers report that when they walk around the corner, police will stop them and interrogate them. On some occasions, police have threatened to arrest male outreach workers on suspicion of being johns (clients), although so far, they have not actually done so. The mayor has maintained a major crackdown on street prostitutes, similar to the sweeps in Milan, and some police have told outreach teams that it is their fault that prostitutes are on the street. It is not surprising that the combined effect of the laws, their enforcement, and the related discrimination and stigma, is such that many people avoid identifying what they do as sex work.

Some health projects have been founded by sex workers, or by coalitions of sex workers and allies, including Scot-PEP, in Edinburgh, Scotland, the Comitato per it Diritti Civili delle Prostitute, in Pordenone, Italy, De Rode Draad, in Amsterdam, the Netherlands, Cabiria, in Lyon, France, Different Avenues, in Washington, DC, the United States, the International Union of Sex Workers, in London, England, the Sex Workers Outreach Project (SWOP), in Sydney, New South Wales, Australia, and the International Network for Sex Work Projects, in Cape Town, South Africa. Some projects originally set up by social workers or health professionals, such as the Working Men Project, in London, recruit sex workers as staff, peer educators or cultural mediators, or at managerial levels. Some projects such as Pro-Sentret, in Oslo, Norway, and the Sonagachi Project, in Calcutta, India, encourage sex workers to form independent organizations, both to advise the projects and to act independently. The alliances have not always been easy, however. Although the interests and agendas of sex workers and non-sex workers are allied in some ways, they can be quite divergent in others. Early in the AIDS epidemic, the interests were quite divergent, as the funders were interested in preventing the spread of HIV, and sometimes other sexually transmitted diseases, from sex workers to other populations, while sex workers were more interested in finding out how to protect themselves from these diseases, as well as from violence, bad working conditions, and arrest. Funding for sex work projects still comes from government or private sources more interested in reducing the spread of HIV and other sexually transmitted and/or blood borne infections, reducing public disorder on the streets, improving access to health care or social services, reducing drug use, or helping people change their occupations, rather than improving the context and conditions of sex work. Indeed, the US Department of State has barred the funding of anti-trafficking projects that recognize sex work as work, which could affect AIDS prevention and other health projects for sex workers, as well. Sex workers, on the other hand, are more likely to think in terms of how to change the context of their work: how to avoid getting arrested, deal with dangerous customers, organize a union, or change the laws, with specific health issues as a subtext.

There continue to be serious barriers to improving sex workers' health when some or all aspects of their work are defined, by law, as criminal. No matter how supportive projects are, and how much they agree with sex workers on the need for legal changes, any improvements in sex workers health will be jeopardised by repressive laws that remain on the books. As the experience in Edinburgh demonstrates, unofficial or local policies of toleration can easily be reversed by new policies. Similarly, the Dutch government has been slow to enact the necessary provisions regarding health care, social security, integration into the work force and other provisions in the new law. This suggests to me that the state is quite happy with the new law as a means of oppression, and in enacting the new law, has exploited sex workers' concerns rather than responded to them.

Why does it continue to be so difficult to change prostitution laws? One factor is the continued assumption that prostitution and other forms of sex work, per se, involve women providing sexual services to men. Prostitution therefore creates anxieties about the proper role of women. Despite thirty years of the second wave of the women's movement, women are still expected to assume primary responsibility for the care and management of the home, not the workplace. Women continue to earn less than men doing similar work everywhere in the world, at the same time as they are expected to work in effect a second full-time job when they go home at night. Moreover, women are still supposed to wait to be asked, not to assert their own desires (sexual or economic). Although in many countries the old laws that punished women, but not men, for adultery and fornication, have been repealed, in other countries, women are still being condemned to death by stoning for engaging in sex without marriage, even when the sex was without their consent. Even though the laws about prostitution in many countries have been made gender neutral, the primary focus of law enforcement is to identify, arrest, and lock up female and transgender prostitutes and, for the most part, to ignore male prostitution. There are numerous reports of police misconduct with transgender workers, which is often more severe than with women, which only confirms this deep-seated fear of female sexual expression.

Male migration for work tends to be recognised as rational, but female migration is often defined as inexplicable, and therefore it must be coerced. The image of women who should stay at home produces a kind of hysteria about female migration that is manifested in panics about prostitution, which is continually defined as sexual slavery and trafficking, not labour. Thus, media depictions of men standing on street corners seeking employment as day labourers have a completely different character than depictions of women standing on street corners seeking employment as day or night sex workers. It is this gendered picture of prostitution that causes countries to deny prostitutes the right to work together in small groups even as they permit managers the right to obtain permits to operate brothels. The assumption is that female sex workers are out of control, out of order, and must be supervised if they are to be allowed to work at all. The other side of this view, of course, is the idea that the exploitation of female sex workers by managers (overwhelmingly seen as male, even when they are not) is categorically different from any other workplace exploitation.

Looking back over the twenty-two years of this epidemic, we have made significant progress in integrating the concerns of the public health establishment and the concerns of the sex workers. When we started working together, hardly anyone but sex workers talked about the problems with the laws and the need to change them. That is beginning to change, but we still have a long way to go.

Notes

[1] Approved by General Assembly resolution 317(IV) of 2 December 1949.
[2] WorkCover is Australia's Workers' Compensation Agency.
[3] In the United States, each state has its own laws governing prostitution, and law reform has to be accomplished on a state-by-state basis, in contrast to both Canada and Europe, where the basic laws governing prostitution are national.

Index

276

279

126, 129-131, 133, 147, 154-155, 157, 215, 233, 242, 244, 246-252, 254-255, 261, 263, 266, 268, 270-271

Trafficking – 3, 5-, 8-10, 13, 20, 25, 33-7, 52, 60, 62, 66, 79, 87-88, 90, 93, 111-112, 118, 136, 139, 146, 155-159, 180, 187, 222, 226, 230-231, 234, 241, 243, 245, 248, 249, 252, 255, 263-264, 266, 268, 272-273

See also Feminism, Migration, State, Violence

Trades unions – 5-6, 8, 39, 42-49, 51, 60, 174, 225-227, 266, 272

Associacion de Mujeres Meretrices Argentinas (Anmar) - 44

Exotic Dancers Union (USA) – 44

GMB (UK) – 47-50

International Labour Organisation – 52, 86

International Union of Sex Workers – 8, 39-52, 271

Red Thread / Rode Draad (The Netherlands) – 47, 75, 255, 266, 271

Service Employees International Union – 44

Trades Union Council (UK) – 45, 50

Ver-di (Germany) – 59, 60

UK – 4, 8, 17-18, 21, 23-25, 39-52, 126, 129, 137, 146-147, 153, 163-178, 179-197, 226, 253, 263, 271

United Nations – 16, 27, 28, 77, 228, 256

Beijing - 33

Protocol on Trafficking 1949-256, 265

USA – 13, 40, 41, 44, 67, 75, 156, 157, 229, 262, 263, 268, 271, 274

Violence towards sex workers – 90, 95, 97, 111, 124, 128, 143-144, 163, 165, 170, 211, 244, 246-247, 255

murder – 11, 168, 179-181, 185-187, 189– 195, 197

perpetrators – 12, 112, 179, 181, 185-187, 188, 191-193, 195

prosecutions – 12, 189, 191, 196,

rape – 11, 46, 115, 179, 181, 183-189, 191, 193-194, 196, 197, 202, 204, 218, 233,

reports of – 51, 148, 167, 179, 181-184, 186, 190, 192, 194, 195-197, 210, 223

vigilante – 185, 187, 192

vulnerability – 50, 51, 110, 129, 153-154, 166, 179, 181-182, 187, 189, 194-195, 221

See also Feminism

281